THE CERTIFICATION SERIES

Passage Making

The national standard for quality sailing instruction

Published by the UNITED STATES SAILING ASSOCIATION   Copyright © 2000 by the UNITED STATES SAILING ASSOCIATION

All rights reserved. No part of this publication may be reproduced, stored in a retrieval system, or transmitted, in any form or by any means, electronic, mechanical, photocopying, recording, or otherwise without prior written permission from the UNITED STATES SAILING ASSOCIATION. ISBN 1-882502-86-8.   Printed in the United States of America.

UNITED STATES SAILING ASSOCIATION   P.O. Box 1260, 15 Maritime Drive, Portsmouth, RI 02871-0907 http://www.ussailing.org

Acknowledgments

The complex subjects of this fifth book in *The Certification Series* have involved a spectrum of experts including Passage Making instructors and instructor trainers, weather and electronics specialists, safety at sea authorities, and blue-water sailors and navigators. Key US SAILING's Committees involved in the creation and review process have been the Training Committee's Keelboat Working Party chaired by David Forbes and Tyler Pierce, the Commercial Sailing Committee chaired by Rich Jepsen and Greg Norwine, and the Safety at Sea Committee chaired by Ralph Naranjo with Sheila McCurdy as its editor and liaison for the book. Dozens of people have contributed input. Unfortunately space does not permit us to list them all, but we would like to give special recognition to Michael William Carr, Mark Ellis, David Forbes, Heather Godsey, Mitch Kramer, Timmy Larr, Warren Mazanec, Glenn T. McCarthy, Sheila McCurdy, Matt Meadows, George Moffett, Ralph Naranjo, Matt Petersen, Tyler Pierce, Karen Prioleau, Rodney Randall, Phil Shull, Ronald Trossbach, and Ray Wichmann. We also would like to thank Ian McCurdy of McCurdy & Rhodes for use of the Navy 44 plans in several Offshore Passage Making illustrations.

This last book in *The Certification Series* is a tribute to the vision and determination of Steve Colgate, James Muldoon and Susie Trotman as well as the constant support of US SAILING's Officers and Board.

And last but by no means least is our extraordinary creative team of experienced sailors, seamen and experts: writer Tom Cunliffe, photographer Ralph Naranjo, designer and editor Mark Smith, and technical illustrator Kim Downing.

Our thanks to all!

Tom Cunliffe, *Author*
Tom brings his vast experience as professional sailor and RYA Yachtmaster Examiner to his writing. His articles appear in major periodicals and his books include a four book navigation series, *Easy on the Helm, Cunliffe on Cruising, Topsail and Battleaxe* and *Hand Reef and Steer*. These last two won BEST BOOK OF THE SEA prizes. He also finds time to cruise in his cutter with his wife Ros and daughter Hannah to such diverse places as Brazil, Greenland, the Caribbean, the U.S., Labrador and Russia.

Mark Smith, *Designer and Editor*
A lifelong sailor, graphic designer, editor and illustrator, Mark is currently Creative Director for North Sails. Mark was editorial and art director for *Yacht Racing / Cruising* magazine (now *Sailing World*) from 1970-83, editor and publisher of *Sailor* magazine from 1984-86, and editor and art director of *American Sailor* from 1987-89. His works include design and illustration for the *Annapolis Book of Seamanship* by John Rousmaniere and published by Simon and Schuster. Mark lives in Norwalk, CT with his wife Tina and daughters Stephanie, Natalie and Cristina.

Kim Downing, *Technical Illustrator*
Kim grew up in the Midwest doing two things, sailing and drawing, so it's only natural that his two favorite pastimes should come together in the production of this book. He has been the technical illustrator for *SAIL Magazine* since 1988 and is the proprietor of *Magazine Art and Design*, which provides technical illustrations for books and magazines worldwide. He and his family enjoy cruising the Great Lakes aboard their 26 foot sailboat and occasionally racing.

Ralph Naranjo, *Photographer*
Ralph has sailed around the world with a camera at the ready. His images have been published in books and magazines, and when not pointing a lens at boats, his passion is wildlife photography. As *Cruising World's*, technical editor and the Vanderstar Chair at the US Naval Academy he spends much time under sail, training crews and evaluating boats and equipment. He and his family have sailed their sloop *Wind Shadow* around the world and have cruised her for over 25 years.

All Passage Making photos are by Ralph Naranjo unless otherwise noted. Cover photo by Neil Rabinowitz.

3

Contents

PART 1: Coastal Passage Making

PART 2: Offshore Passage Making

Introduction

Whether we go to sea for recreation or to make a living, a common thread that binds all true sailors is the recognition that the learning process is life-long. Generally, knowledge builds seamlessly on experience, but for all of us there are several important waypoints which mark our voyage from anxious novice to experienced expert. Of these, possibly the most significant is the day we leave the familiar confines of our home waters or the carefully defined boundaries imposed by a charterer's requirements, to embark on a passage.

At sea, whether under sail or power, we must tackle uncertain conditions and stretch our navigation skills to new limits. We may also discover whether the folks we are sailing with are really the nice people we imagined they were. This book deals with those facets of the sailor's art which separate the passagemaker from his inshore counterpart, beginning with coastal passages and progressing farther offshore.

The Coastal Passage. A coastal passage is generally executed within a few hours' sail of the shoreline. Coastal passages typically run from eight to 48 hours and may include one or two nights at sea, but your boat remains in potential contact with ready shoreside back-up. With modern forecasting at your fingertips, you can make an informed decision about whether to continue with a particular passage or not. Unlike the offshore passagemaker who must make the best of what comes, you retain the option of continuing the passage, waiting for better conditions or abandoning the passage altogether. When things take a nasty turn along your route, there are usually harbors of refuge to duck into, and assistance can generally be anticipated if you come to grief.

Navigation becomes a major issue within twenty miles of the coast. Far more vessels pile up on the shore than ever founder in open ocean, so the coastal skipper must take piloting seriously.

Many coastal passages offer the choice of a series of daylight jumps with nights ashore or at anchor, or transforming the same three-day trip into a single "overnighter." While daylight jumps may seem easier, the dark hours at sea can be safe and delightful in fair weather. The "nights ashore" yacht will also have to enter more strange harbors where the real risk lurks.

Many sailors choose never to progress beyond coastal passagemaking, discovering a lifetime of fulfillment along the continental shelves. Historically, these are the progeny of the schooner captains who worked the U.S. Coasts and Great Lakes. Such people were among the world's finest seamen. As any shrewd observer will tell you, a keen sailor will learn more sailing 500 miles among shoals, islands and anchorages than a dull sailor sailing 5,000 miles offshore.

The Offshore Passage. A passage offshore is a voyage, usually across a substantial expanse of open ocean: a trip to Hawaii from the West Coast, an Atlantic crossing, or a passage to the Virgin Islands from North Carolina. For many sailors it is their ultimate goal, to be savored again and again. For some, it is a challenge which must be endured to reach a far-flung cruising ground. In either case, no compromise can be tolerated. This is the essential difference between coastal and offshore passagemaking.

Offshore, your boat is far from safe haven. Even on a passage that is expected to take a week or less, good weather cannot be ordered up with any certainty. Crews must deal with conditions outside their control in a seamanlike manner. They must accept fair and foul with stoicism.

In an emergency, it can be days before help arrives, if it comes at all. Therefore offshore sailors and their boats must be self-sufficient, self-reliant and able to deal with all eventualities using their own resources. This philosophy is essential to offshore passagemaking. It is not always easy to live by, but when observed, the rewards for the offshore sailor can be grand indeed.

Based on their respective abilities, the sailing experience they seek, boat preparedness and crew experience, two skippers could set out from Newport, Rhode Island bound towards Florida. One might take an offshore route, perhaps via Bermuda. The other might plan a series of short, weather-prompted hops along the coast. Depending on the season, the two voyages can be equally viable and rewarding. To be successfully completed without misfortune, which must be every skipper's ultimate goal, both require a high degree of skill.

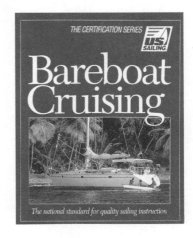

Passage Making is part of US SAILING's Certification Series, including **Basic Keelboat, Basic Cruising, Bareboat Cruising** and **Coastal Navigation.** The Certification Series is based on the US SAILING programs that form the national standard for quality sailing instruction.

The purpose of this book is to consider those elements that separate passagemaking from inshore sailing. Because the challenges presented by sailing are generally more diverse than those of powerboating, we shall concentrate on the sailboat while not excluding power. The power skipper's needs will be addressed where they diverge from the sailboater's.

The vital subject of safety runs through this entire work. Safety is the essence of the seaman's art, whether it be seen in a passage plan that steers clear of a potential lee shore, or deciding on the best bunks to combat Public Enemy No.1: fatigue. Safety may not always be mentioned by name here, but the recommendations in these pages will always keep it in the forefront. The self-reliance of passagemaking requires skippers and crews to make decisions specific to a wide variety of situations. No book can address them all, but the material presented in this one has been selected to form a foundation upon which smart, safe choices can be made based on crew, boat and sailing conditions.

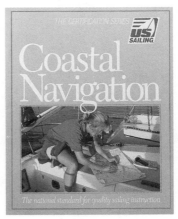

The first part of the book will consider coastal passagemaking requirements. The latter part will take you offshore where the great winds blow and sailors are on their own. Whichever section may seem most relevant to you, read both. Each has a lot to do with the other, and much of the information holds good for both disciplines. Because everyone who has contributed to this work is an experienced passagemaker as well as an instructor, the material is presented in a practical, "hands-on" point of view. We couldn't teach it any other way.

**PART 1
COASTAL
PASSAGE
MAKING**

Coastal Yacht Preparation

Successful coastal passages can be made in a wide variety of craft, and while "the perfect yacht" remains the elusive goal of most sailors, most also make the most of the boat that is affordable and available. A boat does not have to be capable of weathering Cape Horn in winter to carry you safely down a hundred miles of coastline during the right season. In a properly planned coastal context, any well-found, thoroughly-maintained yacht will serve its crew well, so long as she is not being asked to perform beyond her original design.

Hull Forms. Since the 1979 Fastnet Race in which 15 lives were lost when sailing yachts capsized in steep seas driven by storm-force winds, a good deal of research has been undertaken on both sides of the Atlantic on the safety aspects of yacht design and stability. A study of the resistance of different hull forms to capsize in high waves can be found in Chapter 14, but whether you are 15 miles off the coast of California or hove-to south of Greenland, an understanding of the subject is a vital contribution to surviving heavy weather. Even if you have no intention of getting caught in a storm offshore, you should still read this section carefully.

For coastal passagemakers, the bottom line is that while a lightweight boat may be exciting to sail and potentially capable of outrunning a coastal storm, she may prove less able in rough conditions than a heavier, deeper yacht. Many charter boats are designed to provide lively light-air performance, a large cockpit for socializing and capacious accommodations. While there is nothing wrong with this, a skipper should be aware that features that make a vessel a success in sunshine and protected waters might prove less successful in a steep sea and strong wind.

On the other side of the coin, the skipper of a heavy-displacement boat cannot be complacent just because the yacht looks good on a graphic stability analysis. She might be so undercanvassed for her wetted area that she cannot get out of her own way in lighter winds. Investing in an asymmetric cruising spinnaker (poleless) might do far less for her downwind performance than it would for a more easily driven vessel, so her auxiliary power will be a more important factor.

Both yachts have features to recommend them, and there is a range of options in between; what is best depends only on what you want the boat to do. It pays to look beyond the brochures. Try to talk to owners of similar boats. If in doubt, ask a surveyor or some marine professionals.

Cruising multihulls are becoming a common sight in many areas. Their

For ocean sailing, heavier-displacement monohull offer higher load carrying capacity and generally are more able in steep seas and strong winds.

downwind performance — typically 30 to 50% faster than a monohull — increases their daily sailing range. Their shallow draft also makes them accessible to more cruising grounds. Overloading them with extra equipment, however, can noticeably reduce their performance.

Multihulls have high initial stability, which translates into a stable platform with minimal heeling and rolling on all points of sail. This facilitates steering, makes broaching unlikely, and opens up the possibility of anchoring in exposed areas. However, if the windward hull lifts too high out of the water in heavy weather conditions, there can be a serious risk of capsize.

Carrying the right amount of sail area in these conditions is obviously important, but any multihull skipper should know how his or her yacht will behave in different conditions. Will the engine(s) need to be turned on when tacking in heavy seas or in light conditions? What proactive or passive methods will work best to keep the multihull under control in a storm? Talk with other multihull owners and determine the methods that work best for your boat.

A skipper of a power-driven yacht should imagine having to take seas on the beam for 24 hours. Does she really have the guts to cope? How uncomfortable will she be punching upwind into a head sea?

Prioritizing. Given an understanding of your boat's inherent strong and weak points, you should list every possible piece of rigging, gear and hull equipment that you may need to inspect, repair, upgrade or purchase before embarking on a passage. Assign a priority for all the items on the list. As the list grows, you may realize that you can live without a good proportion of it.

Priority number one is the watertight integrity of the hull, coupled with pumps to return the water to the outside of the hull when integrity is breached. Number two is the trouble-free functioning of motive power, be it sail or engine. Number three is steering. If any of these fail, all else will be irrelevant.

Next come the basics of life for the crew. Like the vessel herself, the people aboard must be maintained at full working efficiency. They must be fed, watered and well rested.

Once you are confident of venturing forth with rig, engine, steering and crew in good working order, you need to consider how you will navigate boat and crew securely from departure to destination, avoiding dangers along the way. All you need to pilot a coastal passage is a compass, a parallel rule, a pencil, a distance log, a chart and a set of tide tables.

Looking for something beyond basic? A pair of dividers and a GPS will certainly make life easier. Many people consider a VHF radio to be a minimum safety requirement, but if the boat holds together and you keep your weather eye open, you may not need it to call for help.

From here, we move into the realm of less-than-vital gear. Radar is priceless if you operate in an area of likely fog. Electronic chart plotters are great fun and can save time and trouble. A freezer is handy and a shower is a great comfort. So are a watermaker and blown-air central heating. The capacity to take satellite telephone calls and download Internet pages can make some people's day, but lack of these is hardly going to stop you sailing safely from one place to another.

For coastal passagemakers, the bottom line is that while a lightweight boat may be exciting to sail and potentially capable of outrunning a coastal storm, she may prove less able in rough conditions than a heavier, deeper yacht.

Engine exhaust — Cockpit lockers — Companionway hatch — Dorades — Hatch — Opening ports — Hatch — Chain locker

Manual bilge pump outlet — Stern tube — Cockpit drains — Rudder tube — Raw water engine intake — Sink drains — Bilge pump outlet — Head discharge seacock — Depth sounder/knot meter through-hulls — Head intake

Hull Openings on a Typical 40-footer
Any of these openings is capable of causing problems. Always keep plugs attached to all through-hull fittings to plug leaks if necessary.

If any non-essential item really matters to you, make a decision. But remember there are boats rotting in every marina while their owners await delivery of that replacement circuit board to interface the autopilot with the ice-cream maker. On the other hand, winch pawl springs and spare injectors for popular diesel engines are available just about everywhere, and any sailor should be able to stitch a blown sail. The folks whose needs are simple can generally be found way out at sea, enjoying their uncomplicated boats.

The Hull. It is rare for a modern cruising hull made of fiberglass, composites or steel to fail due to stress of weather alone. While a traditional timber plank-on-frame hull requires careful inspection for deterioration, most wooden yacht owners are enthusiasts who understand the requirement to monitor the condition of their hulls.

When water enters hulls it is usually through holes that are supposed to be there, but also supposed to be closed off. In preparing for coastal passagemaking, therefore, all apertures must be inspected to determine their potential for generating trouble. Here are some common examples:

Stern tubes. The propeller shaft passes through the hull at the stern tube. There are various arrangements for keeping this delicate joint watertight, one of which is the increasingly popular Deep-Sea seal. In a medium-sized yacht, the shaft is supported by the gearbox flange and one or more water-cooled rubber "cutless" type bearings. So long as the shaft is properly aligned, these are unlikely to fail without warning, and even if they do, the shaft won't drop out.

Stuffing box seal. In the conventional stern gland the shaft passes through a stuffing box on the inside of the hull. A packing nut on the stuffing box is tightened against the packing material to keep out the water. This packing is usually a thick oily cord with a square section. A healthy stuffing box may drip every few seconds while turning. Should more water appear at the shaft, carefully tighten down the packing nut until the dripping stops. If you tighten too much, you'll lock the shaft or cause overheating. There may be two adjusting nuts at 180 degrees to one another, or a single adjustment. You should know which arrangement you have and make sure you have a wrench that fits. You don't want to start this homework when the packing fails in the Gulf Stream.

If tightening down the gland does not succeed, back off the packing nut and stuff in a length of packing cord (it's in your spares kit, right?) equal to one circumference of the shaft. The leak probably won't deteriorate while you do this. Now replace the packing nut and tighten down. If that doesn't do the trick, start pumping!

Deep-Sea ("dripless") seal. In this other sealing system the seal is achieved by a stainless steel collar on the shaft interfacing with a carbon ring which closes off a tubular neoprene bellows clamped at its aft end to the stern tube. The carbon slips without significant friction on the spinning stainless collar and the inherent spring in the bellows keeps the two faces pressed together. Such seals are reported to be reliable and maintenance free. If you have one, inspect it and understand it (try moving the carbon ring away from the collar on the shaft and see what happens), so that if anything should go wrong you're familiar with the pieces.

Seacocks. These should be readily accessible on all through-hull openings with hoses. Make sure they are quality fittings of the ball-valve type with no mixed metals to encourage electrolytic failure. If they are seized, free them at the next haul-out.

Every seacock should have a tapered wooden plug at hand to drive in with a hammer in an emergency. These should be attached or mounted adjacent to the seacock, but if this is impractical, note where you have them stowed.

Cockpit Drains. You can't enlarge these without major surgery, but you can make sure the drain pipes are clear and not kinked or compressed by stowed gear.

Cockpit Lockers. Make sure lids can be secured in heavy weather. A locker full of water not only soaks its contents but reduces a yacht's stability, especially if it drains into the bilge.

Hatches. For coastal passagemaking, the main companionway should be set up just as it would be for offshore work; securable in the fully closed position, yet capable of being opened from on deck or down below. It must also be robust enough to resist a sizeable blast of seawater. The same applies for other hatches and opening portlights.

Bilge Pumps. All coastal yachts should have generous pump capacity. At least one high-capacity power-driven or electric pump is a must. These will keep going after you become fatigued with manual efforts. An electric pump requires a high "swan-neck" discharge pipe with a siphon break as well as a non-return valve, since the pumps do not stop water

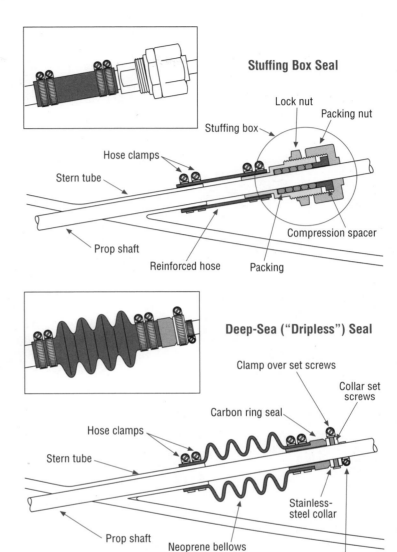

Stuffing Box Seal

Lock nut
Packing nut
Stuffing box
Hose clamps
Stern tube
Compression spacer
Prop shaft
Reinforced hose
Packing

Deep-Sea ("Dripless") Seal

Clamp over set screws
Collar set screws
Carbon ring seal
Hose clamps
Stern tube
Stainless-steel collar
Prop shaft
Neoprene bellows
Safety clamp around shaft

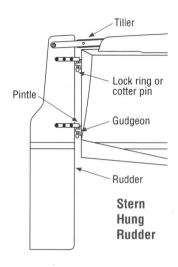

Tiller

Pintle

Lock ring or cotter pin

Gudgeon

Rudder

Stern Hung Rudder

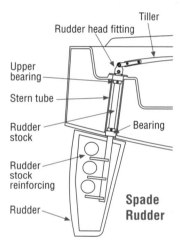

Tiller

Rudder head fitting

Upper bearing

Stern tube

Rudder stock

Bearing

Rudder stock reinforcing

Rudder

Spade Rudder

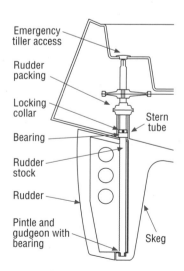

Emergency tiller access

Rudder packing

Locking collar

Bearing

Rudder stock

Rudder

Pintle and gudgeon with bearing

Stern tube

Skeg

Skeg Hung Rudder

running back though their discharge pipes, and seacocks are not recommended in order to ensure the pipes are always operable. This applies to hand pump discharge pipes as well.

In addition to power pumps, two large hand pumps are recommended, one activated from on deck and the other from below. The pump mechanisms should be easy to access, their suction pipes should have strainers (strum boxes) to filter bilge debris, and their handles should be stowed for fast access. Everyone on board should know where these handles are stowed.

One final thought: carry at least two stout rubber buckets, plus a spare, with lanyards attached. Not only do they double as fire extinguishers, deckwashers and emergency heads, they may also save your life if the pumps clog or fail.

Sails. Sails and their use at sea are a major topic and have the next chapter to themselves.

Engines. U.S. Coast Guard and independent rescue services pick up more sailors whose auxiliary engines have quit than from grounding or sinking combined. Given regular service, clean fuel, a modest spares kit and a skipper who has taken a modest effort to learn a bit about how diesel or gasoline engines work, a yacht auxiliary is most unlikely to refuse to start, quit while running, or achieve a state of dysfunction beyond expeditious repair. No engine upgrade need be necessary for passagemaking, just a seamanlike attitude toward what is generally a fine piece of equipment.

Rudders. There is no ideal rudder for coastal passagemaking. spades, skeg- and stern-hung rudders are all out there doing their jobs reliably, day after day. So long as the boat they are steering does not have a history of rudder trouble, and their owners have ensured that all attachments, bearings, pintles and gudgeons are in good order, they should continue to do so.

Once again, success is a matter of preparation. It is unusual for a coastal cruising yacht to lose her rudder, but if you have any doubts about yours, ask a surveyor to take a look. Your job is to carefully check the pintles (particularly the bottom one of a skeg-hung rudder) and gudgeons, to make sure the bearings and gland of a spade rudder are in first-class order with minimal play, and to have a plan if rudder failure should occur.

Steering. Any boat with wheel steering needs to carry an emergency tiller in case steering cables break or the hydraulics spring a leak. If you have a direct-drive mechanical gear, such as a rack-and-pinion or worm, you'll be less likely to suffer this particular disappointment. In any case, inspect your system to be sure of what you've got.

Don't leave your emergency tiller lying around under the double bunk until its moment of glory. Try it out on an average sailing day. You just might find it doesn't fit properly, or is difficult to use. There has been at least one case of an emergency tiller that could only be operated from the aft cabin shower compartment, demanding crew members on deck and below to keep watch and convey helm orders.

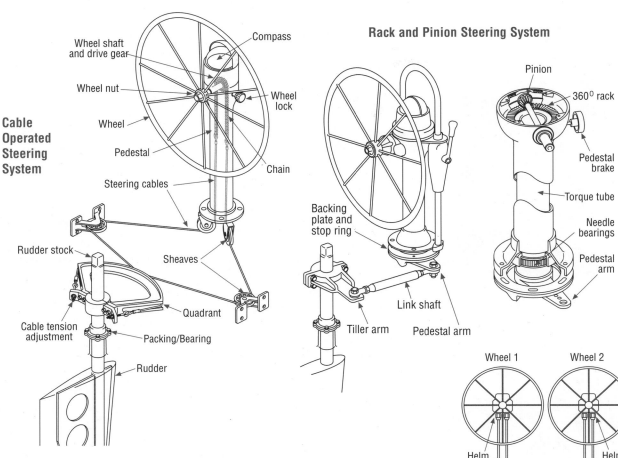

Rack and Pinion Steering System

Cable Operated Steering System

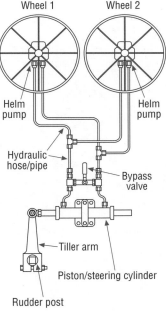

Hydraulic "Dual Station" Steering System

Crew Welfare. There will be much more on this subject in Chapter 4, but in the meantime, here are one or two details that can be attended to when preparing a boat for coastal passagemaking.

Bunks. On any passage, fatigue is the enemy. It is essential you have sufficient sea berths so that the entire watch below can relax properly while the boat is under sail. If your yacht has no serious sea berths with solid boards, no pilot berth or tunnel quarter berth, perhaps one of your settees located amidships or further aft will serve adequately with the addition of a strong canvas leecloth. While at sea, the use of a settee can be rotated by two people who are on different watches ("hot-bunking") for a night or two. But the leecloth must be strong, easily adjustable and easy to secure. Nothing is worse than wrestling with a seized slip-knot when you're tired and a little seasick.

Galley. Most galleys feature a gimbaled stove that has been installed by a professional (see Chapter 9). At sea, the system is liable to be tested more

A well-designed sea berth is vital to crew effectiveness. Without proper rest, efficiency and safety rapidly deteriorate.

A crash bar mounted between the cook and the stove prevents a lurching cook from launching a hot meal before intended.

Batteries should be readily accessible for inspection and secured from moving in all directions.

strenuously than in sheltered water so, if it burns propane, check all pipe unions for leaks with a strong soapy water solution when the boat is bouncing about. Apply the suds with a paint brush and watch for bubbling. If there is even a hint of a leak, tighten the joint. If this doesn't work, call an expert. Also check that the stove won't come free if the boat takes a knockdown or capsizes.

Race boats generally have a stout crash bar rigidly mounted between the cook and the stove. This is the sort of upgrade that makes sense for passagemaking. While you're at it, rig a stout "bum-strap" to lean back into when the galley is to windward, then make a thorough inspection of your stove's fiddle rail and pan clamps. If they look like something from a Toytown movie (many do), beef them up now before the soup makes a dive for your shirt on a rough night.

On deck. Bimini tops are a pleasant luxury at anchor, but at sea a much more vital piece of gear is an effective spray dodger. In more than 15 knots of wind from forward of the beam, you are likely to experience spray or more concentrated forms of moving water on deck. Nothing demoralizes crew quite as fast as being wet and cold. Tuck yourself in behind a good dodger, click on the autopilot or engage the windvane and life is much better.

An effective spray dodger is a vital piece of gear offshore.

Securing gear. Before setting out on passage, make sure that the heavy items down below can't take flight. The obvious culprits are batteries and stoves, but there are many other gremlins lurking if they have not been made fast. Spend a day rigging lashings, strongbacks, leecloths on forward bunks (great for stowage but only a last resort for sleeping at sea), tightening nuts. Devise a means of keeping the ballast in the bilge and the lead crystal decanter in its locker. It can save the Coast Guard a call and you a spoiled passage.

Seasonality. One final consideration when preparing for a coastal passage is that sailing conditions can vary greatly with location and season. Sailing the coast of Alaska or Newfoundland in early fall can be a very different kettle of fish than the West Coast of Florida or Baja in mid-summer. In the balmy latitudes you might feel safe making a passage in a boat you would rather leave at the dock up north. Remember that every seaman, however well informed and cautious, is always playing the odds to some extent. If we were all granted a thousand years of life and sailed every day, each of us would sooner or later come face-to-face with adversity, no matter how skilled and careful. So if you take something of a liberty with a boat you know to be less than ideal, be especially aware of your weather. And don't be tempted to make an optimist's dash. If you are justly confident in your boat on the other hand, don't be timid. Out at sea, you'll probably have a great time. If you don't, you'll learn something from the best teacher of all — yourself.

Coastal Rigging and Sails

There is no "best" rig for coastal passagemaking. A schooner might prove superior on a passage with winds on the beam, while a sloop will excel sailing to windward. A ketch is everybody's winner when it blows hard and you are short-handed, while a cutter represents a balanced compromise. The yawl's protagonists will tell you it represents the best of all worlds.

Whatever form your sail plan takes, your number one priority is that the rig and its components deliver reliable power. Preventive maintenance is the key.

Onshore Maintenance. The most important maintenance you can perform on a passage occurs before you depart. Careful, thorough preparation ashore will greatly reduce the demand for solving skills at sea.

Standing rigging. Keel-stepped masts with fore and aft lower shrouds and upper shrouds (cap shrouds) led to the masthead with intermediates are the strongest cruising rigs and have been known to lose a single rig component without the mast falling over the side. In contrast, a deck-stepped mast relies entirely on standing rigging to keep it upright, so the failure of a single wire can spell disaster, particularly if the configuration of the shrouds has departed significantly from the ideal described above.

Your best "ounce of prevention" is regular maintenance. While stainless steel rigging is remarkably strong and durable, over time it is nonetheless susceptible to failure. If your standing rig is seven or more years old, have every inch inspected by a professional rigger who understands your passagemaking plans. Prior to departure, perform your own inspection.

Cotter (or "split") pins. Make sure all cotter pins securing clevis pins and turnbuckles are properly spread, then taped or given a dab of silicone to prevent chafe. Spreading a cotter pin does not require bending it inside out. It is enough to open the ends so that it cannot slip back through the hole. This technique allows for faster extraction (using pliers) in an emergency or if the mast is removed from the boat. In an ideal world, cotters protrude no more than half a clevis diameter, and all cut ends are filed smoothly to a half-round form.

Toggles. Many standing rig failures result from restricted movement at the ends of shrouds and stays. Most terminals allow only two-dimensional motion. Adding toggles that allow full motion in all directions to the lower ends of all stays and shrouds does a lot to reduce long-term stress fatigue. Whenever practical, toggles should also be fitted to the upper ends of headstays and forestays to allow for the diagonal loading of the headsail.

Shackles. If your standing rigging has shackles, they must be wrenched up tight, then seized with wire to prevent them vibrating loose. If you forget to do this, you'll spend your first gale praying nothing shakes loose. The finest seizing wire is monel, but stainless steel is a readily obtainable substitute.

Periodic inspection. At least once a season, have someone pull you

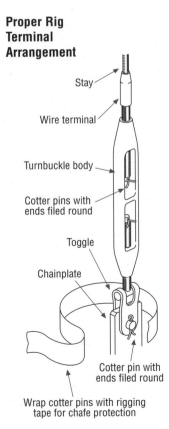

**Proper Rig
Terminal
Arrangement**

Stay

Wire terminal

Turnbuckle body

Cotter pins with
ends filed round

Toggle

Chainplate

Cotter pin with
ends filed round

Wrap cotter pins with rigging
tape for chafe protection

Typical Self-tailing Winch Assembly

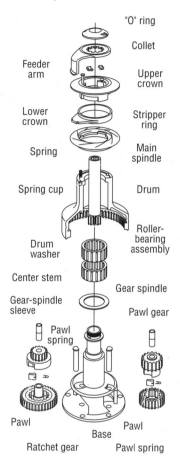

- "O" ring
- Collet
- Feeder arm
- Upper crown
- Lower crown
- Stripper ring
- Spring
- Main spindle
- Spring cup
- Drum
- Roller-bearing assembly
- Drum washer
- Center stem
- Gear spindle
- Gear-spindle sleeve
- Pawl gear
- Pawl spring
- Pawl
- Pawl
- Base
- Ratchet gear
- Pawl spring

The inner forestay on this double headsail rig is not equipped with roller furling so that a smaller storm jib can be hanked onto the stay in severe weather (see page 107).

aloft so you can scrutinize your rig. Check each terminal for signs of stranding wire, cracks in swaged terminals or enlarged tang holes, and the condition of cotters and attachments. Deal with chafe and generally try to second-guess any potential problems. At sea, inspect the rig aloft with your binoculars each day.

Running rigging. Sheaves should run freely. A regular drop of oil on those with no bearings helps reduce friction. The biggest cause of owners feeling their boats are under-winched is friction.

Winches. There shouldn't be a winch on board that at least one person on board can't strip. A regular checkup will almost invariably reveal an internal gear clogged up with grease, or a pawl not functioning. A broken pawl spring can lead to a broken wrist when the winch handle spins out of control, so pre-empt it at the dock.

Roller furling. Roller furling genoa gear is practically universal in modern cruising. Many coastal boats rely on roller furling exclusively, often with a choice of only two headsails to set from them. You simply cannot afford to have this gear go down, and its reliability depends largely on a few seals that keep seawater away from greased bearings. These require diligent maintenance. If you haven't the time or the inclination, pay a professional to inspect your genoa furling gear regularly. Stripping your furling gear at sea may compromise your mast, and even if it doesn't, anyone who recalls lying on a foredeck half under water while the valued assistant drops the crucial wrench over the side knows the job is not fun.

Labor-Saving Devices. Today, all manner of devices are available to make sailing easier. Many are useful, and some make cruising possible for older sailors who might otherwise be struggling to handle the canvas. Keep in mind, however, that none of this gear was available until very recently and many sailors have made many very impressive voyages without it. There are still those who feel that the occasional bout with a difficult mainsail is part of proper seafaring, so don't discount the idea of setting out with nothing but a good suit of sails and a sturdy mast to hang them from. There will certainly be less that can go wrong.

Roller furling headsails are desirable in many ways, but they do represent a compromise of performance in favor of convenience. On a passage, with the ongoing possibility of foul weather, a 150% roller genoa alone will not be up to the job. Reefed down to working jib size it will unlikely be able to drive the boat to windward. Reefed to storm jib size, it may prove totally useless. The minimum requirement is for two different-sized jibs to be used with the roller furling system. The smaller should be flat cut, high-clewed and built specifically to set decently when furled down to a small size. Bend it on before setting out if you have the slightest doubt about the bigger jib. Changing down at sea will involve unrolling the currently deployed sail completely in order to drop it, which may be precisely what you do not want in a building wind. In any case, a well-shaped smaller sail of high aspect ratio will drive a boat faster than a big, flabby one that produces more drag and less lift. It is also far easier to handle when tacking.

The over-riding benefit of a good roller furling headsail is that within its limits you can always present the desired sail area to the wind. Any cruiser without a roller furling system is often obliged to sail with too much or too little jib.

A permanently rigged mainsail cover (such as the StackPack®) makes for easy stowing. It also supplies instant sail protection whenever you anchor. There are critics who say that it is unseamanlike to cover a sail while anchored in case it is wanted in a hurry, but this system allows the main to be hoisted quickly. These covers create some additional windage and may not function ideally if the sail must be lowered at an angle other than head-to-wind.

Lazy jacks offer an economical solution to mainsail stowing. A well designed arrangement can be slacked while sailing to prevent chafe or hauled forward altogether so as not to interfere with a sail cover. Like the permanent mainsail cover, lazy jacks can ease the requirement to tie in reef points, but unlike their more expensive cousin, their windage is negligible. Two people can rig lazy jacks in half a day for under a hundred dollars.

A permanently rigged mainsail cover makes for easy stowing.

Doyle Sailmakers photo

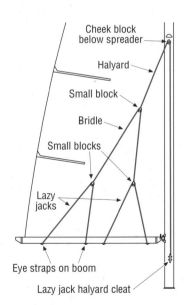

Through-sail controlling lines thread a series of light lines through eyelets in the body of mainsail from the toppinglift down to the boom. When the sail is lowered, it stacks up neatly on the boom. This system can chafe over time, although the amount is usually not significant to coastal passagemakers.

Fully battened mainsails improve sail shape, reduce noise (luffing) and extend sail life. They work well with all the above systems, but can cause problems with lazy jacks and on-boom covers when the mainsail is dropped or hoisted while not head-to-wind. Fully battened mains are heavier and more expensive than traditional mains, and the luff cars required to handle batten compression are another category of potential breakdowns, although reliability has improved much in recent years.

In-mast and in-boom mainsail furling systems save work, if they do not malfunction. Because most in-mast furling mainsails cannot carry battens, they are usually made with hollow leeches (no roach) that reduce sail area and performance (vertical batten mainsails designed for in-mast furling systems are available). The in-mast arrangement also increases weight aloft which increases heeling moment and can compromise ultimate stability (see Chapter 14). If you set out with such a system, you should be satisfied that it will not fail, or that if it does, it would fail with the sail furled or furling, not full or hoisting.

Sails, Rigs and Their Use on Passages. It is an all-too-common sight to see a sailing yacht motoring under mainsail alone in a light breeze when, given a more flexible sail wardrobe, she could be making a reasonable

Harken, Inc. photo

A fully battened main sets beautifully and works well with lazy jacks so long as you can let it feather, but it is harder to depower when maneuvering. Special batten-end hardware (shown) is also required at the mast.

Cheek block below spreader

Halyard

Small block

Bridle

Small blocks

Lazy jacks

Eye straps on boom

Lazy jack halyard cleat

Lazy jacks gather up the sail when needed but can be slacked off and hauled forward when not needed.

speed under sail alone.

On a typical "day-trip" one is sometimes more ambitious for distance than light conditions will allow under sail, and crews are often quick to reach for the ignition switch. On coastal passages, there may not be such a time constraint. If sailors can manage to forget the motorboat philosophy that requires reeling off six or seven knots every hour, the whole process becomes mysteriously more relaxing.

Light-weather specialty headsails are generally larger than standard genoas, made of lightweight material, and are set flying rather than from a stay. An asymmetric cruising spinnaker would be typical. Such sails can be something of a handful if left up too long, so ask your sailmaker to build in a retractable sleeve to encase the sail when hoisting or lowering. The sail is usually hoisted in its sock. Once hoisted, the sleeve is pulled up to the top of the sail, freeing it to open and fly. Before lowering, the sheet is eased and the sleeve is pulled downward, gathering and encasing the sail.

If you are "sleeveless," always remember that the best way to defuse a downwind sail of any sort is to head off to a dead run and lower it behind the mainsail while the main is blanketing it from the wind.

Without a clean bottom, however, all attempts to make the boat move in light winds will be in vain. A slippery bottom is therefore a high priority. If you are not lucky enough to operate in an area with enough tide to dry out alongside a wall, it only costs a few dollars to hang in the slings for half an hour and spray her off. Do it before you leave. Slime alone can cost you a knot of boatspeed, and once the weed takes hold you can lose two or more. While you're scrubbing, make sure your prop is spotless and your through-hulls and shaft zincs are in good condition.

Motorsailing is the light-weather alternative to patience and the right sail. Some heavier boats that do not move easily though the water may find it is the only real alternative to a very slow trip. Try to keep all your sails up and drawing while motoring. It's more comfortable and you'll

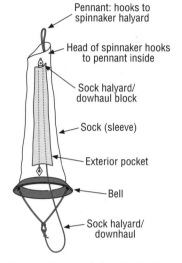

Pennant: hooks to spinnaker halyard

Head of spinnaker hooks to pennant inside

Sock halyard/dowhaul block

Sock (sleeve)

Exterior pocket

Bell

Sock halyard/downhaul

A spinnaker sock (or Snuffer) makes raising and dousing a spinnaker easier and safer, particularly for shorthanded crew.

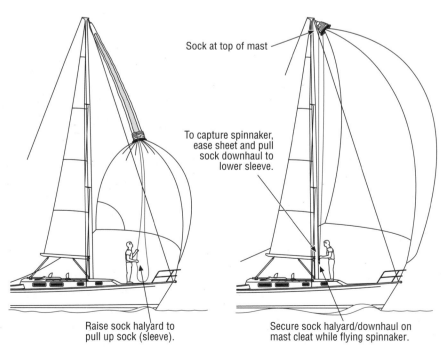

Spinnaker hayard attached to sock pennant.

Spinnaker sock

Sock halyard/downhaul

Spinnaker clew and tack pre-sheeted

Raise sock halyard to pull up sock (sleeve).

Sock at top of mast

To capture spinnaker, ease sheet and pull sock downhaul to lower sleeve.

Secure sock halyard/downhaul on mast cleat while flying spinnaker.

save fuel. When you power up, the apparent wind often swings so far forward that the headsail backs, in which case you must either furl it, alter course slightly to keep it full or drop it. The latter tactic is also advised for the mainsail when the genoa is already doused and the wind is so far ahead that the main is flogging as you power on. (See Chapter 19 for the philosophy of steering comfortably across an ocean.)

Shortening Sail. The basics of shortening sail to suit rising winds by changing headsails and reefing the main (slab reefing or single line reefing) are dealt with in US SAILING's book, *Bareboat Cruising.* Whether your boat should be rigged for slab reefing or single line reefing depends on factors such as performance versus convenience, and agility of the crew. The advantage of the single line reefing system is that it can be executed from the cockpit, but it cannot achieve the well shaped sail of slab reefing. The disadvantage of slab reefing is that someone has to go forward to hook the luff cringle to the boom. On a passage, there are several additional tricks of the trade that may prove helpful.

When reefing a mainsail, it is preferable to de-power the main by bringing the wind forward of the beam, easing the sheet until the sail flaps, and letting off the vang (this is important). While reefing, the headsail is trimmed for a close reach, but the boat is steered on a close-hauled course. The sail will luff slightly and slow the boat with only a marginal loss of control. Bringing her head to wind will result in chaos.

There will be times, however, when bringing the wind forward of the beam proves inconvenient. This happens when you have left too much sail set for too long in a rising wind and want to avoid the drama resulting from the increased apparent wind as you head up to reef. If you have powerful winches and your spreaders are not swept too far aft, some yachts can be reefed by vanging the boom hard down, easing the halyard and dragging the luff down to the next reef. The clew cringle can then be winched out to complete the reef. This unorthodox method won't work with a fully battened main because of the

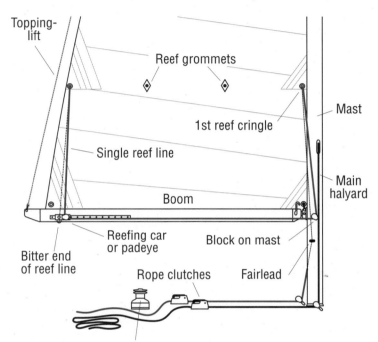

Single-line Reefing

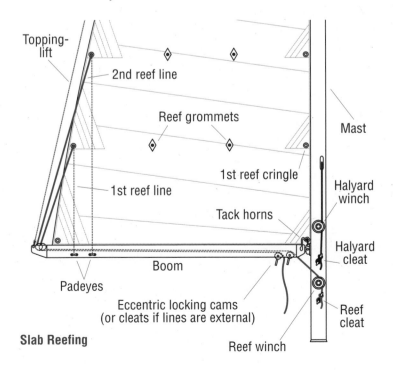

Slab Reefing

increased friction, but it has its place. For example, if you are running "poled out" (see illustration) you may want to reef the main without disturbing the genoa. Afterward, you may find that you are unable to reach the outer reef points to tie in the loose sail. Leaving them untied won't matter if you have a permanent mainsail cover or lazy jacks. If you have neither, you'll probably survive without tying the points at all.

Such lateral thinking horrifies some "by-the-book" sailors, but once you enter the lively world of wind and wave, you tend to discard hard and fast rules. The good seaman assesses the boat's needs for a given situation and decides the best way of servicing them. If this means adapting workable methods for your boat, then do it! In hard going, a headsail will often furl more easily from within the wind shadow of the main. If you are dropping a genoa to change it, leave the sheet trimmed until the sail is well down, and remember you can hoist or drop a headsail on any point of sail at all. Keeping the sheet trimmed will help the sail to slide down sweetly inside the lifelines. Alternatively, it may pay to tack and keep the sheet on the new weather winch so that the sail comes aback. If you now release the halyard and drag the sail down, it will have nowhere to go but onto the foredeck.

These techniques may not work if you have a tight headfoil, in which case flogging the sail may prove the only answer.

In general, try to get into the way of thinking creatively about each maneuver rather than sticking slavishly to one method. The essence of seamanship is flexibility. Have the confidence to try new methods and the self-awareness to accept your error if they do not work. Only this way, will you really develop your skills.

Sailing Downwind

The mainsail. Running square before the wind, the main should be strongly vanged to keep the boom down. This reduces chafe against the shrouds and spreaders which is otherwise inevitable unless you oversheet hopelessly. On a long run, particularly in an awkward sea, a boom preventer should also be rigged. This is simply a line secured to the boom end and led forward to a turning block on the foredeck. From here, it comes back to the cockpit where it is brought to a spare winch and cleated tight. If there is no winch, ease the mainsheet off, harden the preventer up as much as you can by hand, cleat the preventer, then trim the mainsheet back against it. Be sure to cleat the preventer so that it can be released under heavy load.

A boom with a preventer should be held more or less rigid. This not only saves you from the effects of an accidental jibe, it makes you far less likely to jibe in the first place. A preventer is also extremely useful in light airs to stop the boom from slapping and banging

Poling out the headsail and using a preventer on the boom will bring peace of mind as well as making life easier in the long run.

Mainsail

Preventer

Boom vang

Mainsheet

Pole toppinglift

Genoa

Foreguy

Whisker pole

Weather sheet

Lazy sheet

After guy (recommended for extended runs or rolling seas)

about with each roll of the boat.

The headsail. On a run, it pays to sheet the genoa out to the windward side using the technique known as "wing-and-wing" or "goosewinging." In any kind of sea, however, a yacht will roll and an unsupported wing-and-wing genoa will collapse every few seconds. To compensate, you'll need to boom out the genoa to weather with a whisker or spinnaker pole.

To achieve this safely, do not try to poke the pole into the clew of the sail, then scramble it onto the mast fitting. This is the sure route to injury, falling overboard, or at least a shouting match with the denizens of the cockpit. Do it this way instead, step by step:

On an extended run or in rolling seas, the pole can be made more

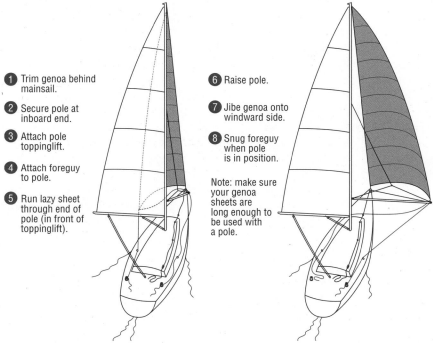

1. Trim genoa behind mainsail.
2. Secure pole at inboard end.
3. Attach pole toppinglift.
4. Attach foreguy to pole.
5. Run lazy sheet through end of pole (in front of toppinglift).
6. Raise pole.
7. Jibe genoa onto windward side.
8. Snug foreguy when pole is in position.

Note: make sure your genoa sheets are long enough to be used with a pole.

stable by rigging it with an after guy. The after guy should be attached to the pole before raising it, and once the pole is up it should be "squared" (pulled aft) into position using the after guy before jibing the sail onto it.

With a furling headsail, the answer to getting rid of the pole is simply to roll the sail away and remove the spar from mast, sheet and foreguy. To de-rig the pole safely with a fixed sail, either jibe the main to shelter the whole assembly from the wind, or trim the headsail and pole back aft as much as possible (don't forget to ease the foreguy), then head the boat up until the wind fills on the other side of the sail and ease the windward sheet, as you take up on the leeward one so that the sail slides across to the lee side between the forestay and mast. If you merely let go the windward sheet, and heave in on the lazy one, the sail will get mixed up with the forestay.

If your sail is hanked onto the forestay, in extreme conditions you can release the halyard and drop the sail, hauling down the luff with the clew still sheeted out. Only when enough of the sail is down for its proximity to the water to become a problem should you ease the sheet and pull the sail inboard.

Sailing "Wing-and-Wing" with Genoa "Poled Out"

Step 1

Run the boat downwind, trimming the genoa behind the main or rolling it away. This makes the foredeck a safe environment.

Step 2

Secure the pole's inboard end to the mast.

Step 3

Attach the pole toppinglift (if fitted) inboard of the lazy weather jib sheet, which must pass over the pole.

Step 4

Attach the foreguy (downhaul) to the end of the pole or the under-pole wire strop which may be there for this purpose.

Step 5

Lead the bight (the middle part) of the lazy sheet through the pole end.

Step 6

Raise the pole on its toppinglift, making sure its outboard end is to weather of the forestay. Leave the foreguy slack. Now come aft, leaving nobody on the foredeck. The pole may wobble about a little, but this won't last long.

Step 7

Next, ease the lee sheet and take up on the windward one, jibing the headsail to windward. If the sail was furled, unroll it progressively onto the pole until you have exposed the desired area.

Step 8

Once the pole is in position with the genoa winged out to weather, snug the foreguy and cleat it.

Coastal Passage Planning

Sailors who plan their passages thoroughly generally have an easy time of it at sea. Those who don't, appear consistently unlucky with the weather and are often surprised to arrive at a major tidal gate at the peak of a foul current. They tend to run out of fuel at critical times and seem to be unlucky in their choice of shipmates. Foreign harbors find them unprepared for the official necessities of entry, they run out of AA batteries for their GPS sets and are obliged to ration toilet paper.

While the final responsibility for a good plan rests with the skipper, he or she is best advised to include the whole crew in at least the domestic side of the process. More minds are less likely to overlook an issue, and an involved crew is well on the way to being a happy one.

The most telling items in an overall plan are strategy regarding weather, and navigational tactics. The latter subject is considered in US SAILING's *Coastal Navigation* book, but since one or two of the items are so key to subjects covered here, they will be reiterated.

A successful passage plan doesn't have to take all night to prepare. Indeed, if the trip is short and you are familiar with the waters, it may be merely a question of waiting for the green light from the weatherman, checking the tide tables for the right time to leave, topping off the fuel tanks, loading drinks and sandwiches, then shoving off. On the other hand, a longer voyage of many stages — from San Diego to the Columbia River, or from Charleston, SC to New York, for instance — could take a day to consider.

Don't rush your planning. After a few years it becomes second nature, but it's always preferable to be over-prepared than be caught in one of the many traps waiting for those who simply let go their docklines and hope for the best. Using a checklist is a great help, and on a longer passage, paying attention to such things as starting early in the day rather than late to allow people to become accustomed to on board motion before nightfall will make a difference.

On the navigation side, reviewing your charts and distances is the first and important step, not just for working up a route, but because they answer the critical questions, "How far is it?," "How long is it likely to take?" These data are the base on which all plans are built.

Next, study coast pilot books, alternative destinations and harbors of refuge. Identify your waypoints and check tidal information, noting any relevant tide considerations or potential danger points. Piloting plans must be developed thoroughly, but running through every thought is the most important factor of all — the weather.

Weather. **Climate, clothing and bedding.** The U.S. is a vast country with widely diverse climates with an equally wide range of predictability. At different times of the year, passagemakers must be aware not only of short term weather predictions, but also a broad overview of conditions in their locality. If you are travelling to an unfamiliar region, make sure you know what to expect. Don't take "ocean grade" foul-weather gear for a coastal trip down the west coast of Florida in springtime, but make sure you pack your fleece if you're

If you plan right, you'll enjoy the full benefit of this strong current. Four hours later, and an adverse current could slow you to two knots over the bottom.

bound for San Francisco in the surprisingly cool months of summer. In short, ship out with the right gear after considering likely air and sea temperatures. Think hard about it. Because of stowage limitations, experienced sailors travel light.

Another climate-oriented question is that of bedding. A sleeping bag suitable for high-altitude mountain climbers will be unbearably hot on a mid-latitude passage in summer. For an early season trip to Alaska, however, you'll be the envy of your shipmates.

Comforters are perfect for most cruising, so long as their fill is synthetic. A mid-weight comforter can be as warm as you want it to be, depending on how far you pull it over you. It stays put and you don't have to struggle into it. You just hit the bunk and drag it on top. The flip side is that comforters don't pack small and require a bed sheet.

Typically, the best compromise for most coastal passages is a cheap, "zip-all-round" sleeping bag containing 38 oz. (approx.) insulation. Much of the time you'll use it opened up like a comforter, adjusting your sleep clothing to suit the temperature. If it's cold, you can zip it up and crawl in easily because it's a sloppy fit. If you're still chilly, wear a sweater in bed.

Forecasting. Any coastal passage of up to 48 hours will be weather forecast dependent. Fortunately, when you're planning a coastal passage you are generally in a position to augment any receiving information with shoreside weather reports. Make sure you have the right radio equipment for receiving regular and comprehensive forecasts at sea, and keep in mind that withstanding whatever weather comes along is not a necessary part of your brief on a coastal passage. Only by sensible preparation and continuous monitoring can you enjoy reasonable conditions and be in a position to alter course towards a safe haven when a filthy day promises to turn worse (see Chapter 5 for more details).

Fuel. Fuel supply is a critical consideration for a powerboat, but it is also important for the sailor. Powerboaters usually factor a 33% safety margin beyond probable fuel consumption.

Ideally, a sailboat will carry enough fuel to make the entire passage so that she can keep moving if the wind lets her down. Depending on how much sailing is done, sufficient fuel should be carried to reach a harbor of refuge from the furthest-out point her planned route will take her — plus 33%. She can then look after herself without enlisting emergency services in case of a problem aloft or even a dismasting.

Real and imagined fuel capacities. While boat manufacturers often encourage buyers to order large fuel tanks, it is up to the skipper to decide how much of the fuel put into them will actually be available to the engine at sea. The ideal shape for a tank is deep and narrow, so that only a minimum will be left when the tank "runs dry." Many modern fuel tanks depart radically from this, however, with flat, shallow tanks being

Nobody looks for this kind of weather. Fortunately, with sensible use of all available forecasting services, it need only rarely happen on coastal passages.

Passage Planning Items

- ☐ Review relevant charts and any updates.
- ☐ Review relevant updates to Coast Pilot and/or cruising guides.
- ☐ Determine distances and estimated times.
- ☐ Determine viable alternatives and ports of refuge.
- ☐ Identify suitable waypoints and double check their latitude and longitude.
- ☐ Check short term weather forecast and developing trends.
- ☐ Determine tides and currents and use them to your advantage.
- ☐ Identify any tidal height considerations relevant to harbor entrances and exits.
- ☐ Identify dangers and obstacles.
- ☐ Note approximate basic courses.
- ☐ Prepare appropriate foods.

all-too prevalent. It is necessary for the draw-off point inside the tank to be a short way up from the bottom to allow sludge and water to collect beneath it. If a tank is only a foot deep, a measurable proportion of its contents will therefore be inaccessible. Such a tank is also more likely to suck air well before it has reached its lowest point of delivery, which will be unhelpful if the engine is a diesel. Even if a tank is the right shape to

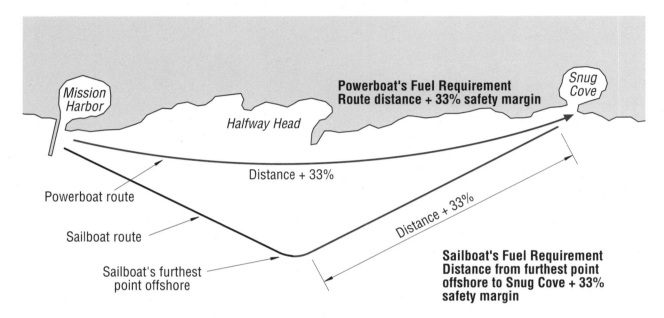

Powerboat's Fuel Requirement
Route distance + 33% safety margin

Mission Harbor

Snug Cove

Halfway Head

Distance + 33%

Powerboat route

Distance + 33%

Sailboat route

Sailboat's furthest point offshore

Sailboat's Fuel Requirement
Distance from furthest point offshore to Snug Cove + 33% safety margin

Powerboats require enough fuel for a full passage plus a 33% safety margin for contingency. Sailboats must be able to make it to the nearest safe harbor under power should their rig be lost. If sailing off the coast, estimate the amount of fuel needed from the furthest point offshore to the closest harbor and add a 33% safety margin.

give full value for your fill, you still won't want to run it dry, as the last few hours can become increasingly nerve-wracking as you motor along waiting for the engine note to falter.

At some point prior to your passage, it's a good idea to run the tank as dry as the engine can make it, then refill it and measure its real capacity. If you can't do this, be conservative and always leave an ample safety margin.

Water and Ice. It goes without saying that a guaranteed supply of drinking water is paramount on any passage. Standards for offshore passages are described in Chapter 16, but on passages less than 30 miles from shore, running out of water will be more of an inconvenience than a catastrophe. Nevertheless, make sure your tanks are clean and their capacity is more than adequate. Then bring one or two gallon bottles of drinking water aboard as a standby in case tanks leak or the contents become contaminated. It makes a better cup of tea than most tank water, and certainly tastes better in your drinks at the end of the trip.

As for ice, you know your own requirements best, but remember if you initially stock the ice box with pre-frozen food, the ice will retain more of its cooling capacity for items that come aboard later at ambient summer temperature.

Medical Requirements. Before your passage, ask all crew members whether they have any specific medical conditions or unique requirements. Ask about serious allergies or conditions (including asthma, shortsightedness, pregnancy, and chronic problems such as a weak back). Check whether anyone requires regular medication for ongoing conditions such as diabetes or a heart problem. The administration of specific medications should be understood by someone other than the person taking it. Crew members who are taking medication are responsible for bringing a sufficient supply with them, with enough extra to last if the passage is delayed. Because some people might be hesitant to reveal certain medical conditions, a skipper may request that crew members provide a brief medical history in a sealed envelope which is either held by the skipper or kept in the crew's seabag. The envelope is only opened if the person becomes incapacitated, and can provide valuable information that a medical attendant (on board or via radio) may need in order to diagnose and stabilize the victim. People should bring along any personal favorite remedies for seasickness, headaches, indigestion, etc. The ship's first aid box must be waterproof, readily accessible, and contain at least the items listed to the right.

Provisioning. The main issue of what food to take and how to prepare it will be dealt with in the next chapter. Before you depart on an overnight trip, however, it's well worth preparing the first night's main meal ahead of time. This will allow everyone to more easily acclimate to life on board without facing the task of preparing a meal. It can be a one-pot stew or other easy-to-eat, easy-to-clear special.

Preparing for Arrival. If your destination is in another country, make sure all hands have their passports and required visas with them. It is up to the skipper and crew to determine such requirements, but if in doubt, call at the consulate concerned and inquire about protocol.

Carry originals of your ship's registration papers and personal documents. Some foreign authorities will not accept photocopies. It is also sensible for owners to carry their boat's bill of sale and purchase receipt to prove property ownership. Many harbors won't let you enter if you aren't insured and you may be asked to prove it. In some countries the skipper may have to produce at least a limited radio operator's license.

Float Plans. A "float plan" is a description of your boat's identity, who is aboard and where you are going. It can be your lifeline. Leave one with a responsible person who is likely to be available if the emergency services call them. This is usually a family member or friend (*not* the Coast Guard) whose telephone number should also be on your EPIRB registration data. Leave a list of crewmembers, your itinerary, dates of departure, estimated time of arrival (ETA) and a means of contact. Make sure you call them as soon as you arrive safely!

The U.S. Coast Guard is experienced at dealing with float plans. If a sailboat is reported missing with an ETA based on 150 miles per day, they may keep the situation on hold until a more realistic time has elapsed. History indicates that for the average sailboat, 120 miles in 24 hours is realistic — even 100 miles or less if the engine fails in light weather or strong headwinds are encountered.

First Aid Items

- ☐ First aid book
- ☐ Seasickness remedies
- ☐ Sunblock
- ☐ Bandages
- ☐ Butterfly sutures
- ☐ Gauze
- ☐ Sterile cotton
- ☐ Sterile strips
- ☐ Tape
- ☐ Elastic bandage
- ☐ Analgesic (aspirin)
- ☐ Antiseptic
- ☐ Antacids
- ☐ Laxatives
- ☐ Anti-diarrhea drugs
- ☐ Anti-itch cream
- ☐ Finger splints
- ☐ Germicidal cleanser
- ☐ Bandage scissors
- ☐ Disposable razors
- ☐ Thermometer
- ☐ Eye/ear drops
- ☐ Resuscitube

NOTE: Some people recommend carrying two First Aid kits: one is for daily use and the other is a sealed trauma kit for emergency use.

Life Aboard a Coastal Passagemaker

A wise sailor once said that there are two things you can't fix at sea: a 6-foot hole in the bottom and a social problem. The first requires no explanation. As for the second, leadership and delegation are the most important keys nailing down the lid before the niggling begins. Leadership is a quality you don't have to be born with. Leaders who develop a limited native ability through careful thought and preparation are often more effective than those who rely on natural talent, real or imagined. Showing confidence in the person designated for a task is crucial to crew self-esteem.

Whether the ship's company is a couple or a full team of diehards, their welfare and happiness is central to the success of any significant passage. It may be possible for a group who truly dislikes one another to move a boat from one port to the next, but the essence of recreational seafaring is enjoyment and reward. Furthermore, friction among crew is likely to lead to bad decisions. This chapter is dedicated to keeping the human element cheerful and safe in an environment where everyone is sharing the same small space.

Competence and Compatibility. It would be wonderful if all sailors were fully educated by book and by experience to fulfill their on board duties to perfection. Unless people have been sailing together for years, this is rarely the case. In any crew, competence is obviously desirable but should not be considered axiomatic. An inexperienced but enthusiastic crew member is often preferable to someone with psychological "baggage," who repeatedly makes a point of how capable he or she is, or constantly questions your decisions.

Listen to your inner voice when considering someone for a passage. If you have even a subliminal nagging doubt, leave the candidate behind. One day out, your gut feeling will usually have proved itself right.

Motivation and Expectation. Given normal, reasonable standards of behavior, the big secret of crew harmony is that their motivations, expectations and desires are in tune. Suppose a skipper goes to sea regardless of the weather to stay on schedule. His teenage son is dreading the seasickness he knows he will suffer, wishing they would wait until tomorrow when a better day is forecast. The boy's mother is caught between two camps, and all three will probably have a trip filled with resentment and recrimination.

Perhaps another skipper doesn't enjoy being at sea after dark and puts in to a noisy port halfway to the destination. His partner meanwhile has been looking forward to a quiet night under the moon with the wake stretching astern and the coast lights winking. There may be a grim silence at "happy hour," or maybe disappointment will be bottled up and add to a growing general incompatibility.

In both cases, if one party had listened to the other or preferences discussed ahead of time, a compromise might have been reached. Even if the skipper's own desires were not immediately met, at least he would have the tremendous satisfaction of running a happy ship.

The crew must bear their own part too. When the skipper is insisting on a tough course of action for the safety of the ship or the overall good of the cruise, then the crew should be ready to put aside immediate wishes for comfort and turn to their duties graciously. Crew harmony depends heavily on generosity of spirit, and making sure from the start that your requirements and expectations are sufficiently compatible to allow better human traits to prevail.

Communication. Another key to on board contentment in a close working environment is ongoing communication. Think before you open your mouth. Would it be better for everyone if something were left unsaid for the time being? Might there be a better way to approach a subject from a more positive direction?

One way to reduce potential strife is to have a ship's meeting each day where all hands come clean about things they like and things that "could be better." With a strong lead and a mutually-agreed positive approach, this session can go a long way toward keeping small differences from growing into big problems.

Good Shipmates. Constantly thinking of others is the watchword in a small vessel at sea. Here are one or two general reminders that may help:

Untidy personal gear is annoying for everyone, even your partner. Socks on the bedroom floor at home may be a minor irritant, but leaving them on the settee aboard makes a much stronger impression. On one sail training vessel, the bosun's rounds included a check for unstowed gear. Anything left out for more than one watch was confiscated and sold to swell the Missions to Seamen charity fund. It may sound draconian, but this was always the tidiest ship in the fleet.

A noisy watch on deck robs the watch below of their sleep, so lift your tether and its clattering hook off the deck as you move around. While you're at it, walk on the balls of your feet, not your heels, unless it's so rough nobody will notice. In light winds, heave in the headsail sheets by hand without rattling the winches, then carefully clap on your three turns and secure them silently. Talk in low voices.

Volunteering for unpopular jobs is a sure way to be asked to come again. Washing up, cleaning the heads and sweeping the cabin sole are all daily chores that someone has to perform. If there is no assignment list, don't hang back. People will notice. If you are a couple, don't assume that one person will deal with all the domestic duties. The less pleasant ones should be rotated around to help generate a sense of shared team spirit.

If no volunteers are forthcoming, the situation can be tactfully defused by posting a "belated" duty assignment. If really in doubt about your shipmates, organize the rotation of duties before you leave the dock. Then there can be no argument.

Standing Orders. In order to be relaxed and confident, people need to know what is expected of them. Crew members shouldn't be wondering whether they should be wearing their safety harnesses outside the cockpit. Questions of protocol gone unanswered can create uncertainty and embarrassment, not to mention their effect on safety. A statement

Roles on board are best decided on the basis of such issues as physical strength and levels of specific education, rather than pre-judged on some other rationale.

Less experienced crew members should be encouraged to improve skills and actively participate in the running of the ship.

from the skipper before leaving the dock would help to solve this problem — as well as others. Propane gas discipline, head seacocks, bare feet on deck…the list can be long. How you handle it is up to you. Some skippers post a standing orders checklist for all to read. Whatever your style of management, one of the skipper's essential duties is to let everyone in the crew understand how you want things done. Your crew will be happier and safer.

Couples with Unequal Skills. On board problems often arise when one member of a couple considers the boat to be "mine" rather than "ours." Less competent crew members must be actively encouraged to improve skills and participate fully in running the ship. A less experienced woman should learn to handle the helm so that the man can deal with the heavy ground tackle on the foredeck. A male may also be more comfortable jumping off onto a dock, so for a female crew to develop the ability to lay the vessel alongside is not only good for her confidence, it's also a sensible use of personnel.

In a man-woman boat ownership where the woman may feel alienated in the early stages, her partner who also takes an active interest in "humanizing the ship" can encourage participation and contribution. Wild flowers on a saloon table in harbor, well-chosen curtains, pictures on the bulkheads and other personal touches make an on board environment more inviting and more comfortable. Most men appreciate the results, but will rarely initiate it alone.

Other women may seek a more active role in the running of the ship, taking as much satisfaction from performing a neat headsail change or a smart piece of navigation as others do from turning up a great dinner in the middle of a storm.

By the same token, it is sad to be aboard a boat where a man with a culinary bent feels excluded from the galley by a female partner. Both men and women should be encouraged and respected for following their natural inclinations, whatever these may be. Most importantly, they need to feel like partners.

Children. The happiness of children aboard is not to be taken for granted. Suffice it to say that a thinking approach is required at all times and at all levels. Don't make a young child's first trip a heavy passage with the wind forward of the beam and long, cold nights. Transform a cruise into an adventure by planning short, achievable goals and lots of new harbors. Build them into longer passages gradually, encouraging them to become a deck-proficient part of the ship's team and nurturing a sense of seamanship. By twelve years old, a sensible child can be steering alone on deck in daylight and fair weather. Treated right, a child is just dying for that day when the parents say, "Want to take the first watch after supper tonight and give me a chance to rest?"

Seasickness. There is no simple answer to this sailor's curse, but several time-honored policies can help.

• Maintain morale actively by whatever means you can, even singing crazy songs helps take children's minds off their problems.

• If you intend to use a seasickness remedy with which you are unfamiliar, it makes sense to do your experimenting weeks before you try it at sea. You may not discover how well the remedy works, but it will certainly flag any adverse reaction or allergy. It is far better to discover a problem early and change your medicine than to discover this at sea. Bear in mind that many motion sickness drugs work better if you start them the day before you set out on passage.

• Seasickness sufferers will do almost anything to avoid going below, yet this is often the best place for them. Exposure to wet and cold will exacerbate seasickness by adding to a state of fatigue. A well-planned move from the cockpit to a bunk is the answer. No hanging about to undress. Tell them to lie down as quickly and as far aft as possible, then pull the comforter over their head until it's watch time again. Their oilskins might moisten the bedding, but this is a small price to pay for keeping lunch where it is doing most good. If there is any doubt, give them one of those stout buckets for company.

• In cases of chronic seasickness, dehydration becomes an issue, and sufferers should be encouraged to drink water. Note also that there is a brief period after vomiting when a victim can often be persuaded to take light sustenance and fluids. But however bad the victims may feel at the time, on a coastal passage, dying is an unlikely outcome.

Provisioning and Cooking. **What to take.** Consider how many meals you will require on the passage, imagine cooking them in rough weather, then design your menu and buy accordingly. Be sure to add a couple of extra meals that can be cooked in one pan so the crew can get some sustenance no matter what is happening.

"Easy" is the key to success. While stocking up for a trip, think continually about the difficulties of preparing meals in a rolling boat. Don't buy one of those soft loaves you use at home. Load up on quality, bran-based sliced bread that can be used for an instant sandwich.

If the trip is overnight, prepare at least the first evening's dinner before you leave. Make it simple to serve, appetizing and readily digestible. A good guide for seagoing meals in rough weather is that they can be consumed with no more equipment than a bowl, a mug and a spoon. Where appropriate, the second night's meal frozen from home and stowed in the ice box will maintain its cold level.

Always ship plenty of snack foods, candy bars, fruit, etc. These "naughties" are great at night, or if a queasy crew can't face the spaghetti bolognaise.

Meals on time. Not knowing when the next food is expected to appear is bad for morale, so post times for meals and stick to them. If you have a designated cook, this is easy. When the galley is being run more casually, the skipper should give mealtime logistics serious thought. With planning, a mealtime routine can be achieved.

Another contribution the galley can make to raising spirits in rough conditions is to keep the hot drinks coming all day long. In sultry weather, combat dehydration with plenty of cool ones.

Taking children aboard requires a "thinking approach." Start with shorter outings, gradually building to longer passages.

David C. Forbes photo

Galley safety. Any seagoing craft, sail or power, should have high fiddles (rails) at the edge of galley tops and reasonable ones on eating tables. The stove should be similarly equipped, as well as with robust pan clamps. If any of these are absent, don't go to sea until the situation is remedied. Should the trip be a one-off in a strange boat, buy plenty of non-slip mats from your friendly chandlery. If they have none, use a wet towel laid flat. When in the galley, always think "fiddle." Wedge cups and containers hard against it, don't leave them to slide. Look to the sink as the ultimate temporary safe stowage.

It makes sense at sea to assume that pots will fall off the stove, even if you have taken almighty steps to make sure they don't. When the stove is to windward of you, consider wearing shoes and foul-weather pants with a bib front to protect you against scalding. This is a difficult discipline to enforce in warm weather, but there is more than one cook whose legs bear the evidence of not having done so on the one day it mattered.

Tactical cookery. Managing the galley in rough weather begins with knowing where everything is stowed. Cooking dinner then proceeds as follows:

• Start planning in a safe place such as the cockpit or your bunk.

• Think about what you can realistically cook, then work out where the ingredients will be found.

• Plan your meal, blow by blow.

• When you're ready, take a deep breath and go for it. Get the onions chopped and in the pan, then nip up for a breath of air. Now go down, drop in the rest of the ingredients. Proceed in this manner until the meal is ready.

• Serve in mugs or bowls, and if you can't face eating yourself, leave some in the pan for later. In bad weather it pays to cook too much so the excess can be used as night nibbles or form the basis of tomorrow's feast. It should get better every time.

Clearing away. If one shipmate has cooked, it's a good idea to have another clear away the galley. Cooks and cleaners should train themselves to consider those who will come after them. Leave as little mess as possible, and you'll sail a happy ship.

On a coastal passage, all trash must be stored for shoreside disposal. Bag it up tightly and find a well-ventilated place to stow it. A large, sealed, self-draining propane locker is a winner. You can ease this problem before you leave by dumping any extraneous packaging. On no account should you heave anything plastic over the side.

"Easy" is the key to success for cooking on board. Meals served on a regular schedule have a strong positive affect on the morale of the entire crew. Note cook's harness rig, which allows her to use her hands for cooking even when the boat is lurching.

Watchkeeping and Fatigue. Given the right boat for the passage, the biggest threat to safety is crew fatigue. This creeps up on you, often going unrecognized until you are genuinely tired. Get to know the symptoms. Irritability, laziness, or difficulty in performing small sums of mental arithmetic such as working out an hour's run from two log readings are typical. As soon as you realize what's happening, take yourself firmly in hand and get some rest. Better still, work a watch system that avoids fatigue in the first place.

A coastal passage is often not long enough for a crew to acclimate to a full sea-going routine. Offshore in fair weather, watch follows watch like clockwork, and after three or four days any fatigue that might result from changing sleep patterns has dissipated. Coastal watchkeeping must be

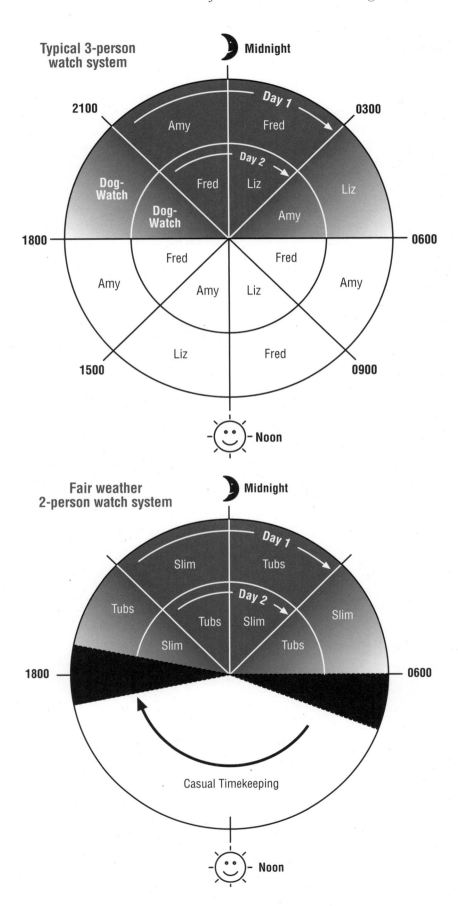

Typical 3-person watch system

Midnight

2100 · Day 1 · 0300

Amy · Fred

Day 2

Fred · Liz · Liz

Dog-Watch · Amy

Dog-Watch

1800 · Fred · Fred · 0600

Amy · Amy · Liz · Amy

Liz · Fred

1500 · 0900

Noon

Note how a "dog watch" is set to include the main meal of the day (dinner on this boat). The watch becomes informal during this period, which enables people to eat in peace and also to clear away the galley. The "dog" coincides with "happy hour" where, in fair weather, all hands have traditionally gathered in the cockpit to yarn. It is also used to cycle the watches so that nobody gets the 0000 - 0300 two nights running.

Fair weather 2-person watch system

Midnight

Day 1

Slim · Tubs

Day 2

Tubs · Tubs · Slim · Slim

Slim · Tubs

1800 · 0600

Casual Timekeeping

Noon

Here is a useful two-person watch arrangement for fair weather. Note the two dog-watches where cooking and clearing away can be organized. The early evening watch is easy and can be rotated each night. In the daylight, whoever is more tired may sleep while the shipmate keeps things going. The night cycle is rigid with no "heroes."

tailor-made for the crew and the length and nature of the trip. Its purpose is to ward off fatigue so that all hands, and in particular the skipper, can perform at full efficiency when required.

On an eight-hour passage made in daytime, it may prove feasible to run no watch system at all, merely ensuring that nobody spends too long on the helm, and people move about periodically to ward off seasickness with activity. Once the dark hours begin, this will not be enough. Even if the skipper does not feel tired, he or she should still make a point of taking an hour or two "off watch." Reading a book, napping, listening to the stereo or putting the trip out of your mind in some other way will refresh the personal batteries. If the passage is an overnighter, some real sleep is important; two nights and it becomes imperative. There are numerous watch systems that can serve on a coastal passage, but rather than supply a long list, none of which may suit the requirements of a given ship and crew on the day, here are some general factors to consider when making watch arrangements:

Steering. Nobody should steer for more than two hours at a trick. Three is the maximum even in fair weather before most people's concentration begins slipping. If you are working a small craft with one person on at a time and no autopilot, the question of attention span will determine the length of the watch. In hard going, an hour is enough for most.

Keeping awake. On boats with an autopilot, most adults can stay responsibly alone on watch for up to three hours. Freed from the tyranny of the wheel, they can change their station, take a careful scan round the horizon, brew coffee, have a snack, perhaps even read a little, so long as they always concentrate on the responsibility to look out. A three-person crew can therefore work "three hours on, six off," an excellent arrangement allowing plenty of time for structured rest. The skipper will miss out from time to time when piloting decisions must be made, but so long as the system can be timed to coincide with meals, it is generally successful.

Some three-person crews work night watches on a "two hours on, four off" basis, starting after dinner and ending at breakfast. The daylight hours are covered casually, "according to conscience."

Couples watchkeeping. With a crew of two, life without an autopilot of some sort is extremely fatiguing and not to be recommended for passages of over 24 hours. On a longer trip with the autopilot functioning, many couples work a variant of the three-person system described above. No watches in daylight, but a good lookout by whoever is around while the other rests up. At night, it's "three hours on, three off" in fair weather, perhaps down to "two hours on" or even less in foul weather. So long as you make sure you get your head down when it's your turn, and there are no "heroes" you can keep going for long spells with such a system.

It can be perfectly seamanlike for the watch on deck to take a short rest below, particularly when conditions are tiring. Indeed, to do so may assist overall alertness. If you adopt such a policy, however, work on the understanding that a ship may come over the visible horizon at a converging speed of up to 30 knots. You don't need a time and distance table to tell you that this is a mile every two minutes. Plan your private on-watch routines accordingly.

Coastal Weather

Three elements make up the interface between the surface of our planet and space. First is the atmosphere, highly fluid and able to move around more or less at random. The oceans also move, but their currents are more predictable and far slower than the atmosphere. Only the land, our datum point along the coast, can be taken as solid and fixed.

The face of seafaring has changed almost beyond recognition in the past hundred years, but two factors remain unchanged by time. The tides will rise and fall around our globe until the moon slips her orbit, and the weather will continue to confound us.

While tides can be predicted for years ahead, weather cannot. Meteorologists provide valuable forecasts of what each day will bring, but despite remarkable advances in the science of forecasting, they are not always right. In order to make the best assessment of developing weather as seen from the deck, a general understanding of what makes it happen is vital.

The atmosphere is not homogenous. It is composed of distinct air masses which move and interact with each other. Movement of air within an air mass, or the drifting of the air mass as a whole, creates wind. Interplay between air masses creates precipitation and other more powerful weather phenomena.

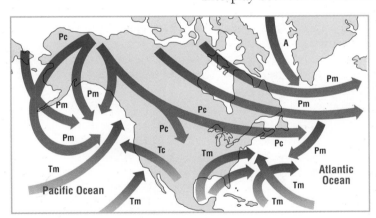

Air Masses in North America
A = Arctic
Pc = Polar Continental
Pm = Polar Maritime
Tc = Tropical Continental
Tm = Tropical Maritime

Air Masses. Air masses take their qualities from their area of origin. Generally speaking, warm air holds more moisture than cold, so parcels moving out of the oceanic tropical regions will be warm and moist. Air that started life out on the continent is likely to be drier, as is cooler polar and cold arctic air.

As these masses pass over an observer, the effects are tangible. So-called "tropical maritime" air coming north to the east coast brings muggy, humid conditions and indifferent visibility. Continental air, particularly that from warmer climes, may well be dust-laden so once again, the air quality will not be good. Polar air, on the other hand, can sparkle in its clarity, particularly polar maritime air, which has a sharp, clear quality. Contrary to what their names might suggest, all these air masses can affect weather in more southern latitudes.

Pressure Systems. Atmospheric pressure is measured either in inches of mercury or millibars, and areas of equal pressure are indicated by lines on a weather chart called isobars.

Natural laws dictate that air pressure tends to equalize, and therefore winds try to blow from an area of high pressure into an adjacent low pressure region. In practice, it's not that simple. As the air in the heart of a high pressure region fans out, it is caught by a force generated by the

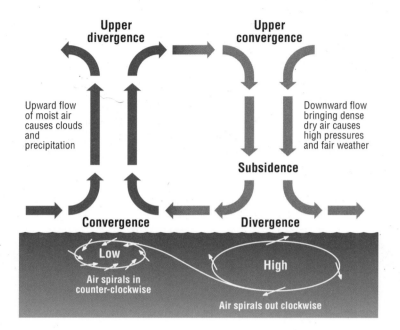

Upper divergence

Upper convergence

Upward flow of moist air causes clouds and precipitation

Downward flow bringing dense dry air causes high pressures and fair weather

Subsidence

Convergence

Divergence

Low

Air spirals in counter-clockwise

High

Air spirals out clockwise

Vertical movement of air associated with high and low pressure areas.

A high pressure system typically has wider spaced isobars than a low, indicating a slacker pressure gradient and lighter winds. Lows often have closer spaced isobars toward their centers, depicting stronger winds. Blue arrows have been added to this chart to indicate air flow, spiraling outward and clockwise around the 1039 millibar high (H) and inward and counterclockwise around the 959 millibar low (L). Only the last two digits of the millibar pressure are indicated on the isobar lines, i.e., 36 (1036 mb), 32 (1032), 68 (968 mb), 76 (976 mb), 84 (984 mb), etc.

turning of the earth known as coriolis force. This causes the air to spiral out of the high in a clockwise direction, (counterclockwise in the southern hemisphere).

A high pressure system, called an anticyclone, is usually much larger than a low pressure system, and has a gentler gradient of pressure (pressure slope). You will notice on a weather map, the isobars in a high are usually well spaced out, indicating a "slack gradient." This means the pressure slope down which the wind flows is an easy incline, so breezes tend to be light.

Usually, falling air in a high is stable, there is little "mixing" going on, so the weather associated with an anticyclone is often fair and predictable.

Weather Fronts and the Mid-Latitude Depression. Where warm, moist air from the oceanic mid-latitudes and tropics meets colder, drier air from higher latitudes, a "weather front" is formed. This demarcation between the two masses of air is called a polar front, even though its actual location meanders around the planet at anything from 35° to 60° latitude.

Frontal depressions, also called "lows," can form along this front when the two air masses interact to produce both a warm front, where warm air is sliding over cold air, and a cold front further to the west where cold air is pushing under warm air.

As air in the low circulates counterclockwise around the low (clockwise in the southern hemisphere), you may experience winds from literally any direction, depending on where your

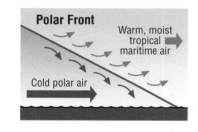

Polar Front

Warm, moist tropical maritime air

Cold polar air

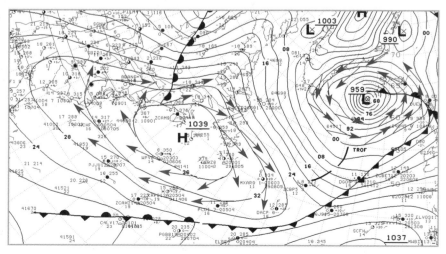

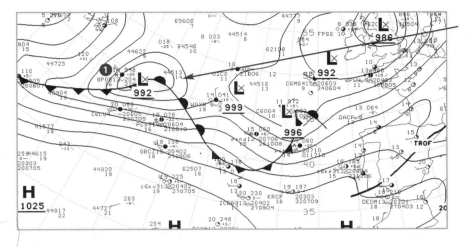

North Atlantic:
1800 Zulu hours, April 17, 2000
The twisting vertical movement of air associated with this interaction causes the polar front to kink (often called a "frontal wave"). In many cases, as the kink or wave increases in size, the system develops "joined-up" isobars (❶) with the corresponding full circulation of a low. At this point, a depression is born. It generally moves in an easterly direction.

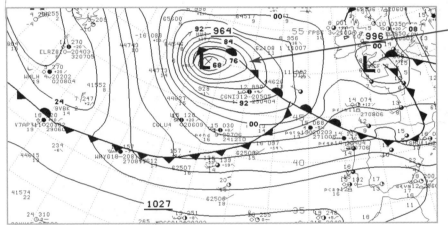

North Atlantic:
1800 Zulu hours, April 18, 2000
A mere 24 hours later, the cold front catches up with the warm front, and the remains of the original warm front are raised hundreds or thousands of feet off the sea. The front is now described as "occluded." A low can still be active in this stage of its life and is able to spin off secondary depressions.

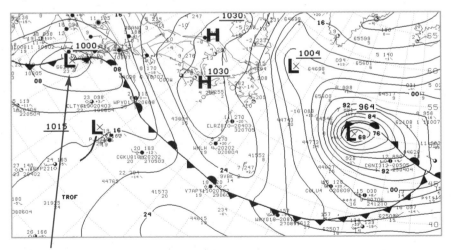

A secondary depression can form on the front trailing behind (to the west of) a "parent" depression. Secondaries are frequently more violent than their parents and are notoriously hard to predict, so be prepared. Watch the sky for cirrus clouds and keep checking the barometer after the main event seems over. In general, secondaries are more likely to form as their parent depression runs towards the lee side of an ocean (except in the winter months). They are therefore more likely to be encountered on the northwest than the east coast of the U.S.

boat is in relation to the center of the system. In the northern hemisphere, you can locate the center of a low pressure system by standing with your back to the wind and extend your arms like a scarecrow. Your left hand is pointing approximately to the center of the system.

If you pass to the north of the low pressure system (see below), the winds will be easterly, the source of the notorious Northeasters of New England. Should your route take you through the middle of the low, you will suffer from "cyclonic" conditions with winds unpredictable in velocity or direction augmented by a confused sea which literally doesn't know which way to turn. It's not a nice place to be.

If your route takes you south of the low, you will experience the fronts themselves, which form the real fairground of the depression.

By taking different routes through a low pressure system, you can encounter dramatically different conditions. A route north of a low ❶, will encounter easterly winds. A route through the middle ❷ will encounter confused "cyclonic" winds and seas. A route to the south ❸ will take you through both a warm front and a cold front with associated changes in wind direction and strength.

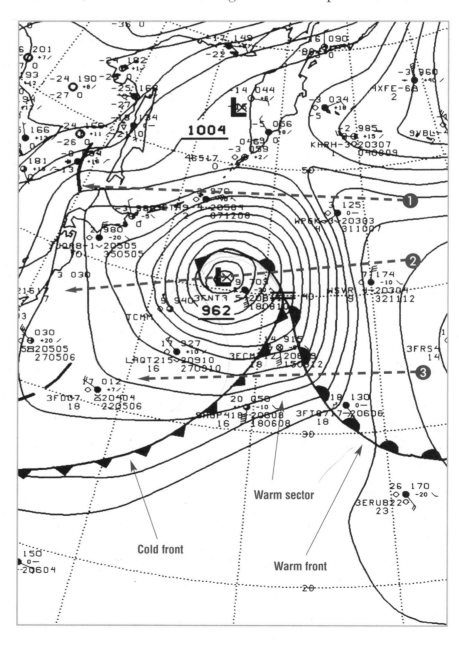

Warm sector

Cold front

Warm front

The warm front. The warm front is the harbinger of bad weather and is often a drawn-out affair. Here is the scenario:

1) Cirrus ("mares tails") clouds are seen high in the west. Sometimes a halo appears around the sun or the moon.

2) From 6 to 24 hours later, the sky clouds over with thin, cirrostratus clouds. The barometer begins falling and the wind may be backing.

3) Cloud cover thickens and wind becomes stronger. Barometer is falling.

4) Nimbostratus and nimbus clouds bring rain as the front drops down to sea level. By now the wind is blowing as hard as it is likely to for a while, as it veers to a southerly or southwesterly direction. The barometer should level out.

The warm sector. Following up the warm front is the tropical maritime air that caused all the trouble. You may feel a subtle temperature change of a few degrees, although sometimes it is more dramatic. The wind now settles down typically to a steady southwest direction, often up to gale force, with rain continuing intermittently until the ensuing cold front brings relief.

The Warm Front

The warm front is the harbinger of bad weather and is often a drawn-out affair. Here is the scenario:

- **Cirrus ("mares tails") clouds are seen high in the west. Sometimes a halo appears around the sun or the moon.**

- **From 6 to 24 hours later, the sky clouds over with thin, cirrostratus clouds. The barometer begins falling and the wind may be backing.**

- **Cloud cover thickens and wind becomes stronger. Barometer is falling.**

- **Nimbostratus and nimbus clouds bring rain as the front drops down to sea level. By now the wind is blowing as hard as it is likely to for a while, as it veers to a southerly or southwesterly direction. The barometer should level out.**

Cirrus Clouds   NOS/NOAA photos

Cirrostratus Clouds

Nimbostratus Clouds

Stratocumulus Clouds

In this vertical section cut through a warm front, note how the warm air laps over the cold air mass in front of it.

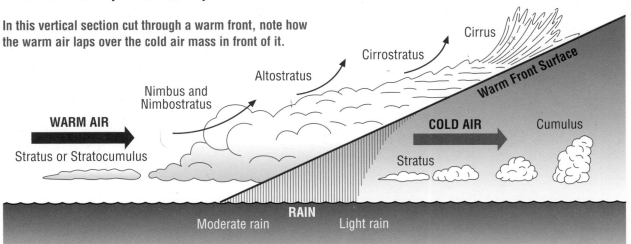

Cirrus

Cirrostratus

Altostratus

Nimbus and Nimbostratus

WARM AIR

Stratus or Stratocumulus

Warm Front Surface

COLD AIR   Cumulus

Stratus

RAIN

Moderate rain   Light rain

The cold front. A cold front is formed by cooler, drier, heavier air shoving its way under the warm sector (see p.35). This is what you see:

1) Very often the first indication of the cold front is a few patches of blue sky.

2) The front is more instantly recognizable than its warm cousin. Because it involves rising, unstable air, associated activity can sometimes be violent. The wind will certainly veer, the barometer rises, the temperature often drops noticeably, and you may see a distinct squall line approaching.

3) The squalls accompanying a cold front involve heavy rain or even hail, as the water dumps from extremely high altitudes where the air is plenty cold enough to freeze water. Wind can be very strong under these squalls, so be ready for fireworks, even if you don't get them.

4) Following the front, the barometer should continue to rise and the wind to veer. You will now see "ice-cream castle" cumulonimbus clouds boiling up to enormous heights as cold air forces the warm up to the heavens. Some of these "cu-nims" can form flat, anvil-shaped tops as the rising air hits a more dense layer higher up and spreads out. Any such cloud may have wind under it, so watch out.

5) Slowly, the clouds thin out as the weather continues to improve. The barometer's rapid rise eases, cu-nims give way to fluffy, fair-weather cumulus clouds and you should enjoy a period of pleasant weather.

A typical squall line   NOS/NOAA photo

Beware if the wind slacks off dramatically as the cold front passes. Don't imagine that the show is over for at least four hours after the barometer kicks up. It may blow hard again. This phenomenon occurs when the isobars are heavily kinked at the front, causing them to have a slack gradient (light wind) immediately behind the front and then coming closer together (stronger winds) as the front moves further away.

Isolated cold fronts. Throughout the world, coastal regions in the mid and sub-tropical latitudes are subject to the phenomenon of isolated cold fronts. These run along the coast, sometimes bringing vicious line squalls, torrential rain and zero visibility as they pass. If one is forecast, do not take it lightly. They are particularly prevalent on the middle east coast in the summer months, with the Outer Banks south of Cape Hatteras and the Chesapeake Bay firmly in the firing line.

Wind strengths and the barometer. Regardless of the forecast, a barometer reading should be part of your hourly ship's log entry. It is then an easy matter to track the pressure readings you have recorded and compare them with the forecast.

If the pressure readings "crash" at a rate of two millibars (0.06 inches of mercury) per hour for three hours or more, stand by for gale force winds of 40 knots. If it suddenly rises as a front passes, you'll see more wind shortly. An old adage states, "Sharp rise after low, you're in for a blow!"

The Cold Front

A cold front is formed by cooler, drier, heavier air shoving its way under the warm sector. This is what you see:

- Very often the first indication of the cold front is a few patches of blue sky.

- The front is more instantly recognizable than its warm cousin. Because it involves rising, unstable air, associated activity can sometimes be violent. The wind will certainly veer, the barometer rises, the temperature often drops noticeably, and you may see a distinct squall line approaching.

- The squalls accompanying a cold front involve heavy rain or even hail, as the water dumps from extremely high altitudes where the air is plenty cold enough to freeze water. Wind can be very strong under these squalls.

- Following the front, the barometer should continue to rise and the wind to veer. You will now see "ice-cream castle" cumulonimbus clouds boiling up to enormous heights as cold air forces the warm skyward. These "cu-nims" can form flat, anvil-shaped tops as the rising air hits a more dense layer higher up and spreads out. Any such cloud may have wind under it, so watch out.

- Slowly, the clouds thin out as the weather continues to improve. The barometer's rapid rise eases, cu-nims give way to fluffy, fair-weather cumulus clouds and you should enjoy a period of pleasant weather.

- Beware if the wind slacks off dramatically as the cold front passes. Don't imagine that the show is over for at least four hours after the barometer kicks up. It may blow hard again. This phenomenon occurs when the isobars are heavily kinked at the front, causing them to have a slack gradient (light wind) immediately behind the front and then coming closer together (stronger winds) as the front moves further away.

Altocumulus Clouds

Cumulonimbus Clouds

Cumulus Clouds　NOS/NOAA photos

In this vertical section cut through a cold front, note how the warm air is pushed rapidly upward, sometimes violently, by the cold air.

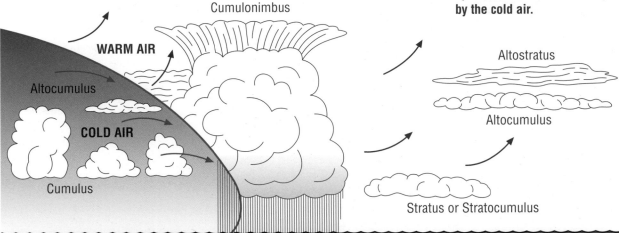

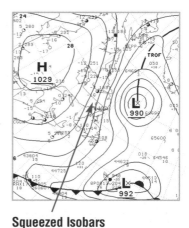

Squeezed Isobars

Squeezed isobars. Once in a while, a section of coast finds itself stuck between a stable high and an area of low pressure which is moving very slowly. If you are directly between such pressure centers, high winds may well be on your menu for days on end. Things won't change until one or the other system moves, fills or declines.

Pressure sometimes builds at prominent corners of continental land masses. A classic example is the northwest corner of Spain in the vicinity of Cape Finisterre, which invariably takes a beating from northeasterly gales.

Tropical Storm Activity. Hurricanes are so well forecast that it is hard to imagine a coastal passagemaker foolish or unlucky enough to come up against the full-blown monster while sailing. However, the remnants of tropical activity can have devastating effects on what might otherwise have been a harmless depression or frontal system. The amount of warm, moist air generated by a hurricane is gigantic, and it does not simply dissipate when the hurricane passes. If it becomes entangled with a forming depression, it can pump it up into a severe gale. If there is a hurricane remnant to the south of your position, monitor its progress with the greatest care while at sea. If you have not yet set out, don't slip your mooring until you're confident you're in the clear. See Chapter 18 for more information on Tropical Revolving Storms.

Sea Breezes. Land warms up quickly as the sun rises on hot days, then cools equally rapidly after dark. The sea maintains a more constant temperature which varies much more slowly with the seasons. The result is that as the land heats up and warm air rises from it, cooler air flows in from the sea to take its place in the form of a "sea breeze." This mechanism can work with a sea/land temperature difference as little as three or four degrees Fahrenheit.

The opposite effect is a "land breeze," which is occasionally experienced at night. It is rarely as strong as its daytime counterpart.

Sea breezes can blow from five miles or more offshore, or they may fizzle out a thousand yards from the beach. A strong "sun-wind" that blows from noon until late evening will often veer (or back in the southern hemisphere) during the time of its duration, following the coriolis effect. Sea breezes are usually at their most obvious in spring and early summer when the still cool water temperature is lagging behind the summer weather ashore.

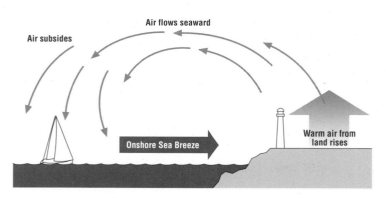

Air subsides

Air flows seaward

Onshore Sea Breeze

Warm air from land rises

Sea breezes are formed as warm air rises above the land, drawing in cooler air from the water.

Fog. Radiation fog, or land fog, generally forms after the ground has lost its heat overnight. Air in contact with the ground is then cooled below its "dew point" (the temperature at which it can no longer hold the moisture it contains). The outcome is fog, usually found near the shore, in rivers and harbors. It will nearly always burn off when the day cooks up or a rising breeze stirs the air layers.

Sea fog, also called "advection fog," is created by warm, moist air blowing over colder water. The classic case occurs on the Grand Banks of Newfoundland, when warm air migrating north with the Gulf Stream meets cool water flowing south from Labrador. The same phenomenon occurs in Nova Scotia, Maine, and down into New England.

San Francisco Bay's famous fog is a local variant of sea fog caused by relatively warm and very moist air moving over an area of very cold deep sea water that has upwelled to the surface just off the coast of Northern California. The fog formed is then carried in spectacular fashion through the Golden Gate on the sea breeze.

Sea fog is formed by warm, moist air blowing over cold water. NOS/NOAA photo

Forecast Availability, Assessment and Self-Help. While you are still at the passage planning stage, the TV Weather Channel can supply excellent overviews, as can Internet downloads from any of the numerous available weather sites. Once aboard, make full use of VHF and Navtex forecasts for your area (if you have the equipment — see Chapter 20), bearing in mind that you must work at the VHF information to get more than a local picture. The overview is broadcast at longer intervals. Of course, if your equipment includes a weatherfax receiver, keeping abreast of the big picture is simple so long as you keep your batteries fresh and are able to interpret a synoptic chart. There is more information about weatherfax in Chapters 8 and 18, but whatever your equipment, never ignore the barometer and what you observe with your own eyes.

If you don't want to invest in a weatherfax for longer coastal passages, a more modest outlay for a "receive-only" Single Sideband (SSB) radio will pay off. These can be small units operated from their own internal batteries. With a little practice, you can keep up with the synoptic situation, and when the set is off-duty it will pick up your favorite FM station.

Continue monitoring all available weather sources on a regular, disciplined basis and make a point of writing down the information. Comparing a forecast with its predecessors enables you to draw conclusions about trends and developments.

When it comes to making decisions based on weather information, never let bravado carry you away. Also beware of being too timid. There is a malaise known as harbor sickness to which we are all prone after hiding from rough weather for too long. Things may not be so bad as they seem. Sometimes, it's better to bite the bullet, even if it's going to be a rough ride.

Above all, become a weather freak. It is only by looking at the sky constantly to compare it with barometer readings and wind patterns that you can develop the mariner's sixth sense for what may be around the corner. Think about weather every day. Scrutinize the clouds from your office window, check the halo round the sun as you drive home, gaze aloft from the church parking lot for something more than divine inspiration. At sea, never, never ignore a wind shift.

Coastal Passage Navigation

This chapter assumes the reader is proficient in the sound methods of plotting a course and determining a yacht's position in most conditions using the traditional navigation tools, and the following information builds on that knowledge. For further information on these fundamental methods, refer to *Coastal Navigation* published by US SAILING.

The instruments used to provide pieces of information to a navigator are only tools, and a broad understanding of how these pieces fit together is essential to safe and pleasurable passagemaking. This philosophy was clearly understood by navigators when their tools consisted of compass, chart, dividers and parallel rules. But even as increasingly sophisticated electronic instruments are put at our disposal, an understanding of overall piloting concepts is vital. It would be a mistake to assume that because an electronic chart plotter can perform every navigation function except sound the depth, that the navigator's job is done.

Almost everyone now chooses GPS (Global Positioning System) with its internal computer as the mainstay of coastal and offshore piloting. Though the universal availability of such navigational accuracy can improve the performance of a good navigator, it can be dangerous in unthinking hands.

GPS and the Coastal Passage. GPS and dead reckoning. When using traditional piloting techniques, the good old-fashioned "fix" appears to be the fundamental tool of position. In fact, it is the final arbiter, a verification of the navigator's estimate of the ship's position (the EP) which has been worked up from the starting point of Dead Reckoning (DR).

In unfamiliar waters, an EP is constructed on a chart using distance run and course steered (DR), taking into account current and leeway. After estimating a position, the navigator determines which surrounding features are most suitable for a visual "fix." When the fix is plotted, the two positions are compared. If there is no obvious discrepancy, the position has credibility. This classical system has the significant virtue that one source of position is constantly being reviewed by another. This is an essential axiom of safe navigation and users of GPS (or Loran C) abandon it at their peril.

Before electronics, the navigator selected the best available sources for a fix. Today, the best source for a fix is GPS (assuming it is functioning properly). "Differential" GPS (DGPS) can be even sharper, because it measures distance to within a yard of accuracy. Currently, even unassisted GPS will fix you to within 20 yards. If the U.S. government decides to re-introduce SA (Selective Availability), this will degrade to 50-100 yards. Unless it is based on two intersecting visual ranges, a fix is unlikely to approach such accuracy.

A further advantage of a GPS fix is that it is instant. This means its position is as close in time to the attendant log readings as it takes you to write them down. This is an important factor in working up the next EP.

For reasons of accuracy and immediacy, one may be tempted to use only a GPS fix, but this would be most unwise. The fallacy of this becomes obvious the first time there is an equipment malfunction or operator error.

The EP is still used by experienced sailors, but on a passage it is no longer plotted on a regular basis. What happens is this:

• Log your departure point, noting time, log reading, course etc.

• Assuming you are in "passagemaking mode" rather than "inshore pilotage," continue for approximately one hour along your planned track. When it's time for your next position, read the log, note set and drift, make a sensible guess about leeway, inspect the chart and make a rough estimate of where you are. Now plot the position as defined by GPS. Does this stack up with your rough estimate of EP?

• It does? Fine. Check the depth sounder as a third source of input. If that adds up as well, you can take it that the position is right. Log it and make a fresh departure from the GPS position as you would have done with the traditional way of plotting an EP.

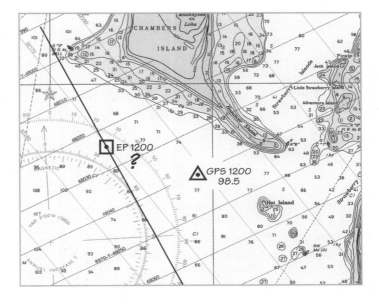

• No? Something's gone wrong. On the face of things, it's unlikely to be the GPS which, if it's working at all, is usually on the button. Obviously, if the readout is warning of poor coverage, or "2-D" navigation, then maybe you should give it a minute or two to sort itself out. But if there is no warning then it's most likely giving you a reliable position. So what could go amiss?

• Your rough estimate of EP might be a couple of miles off. Perhaps you omitted a vital current factor; maybe you misread the log or failed to observe the scale of the chart properly. If this happens a few times, you might be forgiven for thinking you should forget about the EP, but you'd be wrong.

• Far more likely is that you have fouled up your GPS plot, either by making a hash of your lat/long plot or by misreading the actual numbers on the screen. Both mistakes are easy to make. Your first action, therefore, is to double-check the GPS plot. This is the prime reason why the EP is so important, even if it's only in your head. The second reason follows.

GPS and the ship's log. As noted above, once the GPS position is accepted it is immediately logged. Timing of the log entry is as important as the fix itself, because a fix is history as soon the boat moves from the recorded position. Navigators should always treat the log as part of the data-gathering process rather than tacking it on as an afterthought. Even if the reading is not recorded in the ship's log until after the plotting process is completed, it is tied into the fix. It is important to log the fix accurately because without a reasonably accurate measurement of distance run from the last known position, the next EP is adrift before it starts.

So long as you have logged the last fix, be it taken across a spray-clouded hand bearing compass on a rough day, or read to the third decimal place from a DGPS screen, you can work up an EP from it. If you don't log it punctually, or do so carelessly, half an hour down the line you might as well not have bothered.

Should your electronics go down, the first thing you should do (after

Even if you are not running a full, written DR plot, you must still make at least a mental estimate of your position each time you plot a GPS fix. If it doesn't stack up, check the depth sounding, plot a full EP and compare it with the fix. Then start hunting for the mistake. Begin by checking your plot of the GPS readout, and move on from there.

checking the switches and rattling the set) is note the new log reading, refer to the last one for distance, and start a fresh plot.

If, on the other hand, you have been squirting the boat down the GPS track towards your arrival waypoint without noting changes of course or distances run, all you'll know for sure is that you're somewhere between "here" and "there." You are, in a word, lost. The best you can now hope for is to recognize a few shore features for a fix. If land has disappeared in the haze, or all the hills look much the same, you can only heave-to, brew up and read the tea leaves.

If you log all positions, including any buoys you pass close by, you won't need to resort to the occult when the GPS fails. One day, it surely will.

The same principle holds true if you are using an electronic chart plotter. This marvel depicts the chart on a monitor, overlaying the yacht's position, thus moving another stage away from the tried and tested methods of log reading, fix and time. To be strictly safe using a plotter you should have a paper chart on board and at least log the co-ordinates of an hourly position. The fact that the fix is constantly displayed on a "chart" does away with any doubts that you may have physically plotted it in the wrong place, but electronics can't save you from Cousin Egbert as he kicks the aerial off the pushpit while scrambling to leeward. Nor will they help if Uncle Sam shuts down public access to GPS for reasons of national security, or if your main circuit breaker burns out.

GPS and chart datums. Because the globe is not perfectly round,

Use of this type of methodology enables you to make full use of electronics without abdicating responsibility to the machine. If the electronics fail, you can revert to traditional methods of piloting, working onward from the most recent GPS fix.

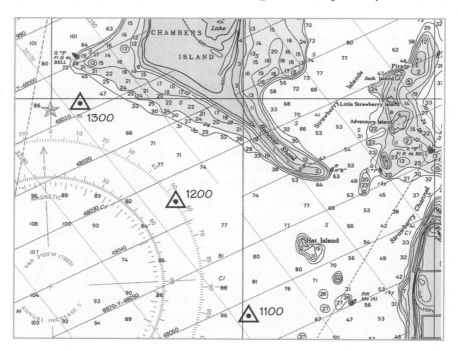

Time	Log	Course	Weather	Remarks	Engine
1100	93.0	325M	10-15 S-SW	GPS fix. Lat 45° 05'-9N by Lo 87° 19'-8W. Hat Island spotted to the NE. RW buoy directly on starboard beam.	Off
1200	98.5	328M	15 S-SW	GPS fix. Lat 45° 08'-0N by Lo 87° 21'-8W. Current table indicates foul set of 0.5 kts. Speed has risen to 5.5 kts.	Off
1300	104.0	324M	15 S-SW	GPS fix. Lat 45° 09'-9N by Lo 87° 24'-3W. Adverse current confirmed. Chambers Island G3 buoy sighted on starboard bow.	Off

A good electronic chart plotter does virtually everything a paper chart and its operator can, until it stops working. Always back up your latest positions.

the question of "absolute position" remains. Different charting authorities relate their positions to marginally varying datum points. If your GPS is reading out its fixes to a "datum" that is not the one your chart was drawn to, the plot could be in error by several hundred yards or more. Fortunately, the majority of receivers now offer a wide choice of datum at the touch of a button.

Check the title corner of your chart. Assuming it is reasonably modern, you will usually note a statement of datum. The most likely one on a U.S. chart is World Geodetic System 1984 ("WGS 84"). Alternatively, there may be an instruction concerning shifting "satellite-derived positions."

In the case of non-differential GPS, failure to take this important question into account may add a substantial error into a situation where total accuracy is assumed. With DGPS, the error will be present where total accuracy is otherwise assumed.

Cross-checking GPS against radar. We have noted the rule of always cross-checking one source of navigational information against another. On boats suitably equipped, this can be achieved electronically by using radar and GPS together. Even if your sets do not interface, noting the distance and approximate bearing to a recognizable charted

Check the datum of your working chart (left) and make sure it's the one you've fed into your GPS (below).

Mercator Projection
Scale 1:500,000 At Lat. 44°00′N.
North American Datum of 1983
(World Geodetic System 1984)

HORIZONTAL DATUM

The horizontal reference datum of this chart is North American Datum 1983 (NAD 83) and is considered equivalent to World Geodetic System 1984 (WGS 84) for practical plotting purposes. Positions referred to the North American 1927 Datum do not require conversion to NAD 83 for plotting on this chart.

Flagging a waypoint onto the radar screen from an interfaced GPS removes the ambiguity that is otherwise inevitable when trying to identify, at a glance, a buoy with other boats in its vicinity. Furuno photo

feature by radar will soon show up any significant nonsense on your plotted GPS position. Many modern sets do interface, however, so that a waypoint can be highlighted on the radar display. It appears as a sort of "lollipop on a stick," which instantly differentiates it from any other targets in its vicinity. Without the interface, it can be awkward to tell the buoy you seek from others in its close vicinity.

If the passage plan involves passing close to a buoy and the boat features non-interfaced GPS and radar, the GPS is used to approach within a mile or so of the buoy, after which the radar blip can generally be identified. Assuming it's foggy, the radar now takes over as the primary aid to navigation. If the day is crystal clear, the best navigational instrument remains the one favored by Noah, a good pair of eyes.

Do not fall into the trap of navigating as though taking part in a video game. Even in fog, make a point of leaving the instruments regularly to take a look outside. This keeps your perspective sound. If you peer into screens for too long and there is an emergency on deck, you will almost certainly arrive on the scene disoriented. If the power goes down and you haven't been logging your positions, you'll be even worse off. Some things never change.

The Range. No matter how sophisticated your electronics, when it comes to inshore pilotage there is no substitute for lining up two known objects along a track in the form of a "range." The benefits of this ancient technique cannot be over-emphasized. The fact that a standard GPS position can jump around by up to 20 yards either side of a safe track can play havoc in close situations when a boatlength of "cross-track error" toward a waypoint can put you on the rocks. A range, on the other hand, will deliver the goods. Where there is no official range available to cover a situation, try to find one of your own.

The Dubious Landfall. Many passages involve a landfall. On most coastal passages you will be within sight of land, but if visibility is poor, it might be 24 hours since you last had a visual fix. If you are running on GPS, there should be no doubt about the land you see. If you have any

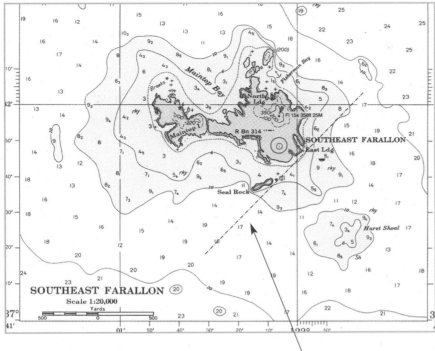

SOUTHEAST FARALLON ⓴
Scale 1:20,000
Yards
500 0 500

14th Ed. June 6/92 ■
13241

Unless you have DGPS, don't imagine that a "cross-track" error function will be as accurate as an old fashioned-range. A well chosen range can be good to a boat's length or less. Even if you do have super accurate DGPS, it's easier to adjust your heading to what you see with your own eyes than to relate a course alteration to a repeatedly changing electronic readout.

Correction dates should be noted in the lower left-hand corner of the chart. Corrections are found in Local Notices to Mariners which are published weekly by the local U.S. Coast Guard District and can also be downloaded from the website of either the National Imagery and Mapping Agency (NIMA), http://www.nima.mil, or the U.S. Coast Guard Navigation Center (NAVCEN), http://www.navcen.uscg.mil.

doubts, you may become subject to one of the oldest piloting pitfalls of them all: forcing what you see to fit the chart. In short, you "invent pictures." If a light beacon doesn't tie up with a landmark the way it's supposed to, don't ignore it or assume that it must have been built since the chart was surveyed. Take another look. If you aren't where you hoped, face the music.

Chart Correction. The reality of owning charts is that although most people pay lip-service to keeping their collection corrected and up to date, few actually sit down and do it. If your charts are not current, be sure you have an up-to-date Light List on board, or at least the latest nautical almanac with buoyage and lights listed for the area you will be transiting. Check important marks against the latest information. It's not as effective as performing a full correction, but far better than nothing.

Calibrating Instruments. Sailing with DGPS doesn't allow you to be unconcerned about the accuracy of the rest of your ship's instruments. Your ship's log may well be inaccurate by ten per cent or more. An echo sounder might read depth below transducer, below keel, or true depth, depending upon how it has been set up. A barometer can easily be 10 millibars adrift from reality, and so on. It remains a skipper's duty to understand how his instruments work, and to ensure they are calibrated so they can be trusted. Study the manuals for all your gear and carry them on board. Make time to do this, or you'll be far less safe than you imagined on the day your GPS goes down. You could also find yourself unexpectedly aground.

Coastal Communications

In the mid-1970s, it was unusual to find a small cruising yacht with a VHF ship-to-shore radio. Communicating between vessels was accomplished by sending signals by Morse code or flags. Boats in distress flew an upside-down ensign and set off flares in the hope that somebody would see them and know what to do. Some text books still recommended the display of a burning tar barrel.

In a single generation, this reality was changed beyond recognition. Today, it would be considered irresponsible putting to sea without a VHF. Yet this recent addition to the list of essential sailing gear is already being supplanted by the universal acceptance of the convenient cellular telephone. But, not so fast! VHF and SSB still have a place in ship-to-ship and ship-to-shore communications.

General Use of VHF (Very High Frequency)

Theoretical range. VHF radio as fitted to most yachts, is a "line-of-sight" communication whereby users can talk to one another. Line of sight means literally what it says. If your eye were at the tip of your antenna and you could see the antenna with which you wished to communicate, you would be able to do so (assuming your set had sufficient power to reach the other). Typically, a moderate-sized sailboat with adequate power output and clean connections can be heard by a lofty shore station up to thirty miles away. In practice, this may drop to 25 miles or less, and two powerboats might only hear each another at seven or eight miles.

Power output. Most permanently installed VHF sets have an output of 25 watts, which is sufficient power for their likely visual range. They can also be switched down to 5 watts for short-range work, which conserves battery power. By reducing the range of your transmission, it also means you won't interfere with valuable airwaves for distance users while discussing the time to light your barbecue. You should put the VHF on the 25-watt setting when on standby or when radio is turned off, so that your signal won't be underpowered in an emergency.

Channels. In North America, the absolute minimum channels you must have remain 6, 9, 13, 16, 22 and 72, plus weather-channel listening capacity. A fully synthesized set will take in all available channels.

Antennas and handheld sets. A sailboat antenna should be well up the mast, but if a sailboat is dismasted, she loses her VHF capability just when she needs it most. For coastal passagemaking, therefore, you should carry either an emergency antenna plus the ability to mount it, a handheld unit, or (preferably) both.

A handheld VHF has an output of 1 to 5 watts and suffers in range through the inevitable limitations in "height of

VHF can span distances of up to 30 miles, given sufficient height of antenna. It's only "line of sight," however, so if there's a mountain in the way, you won't hear anything, and nobody will hear you.

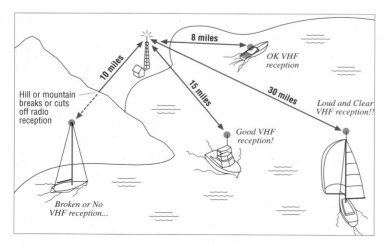

8 miles — OK VHF reception

10 miles

15 miles

30 miles — Loud and Clear VHF reception!!

Hill or mountain breaks or cuts off radio reception

Good VHF reception!

Broken or No VHF reception...

eye." It might raise a shore station from ten miles or more, but its boat-to-boat capability will be limited.

The phonetic alphabet. Failure to learn "Alpha, Bravo, Charlie, Delta, etc." not only makes the novice radio operator sound ignorant, it can also endanger life. Marine professionals worldwide use this system. If you have to spell your vessel's name to the Coast Guard, for example, there will be no doubt if you identify the good ship Sal as "Sierra, Alpha, Lima." If you begin thinking up your own phonetics — "S for Sable, A for Able, L for Label," you may get it wrong.

To learn the phonetic alphabet, transcribe it from your nautical almanac and stick it to the dashboard of your car for study in the next traffic jam.

Who can you talk to, and how?

Ship-to-ship. If you are calling ship-to-ship and speaking with someone you know, make your message brief and to the point. Initial contact in most parts of the world is on Channel 16. Because this is also the distress frequency, make sure nobody is "on the air" with an emergency.

New England and Great Lakes area users should call on Channel 9 unless in distress (commercial users call on Channel 13). Other parts of the country may have different secondary calling and monitoring channels for non-commercial and commercial users. Check your nautical almanac or contact the District U.S. Coast Guard office.

• Call: *"Racer, Racer, this is Chaser, Chaser, Channel 16, over."*
• Respond: *"Chaser, this is Racer. Switch to Channel 6, over."*
You both now switch to Channel 6 and pass your messages as follows:
• *"Racer, this is Chaser. How is the skipper's seasickness? Over."*
• *"Chaser, this is Racer. He's thrown in the towel and we are headed for the harbor. Over."*
• *"Racer this is Chaser. OK. See you there. Over."*
• *"This is Racer. Out."*
• *"Chaser, out."*

If you do not know the ship or cannot read her name, you should work out her approximate position either by deduction from your own GPS or, if appropriate, some shore feature. Then call:
• *"Very large tanker steaming south, 10 miles abeam San Diego, this is yacht Chaser two miles fine on your starboard bow."*

Ship-to-Shore. The shore stations you are most likely to call are the Coast Guard, a harbor authority or marina, a bridge tender, a towboat rescue service or a coast radiotelephone station. The last category is less used by coastal passagemakers than it once was, because cellular phones are replacing calls to special facilities linked to the shore telephone system.

Towboat rescue services are often more easily dealt with via cellular phone, but make sure you know any VHF channel preferences your local operator may have. If you can't raise them on the phone, or don't keep one on board, VHF is likely to succeed.

The primary responsibility of the Coast Guard is marine safety, and can be called any time, day or night, to discuss any safety issue. They are also your first line of defense should you be in distress.

Try to call harbor services before arrival. Once again, a cellular phone can be used here, but many marinas appreciate a VHF call half

Phonetic Alphabet

A = Alfa
B = Bravo
C = Charlie
D = Delta
E = Echo
F = Foxtrot
G = Golf
H = Hotel
I = India
J = Juliet
K = Kilo
L = Lima
M = Mike
N = November
O = Oscar
P = Pappa
Q = Quebec
R = Romeo
S = Sierra
T = Tango
U = Uniform
V = Victor
W = Whiskey
X = X-Ray
Y = Yankee
Z = Zulu

If in doubt that you have been seen it is acceptable to call a ship along these lines:
"Large tanker steaming south ten miles to seaward of Handy Head, this is sailing yacht Uneasy two miles fine on your port bow. Over." Chuck Place photo

Distress, Urgency and Safety Calls

- **DISTRESS CALLS are transmitted when a vessel or person is threatened by grave or imminent danger requiring immediate assistance. The call includes MAYDAY spoken three times; the words, "This is…"; and the call sign (or name, if no call sign assigned) spoken three times, followed by the distress message.**

- **URGENCY CALLS are sent when there is a very urgent message concerning the safety of a vessel or of some person on board or within sight. The signal is PAN-PAN (pronounced "pahn") spoken three times.**

- **SAFETY CALLS are used to send a message concerning the safety of navigation or giving important meteorological warnings. The signal is SECURITE (pronounced see-cur-ee-tay) spoken three times.**

an hour before you arrive to arrange a berth, advise of any special safety aspects, etc.

Before making a shore call, first determine if you should be calling on Channel 16 or if a different channel is designated. The information may be in your nautical almanac, or supplied by the organization concerned. If in doubt, listen for a quiet period, then call on Channel 16. Then proceed in the same manner as ship-to-ship communication.

Selcall. "Digital Selective Calling" (DSC or Selcall) is a feature included in sophisticated VHF sets which enables a shore station or boat to call specific sets individually. The set is given a unique digital identification code after the owner files an application with the FCC. When the shore station transmits this code, the set emits an audible warning or flashes a light. Many sets can also record a missed call, allowing you to call back later. To call someone who has this feature, you would have to program his identification code into your set. VHF with Digital Selective Calling also has a Mayday feature; however, U.S. Coast Guard stations do not have the capability to receive DSC-coded Maydays. You would have to rely on commercial vessels with GMDSS to pick up your Mayday. See Chapter 20 for more information on GMDSS.

What else can you receive? Weather information and navigation warnings are broadcast constantly on their own VHF channel. Tune in regularly to stay in touch with weather developments. Similar information is also available, often in more detail, via Navtex receivers (Chapter 20).

Urgency and Distress Calls

Urgency. Calls concerning serious problems which are not life-threatening, such as dismasting, engine or rudder failure, or medical questions can be given precedence by using the call prefix, "Pan-Pan, Pan-Pan, Pan-Pan."

A typical call would run like this:

- *"PAN-PAN, PAN-PAN, PAN-PAN. U.S. Coast Guard, U.S. Coast Guard, U.S. Coast Guard.*
- *This is motor yacht Hopeful, Hopeful, Hopeful. My engine has seized five miles east of Cape Charles. Request assistance. Over."*

If they can hear you, the Coast Guard will respond and you can take it from there.

When medical assistance or advice is needed, sometimes the words *"pan-pan"* are followed by *"medico,"* creating a *"pan-pan-medico"* message similar to that above. The Coast Guard may "patch" you through to a doctor experienced with on board medical problems.

Distress. The prefix *"MAYDAY"* signals severe distress. Before issuing a Mayday distress signal, these points must be satisfied:

Here is an example. Your boat runs out of fuel outside the bar of San Francisco on a clear, calm, sunny morning. While a worrisome situation, you are not in imminent danger and the lives of all aboard are not immediately threatened. It might warrant a "pan-pan" call if you cannot raise the towboat rescue service.

The same boat runs out of fuel at midnight, two miles east of Nantucket Shoals in a 50-knot northeaster with a west-setting current that's pushing you toward a sand bar. You are in dire straits and a Mayday is definitely in order.

Because a distress call is broadcast to anyone within range, regardless of nationality or tongue, it follows a specific format. You MUST train yourself and at least one of your crew to remember this. Post it by your radio set for good measure.

Use the mnemonic "MIPNANAO" to remember the sequence. It's not the best mnemonic for so vital subject, but it sets out in order the initial letters of the crucial list below. Learn it, and don't forget it. It might save your life.

Receipt and Relay of Distress Messages

Acknowledgement. If you have heard a distress message and are in the vicinity, you must immediately acknowledge receipt. If there is a U.S. Coast Guard station nearby, you may defer for a short interval to allow the Coast Guard to acknowledge the distress. Then other boats may acknowledge receipt of the message. Here's how you acknowledge a Mayday message.

- *"MAYDAY. Lead Balloon, Lead Balloon, Lead Balloon.*
- *This is Silver Knight, Silver Knight, Silver Knight.*
- *Received your MAYDAY."*

As soon as possible, you should transmit Silver Knight's position, speed and approximate time to reach Lead Balloon to help determine which vessel is best to respond.

Mayday Relay. There may be a situation where you have heard a

MAYDAY Requirements

- **The danger must be imminent, not something which may happen a number of hours in the future. The disaster must be actually happening, or inevitable within the next few minutes.**
- **The vessel herself must be in danger (dismasting does not necessarily qualify, but a fuel fire does), or the danger must represent a grave threat to the life of a person on board (appendicitis may not be an immediate life-threat, but a person overboard in unkind conditions is).**

Proper MAYDAY Call (Remember the mnemonic "MIPNANAO.")

- *"**M**AYDAY, MAYDAY, MAYDAY"* (French pronunciation of *"m'aidez,"* or *"Help me!"*)
- **I**dentity: *"This is yacht Lead Balloon, Lead Balloon, Lead Balloon."*
- **P**osition: either a GPS readout of lat/long, DOUBLE-CHECKED, or *"5 nautical miles east of Cape Fear light."*
- **N**ature of distress: *"Sinking," "On Fire and Taking Water,"* etc.
- **A**ssistance required: *"Request immediate assistance,"* or perhaps, *"Request a pump."*
- **N**umber of persons on board
- **A**ny further information: boat length, color and type of vessel, *"sending up red parachute flares,"* or *"activating EPIRB;"* anything that may help you to be found or identified.
- *"**O**VER."* Pipe down now, and wait for acknowledgement. If none comes and you are still afloat, try again after a minute or so. It will seem a long wait.

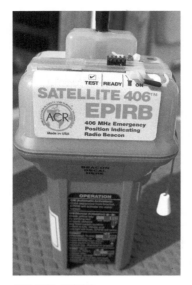

406 MHz EPIRB

Ocean capable SSB transceivers no longer have to be large and unwieldy. Their cost is within many budgets, and they can be an important safety factor if cruising beyond the limits of coastal VHF stations.

Mayday that has not been acknowledged, but you are not in a position to assist. If that happens, you must notify the Coast Guard, or others, by forwarding the distress signal with the Mayday Relay call prefix.
- *"MAYDAY RELAY, MAYDAY RELAY, MAYDAY RELAY.*
- *This is Silver Knight, Silver Knight, Silver Knight. "*

Control of Distress Messages. When a Mayday occurs, all messages relating to the immediate assistance are controlled by the boat that sent the distress message, unless she delegates control to another station. If there is a Coast Guard station or Rescue Coordinating Center involved, that station controls the distress traffic. The boat in distress or the station in control may impose silence on any or all stations in the area by issuing a Seelonce Mayday ("silence" as pronounced in French) signal. This is done with the call, *"SEELONCE MAYDAY to all stations."*

When silence is no longer necessary, the control station will issue a Seelonce Feenee (French for "silence finished") message.
- *"MAYDAY. Hello all stations, Hello all stations, Hello all stations.*
- *This is U.S. Coast Guard."*
- Time (of handing in of the message).
- Name and call sign of vessel in distress (Lead Balloon).
- *"SEELONCE FEENEE."*

Further Emergency Radio Equipment.

The EPIRB. For longer coastal trips that may pass outside probable VHF range, a 406 MHz EPIRB is considered required equipment by the Offshore Racing Council (ORC) in its *Safety Recommendations for Offshore Sailing including ORC Special Regulations*. The acronym EPIRB stands for "Emergency Position Indicating Radio Beacon," a compact, self-contained, floating radio transmitter that broadcasts a distress signal once activated. This signal can be accurately located via satellite. An EPIRB transmits for up to several days on its own batteries. It does not receive. A 406 MHz EPIRB broadcasts essential information dedicated to the boat and her shoreside contacts. An EPIRB is a MUST for offshore sailing. Older EPIRB types (i.e., 121.5 MHz) put out non-specific distress messages that are generally picked up by aircraft flying overhead. These have occasionally been ignored due to numerous hoax calls and accidental deployments. These older EPIRB units are being phased out but are still useful.

A 406 EPIRB must be registered, and registration information requested will include the type of the vessel, her likely number of crew and two telephone numbers. One of these should be the person with whom you leave your float plan.

Single Sideband Radio (SSB). Although a SSB transmitter requires a higher degree of user skill than VHF, and its equipment and installation are not inexpensive, many people feel that carrying a SSB is a responsible safety precaution if they expect to sail beyond VHF range. One form of SSB is amateur (ham) radio. Distress and urgency calls can be made on 2182 kHz frequency and the U.S. Coast Guard also continuously monitors and handles emergency traffic on 4125 kHz, 6215 kHz, 8291 kHz, 12290 kHz and 16420 kHz. There are additional frequencies for weather information by voice or fax.

Computers Aboard a Coastal Passagemaker

Since 1990, there has been a revolution in marine weather information, navigation and communications. At the root of this revolution is the computer, and new uses for it are being developed at an ever increasing pace. It is now the individual sailor's duty to keep up to date with this progress. This book cannot begin to describe in detail which buttons to punch to achieve a given end, but we shall discuss some of the more important uses of on-board computers in broader terms.

Navigation Computers. It is no longer prohibitively expensive to equip a coastal passagemaker with a fully integrated navigation computer system such as the following:

The core of the system might be a handheld, fully environment-proof unit that can be used at the chart table, in the cockpit, or even taken home for pre-planning a passage. On board, this unit slips into a "docking station" which connects it to a power supply, as well as a mouse, keyboard, GPS and, if desired, a cockpit repeater screen. Away from the docking station, the unit runs on a rechargeable battery.

Such a system would include full chart plotting capability plus access to "plug-in" chart modules for world-wide use. Its capacity to zoom in for detail might go down to the pontoons in a marina. The days are over when an electronic chart looked more like a child's depiction than a serious piece of primary navigation data. Today's charts are typically taken from NIMA, or other national authorities such as the United Kingdom Hydrographic Office.

The real magic is not that the computer simply depicts a digital navigation chart, it lies in its interface with the boat's GPS, which plots your vessel's position onto the chart...instantly. Today you can create waypoints and routes with the click of a cursor.

Some dedicated navigation computers combine these features with a nautical almanac. For example, the "Seafile Electronic Almanac" is designed to plug into the "Point 16 Pen Computer" system, giving you all the basic data you need to navigate the U.S.,

Below is an example of port information available on the Internet, which shows tidal heights and current for the entrance of San Francisco Bay.

http://co-ops.nos.noaa.gov

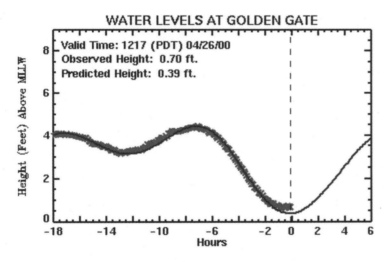

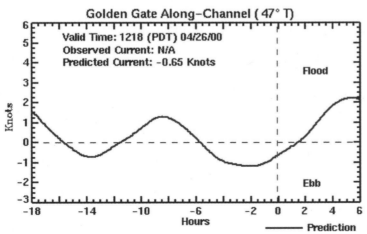

In this station plot, the wind is northwest at 40 knots, the pressure is 997.0 millibars (in the plot the first 9 or 10 as well as the decimal are not shown), the pressure has gone up by 3.0 mb (decimal is not shown) in the last three hours, and the cloud cover is completely overcast (an empty circle would indicate a clear sky).

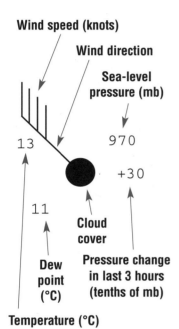

The half barb represents 5 knots, each long barb is 10 knots, and each pennant flag is 50 knots. The direction of the staff indicates the direction the wind is coming from. In this example, the wind is from the west at 75 knots.

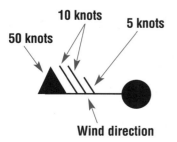

the Caribbean or Europe. The information, including information on tides, general weather, port plans, and lights is accessed by interacting with the chart using a mouse and cursor. Additional information on first aid, safety, waypoint lists and more is also available.

A reasonably capable computer can overlay tidal stream information, corrected for the hour and specific day, directly onto the chart you are using. Secondary port tidal heights are merely grist to its mill.

A computer coupled to a SSB radio with an interface can serve as a weatherfax and long-range email. More advanced computer units can also layer a synoptic weather map onto the current ocean chart, making it possible to project the boat's position in various "what if" scenarios generated from alternative courses and possible weather system movements.

This is the future of navigation. For many, it is already here, but we should never forget the principle spelled out in Chapter 6 concerning the enduring importance of the ship's log. The same principle applies to maintaining a stock of paper charts, almanacs, light lists and coast pilots, because it is more than likely that somewhere, sometime a boat's electronics will fail. Everything that can be backed up should be backed up so that the boat is in a constant state of readiness to revert to navigating with traditional tools.

Autopilot Interfaces. Many autopilots can be interfaced with a GPS system that is running a predetermined route, or "sail plan." The autopilot will automatically adjust course to bring the boat to the vicinity of her first waypoint. Thereafter, it adjusts towards the next, and so on until the boat arrives at the final destination. Such a system is unlikely to be of interest to sailboat skippers, who must attend to sail trim at every alteration of heading if, indeed, the boat can hold the course. Powerboat users, however, may find the possibility interesting.

It seems odd to most sailors that someone going to sea for pleasure should want to hand the full responsibility for steering the ship over to a printed circuit board, but if that turns you on, bear in mind the following:

• *You are obliged by international law to maintain an alert lookout at all times.* It is tempting not to do this if you are under autopilot even in the simple mode, let alone with the device programmed to do all your navigational thinking for you. Make sure a formal lookout is set and that he or she understands the 72 COLREGS (International Regulations for Preventing Collisions at Sea) as well as how to disengage the autopilot.

• *Beware of GPS-induced collisions.* If two or more boats are proceeding from one commonly used waypoint to another, they may at some time pass extremely close to one another.

The possibility of collision increases if both skippers have used the same published waypoint list instead of deciding upon positions suitable for conditions on the day. A two-decimal-point definition of a station is little more than a boat length.

Both the preceding items are doubly imperative if you are travelling at high speed.

Weatherfax. A weatherfax printer runs off a SSB radio. The operator must have the knowledge to tune and use it, and a modicum of computer skill. In addition to delivering synoptic charts, many weatherfax machines can work in a "Navtex" mode, enabling the operator to make the most of this valuable service for text weather data and navigation warnings within 150 miles or so of a transmitter. Other systems with specialized antennas and software can receive imagery directly from the weather satellites as they pass overhead.

These weatherfax sources give sailors something they always wanted but could never have before the electronic age. At set intervals, you can view up-to-date images, and analysis and forecast charts. Assuming you can interpret these (a basic user requirement), they will tell you why you are experiencing the weather you are, and provide a good chance of predicting what will soon arrive. On an offshore passage either system can deliver enough data for you to form a strategic policy for achieving fair winds while minimizing your chances of being clobbered. Along the coast, it advises you about when to duck in before it's blowing 40, and if

This Surface Analysis Chart indicates the actual positions of weather systems, isobars and data observations (i.e., station plots) for the northern Pacific Ocean at 1200 Zulu (12 Z) hours on April 16, 2000. New charts are prepared every six hours at 0000 hours (00 Z), 0600 hours (06 Z), 1200 hours (12 Z) and 1800 hours (18 Z). A polar stereographic map projection is used in this example.

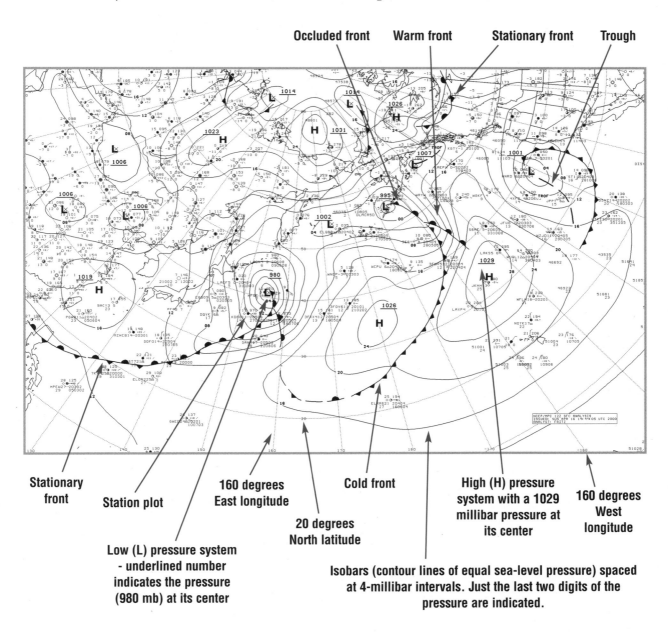

Occluded front   Warm front   Stationary front   Trough

Stationary front

Station plot

160 degrees East longitude

Cold front

High (H) pressure system with a 1029 millibar pressure at its center

160 degrees West longitude

20 degrees North latitude

Low (L) pressure system - underlined number indicates the pressure (980 mb) at its center

Isobars (contour lines of equal sea-level pressure) spaced at 4-millibar intervals. Just the last two digits of the pressure are indicated.

you are anchored behind some obscure island in a gale that seems never-ending, it offers the opportunity to assess whether you will be able to escape to sea before the soda runs out.

However, a weatherfax must be interpreted. If a sailor buys one who doesn't know a cold front from an icicle, they'll have wasted their money. Get used to synoptic charts. They might be your lifeline one day.

E-mail. A laptop, an installed PC or many navigation computers are capable of handling e-mail along the coast. So are an increasing number of cellular phones and Palm computers. The big question is how to hook them up to the telephone system.

This 48-hour Surface Forecast Chart shows the predicted positions of high and low pressure systems, fronts and isobars at the "valid" time as well as the predicted movement of highs and lows 24 hours prior to and after the "valid" time.

"Valid" time for this chart is 0000 Universal Time Coordinated hours (00 UTC) on April 18, 2000. UTC is the same as Zulu (Z) time (formerly Greenwich Mean Time, GMT).

Predicted location (X) of low 24 hours prior to "valid" time

Predicted location (X) of low (L) at "valid" time with a predicted center pressure of 977 millibars

Predicted location (X) of low 24 hours after "valid" time

Storms and gales are highlighted in caps inside a box.

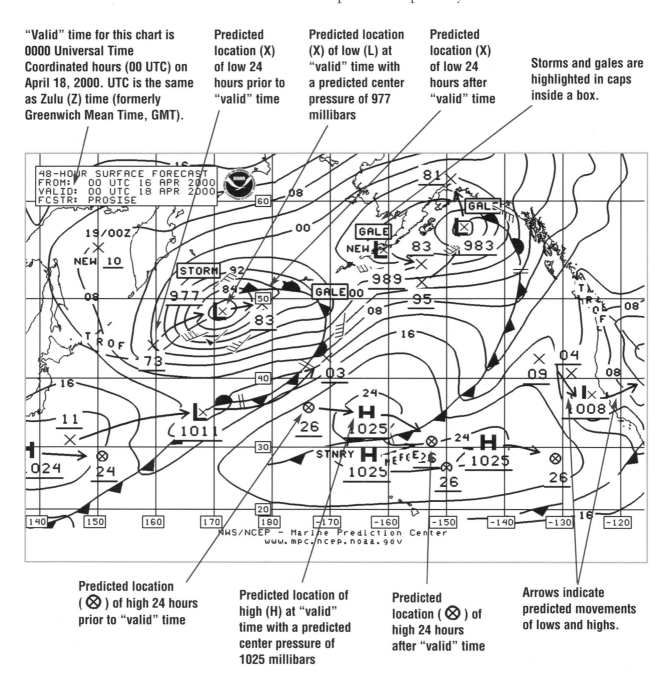

Predicted location (⊗) of high 24 hours prior to "valid" time

Predicted location of high (H) at "valid" time with a predicted center pressure of 1025 millibars

Predicted location (⊗) of high 24 hours after "valid" time

Arrows indicate predicted movements of lows and highs.

The best way of handling e-mail might be a cellular phone tapped into an infrared compatible Palm computer. The Palm computer typically uses two AA batteries and lasts for 20 to 40 hours. Most currently do not use rechargeable batteries. You just pop in two new ones and off you go again. This is actually a "plus" if you are becoming tired of yet another charger to clutter your ever-expanding bag of electrical gizmos. The system is set up with your established service provider and also enables you to access the Internet with all its potential for weather sites.

E-mail communication is sure to grow at sea, as long as the essential on-board telephone is within range of the shoreside net. As this will be the case for much of your coastal passagemaking, e-mail is a realistic proposition. In the year 2000, receiving and sending e-mail via satellite (Inmarsat, etc.) remains expensive and very slow. Doubtless this will change, so keep up to date on the latest developments.

Internet Sources. Weather. The Internet is a major source of weather information around the globe. In addition to sites with local and national forecasts, public and private hurricane sites are an important way of keeping informed during hurricane season.

Pilotage. Some ports run their own websites with up-to-the-minute data about changes in navigation marks, docks, available small-craft moorings, and all manner of other information. These are well worth downloading during the passage planning stage. Finding out where they are is easier each year. In addition to ever improving search engines, you will find a website address included on most port letterheads and advertisements.

Synoptic weather charts and weatherfax (above) deliver fascinating insights into what is going on around you, as well as being a great forecasting tool. Learn to read them!

The information available on the Internet is virtually endless. So long as you have the time, patience, and perhaps a useful collection of CD-ROMs to back it up, your computer can provide access to almost anything you will ever want to know about the technicalities of running your boat and keeping your crew safe. The trouble is that each minute we spend peering into the screen is a minute we aren't looking round the horizon or developing a feel for the sky, the run of the waves, and how the boat is feeling. One of the reasons most of us go sailing is because it establishes a direct connection to the natural forces that rule our planet. This reality will not change, no matter how we try to insulate ourselves from it.

An old-time coaster-skipper once observed, "If the tide's ebbin' at the narrows, the tide's ebbin' at the narrows. You don't have to like it, but there's nothing you, or me, or anyone else can do about it."

Not even the Internet has altered that unshakable truth.

Kim Downing photo

The increasingly useful palm-type computer will not only receive e-mails via a cellular phone, it can also download material from the Internet, giving access to all manner of information.

Systems Aboard a Coastal Passagemaker

The systems aboard the average modern cruising yacht would have boggled the imagination of sailors not too many years ago: reliable engines, watermakers, telephones, propane stoves, computers, holding tanks. The list seems endless. But all these wonders must be seen in the light of what they really are: devices ancillary to the ultimate running of the boat, and without which she must still function.

Systems involve technology, and as such are subject to failure, but if they are maintained on a routine basis, many are quite reliable. At sea or in remote harbors and anchorages, outside assistance for fixing them may simply not be available. Passagemaking sailors must be self-reliant enough to attempt system repair at sea and prepared to carry on without these systems if they are lost.

Some people have a natural affinity towards machinery. Back home, they may have an old motorcycle in pieces in the garage, a plumbing job successfully completed in the loft, and when the washing machine breaks down, their first reaction is to reach for the screwdriver. Direct action should be the sailor's immediate response to any mechanical problem on a boat, although it's harder for those who are not natural born mechanics.

It takes years to develop the skills that can fix most anything on board, so start working on it now. Ultimately, successful problem solving (mechanical or otherwise) is the result of positive attitude. If you're still having trouble, try this maxim: "Some guy made this. Now it's failed. If I can't fix it, I'm as stupid as he was."

Any skipper who cannot sort out system problems must delegate this responsibility, and give it a high priority.

Prioritizing. Assuming that the gear above decks is reliable, by far the most important systems on any boat are the engine, its drive train and propeller, and the batteries. The stove and sewage discharge system are also important. All these are dealt with in this chapter and they, together with any other items you may regard as indispensable should be backed up with spares, manuals and the tools needed to fix problems you can anticipate. The four essential procedures for keeping any system up to speed are "Understanding, Operation, Maintenance and Troubleshooting."

The Engine. Understanding. Trouble-free operation for any piece of machinery begins with comprehending how it works. A boat where nobody understands the four-stroke engine cycle or how an engine is fueled, cooled, exhausted and lubricated is helpless when even the simplest malfunction stops it from running. These functions are as essential to the operation of a boat as her sails, and are more important to her safety than ship-to-shore radio. If the crew can stop a potential problem from occurring, they will not need to call for help.

Operation. While the diesel remains a safer option for reasons of reduced fire risk and long-term reliability, gasoline engines continue to

A good engine installation allows access for repairs and routine maintenance. Some owners use computers to keep a log of maintenance schedules and reminders for their yacht's equipment, ranging from engine to fire extinguishers.

be used because of lower cost and a high power-to-weight ratio. However, because their use is declining on sailing auxiliaries, this section will deal mainly with the diesel.

When starting the engine, don't give any more throttle in neutral than experience teaches you is required. Although the oil should circulate instantaneously, it is a kindness to apply throttle gently and give it every chance. A turbo-charged diesel should generally be started with no extra revs above idle.

Whichever fuel it uses, the engine must be warmed up before demanding higher power. Ignoring this causes premature and unnecessary wear. If the engine is gasoline powered, the engine-room blower should be activated for a few minutes before starting up. This will vent out any gasoline vapor that has built up. It does no harm to adopt the same policy for diesel.

The question of how hard an engine can be run is sometimes covered in the owner's manual. A gas engine pulling at half-throttle is generally a happy engine, though it will certainly manage more when asked. Diesel engines thrive on hard work. A healthy diesel can be driven at three-quarters of maximum revs all day and all night, and many can stand close to full power for extended periods. Running one at low revs for long periods of time is not doing it any favors, particularly if out of gear to charge batteries. Operating a diesel "under light load" has the effect of

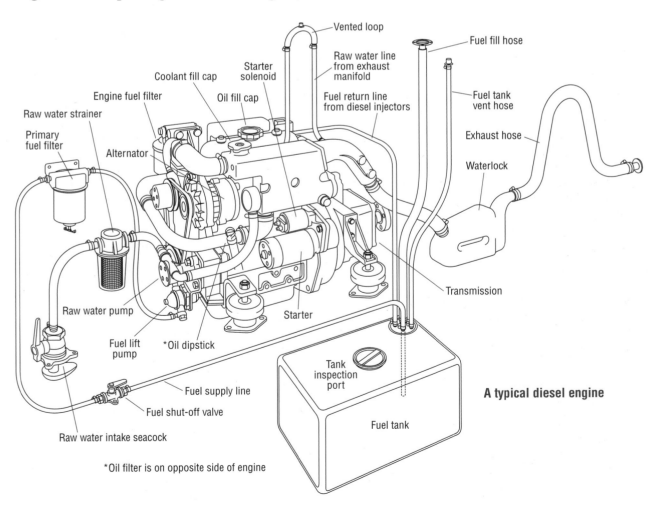

A typical diesel engine

Vented loop
Fuel fill hose
Raw water line from exhaust manifold
Starter solenoid
Coolant fill cap
Oil fill cap
Fuel return line from diesel injectors
Fuel tank vent hose
Engine fuel filter
Exhaust hose
Raw water strainer
Waterlock
Primary fuel filter
Alternator
Transmission
Raw water pump
Starter
Fuel lift pump
*Oil dipstick
Fuel supply line
Tank inspection port
Fuel shut-off valve
Raw water intake seacock
Fuel tank

*Oil filter is on opposite side of engine

"glazing" the cylinder bores. This allows lubricating oil to bypass the piston rings and enter the combustion chambers. Here, it lowers injector efficiency as well as spilling out into the exhaust to generate pollution. Therefore when charging try to keep the engine in gear whenever possible, and if you have reason to believe your unit is suffering from glazed bores, give it a long run under working load as soon as possible.

Always listen to your engine. If it is water-cooled, like most, the exhaust note will change should the water stop coming through. This can be an early indication that the engine is about to overheat, so take a regular glance at the temperature gauge and keep your ears open. You might save yourself an expensive rebuild and relieve the Coast Guard or towing service of another rescue job.

If you have engine gauges, get to know them all. Note the normal temperature and the working oil pressure after warm-up. If the latter starts to drop, either unexpectedly, or over a period of weeks or months, it is telling you something. If it falls over a single running period, stop the engine and find out what's wrong otherwise it will stop itself. If losing oil pressure is a slow, steady process, something moderately expensive is wearing out. With luck it'll be the oil pump, but it might be the big end bearings. Find yourself a marine engine mechanic in the next harbor and have the problem investigated. If you don't take such signs seriously, the engine can die in the relatively near future, and the laws of inconvenience state that the weather won't be pleasant when it happens.

Maintenance. To run forever (more or less), a marine diesel needs clean fuel, regular oil changes, air and a plentiful supply of cooling water. It also needs volts, amps and a reliable electric motor to start it, but more of this later in "battery management."

Fuel. Water or dirt in diesel fuel blocks the injectors which spray diesel oil mist into the combustion chambers. Clearing clogged injectors is a specialist's job, so the engine builders have taken steps to prevent clogs from occurring. All engines have at least one fuel filter in the line.

Most good installations have a filter mounted on the engine itself, generally between the fuel "lift pump" and the injector pump. The lift pump is a small unit that transfers fuel to the larger high-pressure pump that supplies the injectors. The filter between them generally features a disposable element. If this clogs, it will stop the engine as surely as a rope round the propeller. It must therefore be changed at regular intervals, whether it looks dirty or not, and in any case at least once per season. If there is an additional filter it will usually be found between the tank and

Fuel lift pump

Diesel Engine Fuel System

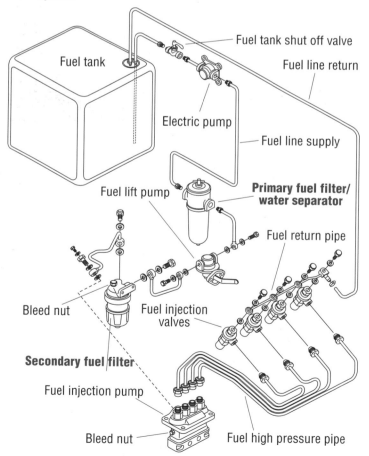

- Fuel tank
- Fuel tank shut off valve
- Fuel line return
- Electric pump
- Fuel line supply
- Fuel lift pump
- **Primary fuel filter/ water separator**
- Fuel return pipe
- Bleed nut
- Fuel injection valves
- **Secondary fuel filter**
- Fuel injection pump
- Bleed nut
- Fuel high pressure pipe

the lift pump. This filter may have a water trap with a tap on the bottom. Drain this on a regular basis, letting the fuel run until it comes clean. The unit may also have a disposable element, and since this is in the front line of defense against the forces of darkness lurking in the tank, change it more frequently than the one on the engine.

Lube oil. Marine engine oil breaks down just as it does on your car, so change it (and the oil filter) as per the manufacturers instructions. Typically, this will be every 100 hours of running. Changing the oil is one of the reasons why engine hours must be logged, so mark when the next change is due on the new filter. Lifting the engine out of a boat is a major task. Spending a little time and money on oil and filters will greatly reduce the odds of this happening to you.

Changing oil is not difficult, but you should research what you need for the job. Some engines have convenient dedicated sump pumps, others must suck their oil out via a stirrup pump with a long snout introduced into the dipstick hole, a messy business. Occasionally, there is room to dump the oil straight out the bottom of the engine via the sump plug, but this is a rare bonus.

If you run beyond the recommended oil-change period while at sea, empty the sump at your next anchorage without fail, stow the waste oil in the container it came in and dispose it at the first available facility. Every boat on passage should carry enough oil for a full change plus some extra for topping off. Carry at least one spare oil filter.

Engine air filters should also be changed as per manufacturer's recommendation.

Cooling water. Because a boat has no airstream to cool a radiator, most maintain their engine coolant at the designed temperature using a "heat exchanger" chilled by seawater. A typical cooling system requires little maintenance beyond checking the "header tank" or externally mounted reservoir. This should only be done with a cold engine to avoid a blowout of scalding coolant. Top up with water/antifreeze mix as necessary, and change the coolant annually to ensure that the mix stays balanced. Be sure to read the manual. Some heat exchangers have a sacrificial zinc element that requires regular replacement.

On some boats with a hot-water system for sinks and showers, you may notice a valve near the heat exchanger. This valve allows the hot water tank to be removed for maintenance without disabling the engine.

Seawater is sent round the heat exchanger by a small pump which will be described in "troubleshooting." The water enters the boat via a seacock which should incorporate a strainer to catch matter such as weed before it enters the heat exchanger. Check and clean the strainer at least once a week, but don't forget to shut the seacock first (see "Flooding" in Chapter 22).

Engine Water Coolant Reservoir

Troubleshooting. There are two types of engine failure. Refusal to start, and fading out on the job.

Failure to start. This is caused either by an electrical fault or a lack of fuel.

Electrics. If your starting batteries are too low to turn over the engine, try starting the engine with the master battery switch in the ALL (BOTH) position. If that fails, you've still got your sails as an option. (Battery management is covered later in the chapter.)

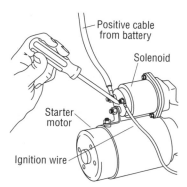

Hot Wiring the Solenoid

Solenoid Electrical Connections

Above is a remotely operated engine stop solenoid.

If you have reason to believe your batteries are in fair shape, but the starter emits an infuriating "click" instead of delivering the goods, you may have a loose or dirty electrical terminal.

Check all the major connections for tightness or white powdery corrosion, including the batteries themselves. If you find any deposit, switch off the power, disconnect and clean. Another explanation for this symptom is that the starter motor solenoid, a small unit piggy-backed onto the starter, could be malfunctioning or that the wiring is not delivering enough power for the big punch. This could be a result of switching problems. Try turning on the power then firmly laying a screwdriver (which must have an insulated handle) across the two terminals on the solenoid. This will "hot-wire" the solenoid and sometimes produce the desired result.

Fuel. When the starter spins a diesel engine in fine style, but the engine will not fire up, you almost certainly have a fuel problem. The first place to look is the fuel cut-off valve by which the engine is stopped.

A diesel is not brought to rest by switching off its electrics like a gasoline engine. Instead, the injector pump is shut down. This is achieved either by a "stop cable" which is pulled manually, or by means of the ignition key. The danger of the latter system is that the uninformed might assume they are switching the engine off, but they are not. They are activating a solenoid switch that does the same job as the older-style stop cable. If your engine will not start, don't keep cranking till the batteries are flat. First, check that the stop cable was been pushed back again after stopping the engine. If you have a solenoid cut-off, make sure it is functioning correctly and that the wiring is not corroded. Sadly, some solenoids fail with the fuel off, so what is imagined to be "fail safe." may prove to be "fail dangerous" depending on your point of view.

Failure under way. Unlike a gasoline engine which stutters and misfires before quitting, a diesel will fade steadily before giving up the ghost. If your cutoff arrangements are in order, and assuming your fuel line is intact, it is possible that one of your pumps has gone down, but it is most probable that you have run out of fuel or have a blocked filter. The former can be solved with your emergency fuel supply. If you have spare fuel, however, you must still bleed residual air out of the fuel system before the engine will run.

Bleeding a diesel. If the engine won't run and there is fuel in the tank, air in the fuel line is almost certainly stopping diesel from reaching the injectors. This usually results from dirty fuel fouling the filters or a break (loose joint or split) in the line. Clear the filters as described earlier or repair the break, and you are almost there. The final job is to bleed air from the line.

Most modern diesels have a bleed point for air on top of the engine filter, which is often arranged to be the highest point of the fuel system. Look here for a bolt head, usually a hexagon, and slacken it off a turn or two. Now find the lift pump on the engine block by following the feed pipe back towards the tank. Operate the small handle on its side which activates it with the engine at rest. Bubbly fuel and air should now be expelled from the bleed point. If nothing happens, make sure all taps are on then try another bolt head to make sure you have the right one.

In due course, the bubbles will be replaced by pure diesel. Tighten the bolt, crank the engine for several seconds to give the clean fuel time to reach the injectors and away it will go. Some engines also need to have their injector pump bled, in which case you will find one or more bleed screws on its body.

The ability to bleed a diesel is critical. Some engines self-bleed after thirty seconds or more on the starter motor, though many do not. Even with a "self-bleeder" you can help your batteries by clearing the lines as described. If you have never attempted it, try the job alongside the dock one day when you have a spare half hour. You'll discover how much paper towel you need for mopping up, whether or not your wrenches fit and if you can actually worm your way in there to get at the bleed screws. Only by this means can you be sure you'll manage at sea. One day, those thirty minutes will save you a tow, which makes it a good rate of pay for your trouble. It might even save your life.

Overheating. This happens when the cooling water fails to circulate, and the problem is usually in the raw water supply. Either the intake is fouled, or the circulating pump has packed up. The former is easily sorted out by clearing the seawater strainer. If this does not work (check for water coming out of the exhaust), the pump is probably to blame.

The water pump is found by following the pipe that leads to the engine from the seacock. First, look to see if it is belt driven. If so, check the belt and replace or tighten as required. If not, the overwhelming likelihood is that the pump impeller has disintegrated, usually due to overheating.

Shut the seacock, then back off the machine screws securing the inspection plate. Remove this carefully to save the gasket, then withdraw the impeller which looks like a rubber windmill. If damaged, replace it with a spare. Should you have broken the gasket, make a new one by placing the inspection plate on a cereal box. Now tap it all round with a hammer to leave an impression on the cardboard. Cut the new gasket out carefully and hoist your shingle as a jungle mechanic. If you've no cereal boxes, use gasket "goo" (aka: Permatex), a tube of which should form part of your spares kit. In either event, you'll be pleased with the results.

The Gearbox. Understanding. Unlike its land-based cousin, a marine gearbox has neither clutch nor torque converter to protect it from the operator's heavy hands. It is designed for direct shifting at low engine speeds and minimum loadings.

Operation. Be gentle with your gearbox. Always throttle down before shifting and never, never, slam the engine from full ahead to full astern. Always wait for a second in neutral. The time lost won't affect the outcome of a situation, but stripping the teeth off your gears certainly will.

Maintenance. Follow the manufacturers' recommendations for transmission fluid changes. These are not so frequent as oil changes for the engine and can often be attended to at leisure during a winter lay-up.

Troubleshooting. The ideal gearbox is designed to fail safe in "forward," but many do not. If your gearbox stops working, first check the control cable. Fix it, or at least disconnect it and operate the gear lever (side of the gearbox on the back of the engine) manually. Should this prove awkward or dangerous, throw the lever into forward with the motor stopped, crank up and enjoy a safe ride to the nearest mechanic. Don't forget to stop the engine well short of the dock and coast in.

Propeller Shaft. Stern tubes and glands for the shaft have been

Raw Water Intake Cooling Strainer

Water Pump Access Cover

Replacement Water Impeller
Be sure to remove all of the old impeller before installing a new one!

discussed in detail in Chapter 1. One final item to add to your checklist is that your shaft should have a zinc collar in good condition to protect the shaft from pitting and corrosion.

Battery Management. Without going into the chemistry, a battery can be considered as a reservoir of electrical power which flows like water. The amount of power required to run an electrical "appliance" is measured in watts. The actual flow of electrical current is measured in "amps," and the state of the battery's potential to push current (through resistance) is calculated in "volts." The amount of current stored in the battery is measured in "amp-hours."

Most small craft electrical systems come in the 12-volt variety, although some employ 24-volt systems.

Systems On	Amp-Hours Required
Navigation tricolor light	15 amp-hours
Instruments, radio etc.	5 amp-hours
Cabin lights	5 amp-hours
Autopilot	25 amp-hours
total	50 amp-hours

If one amp flows from a battery for one hour, the job is said to have consumed one "amp-hour." Every battery has a maximum number of amp-hours it can contain. When a 100-amp-hour battery is full to the brim, it can deliver 50 amps of current for 20 hours. However, it is not able to deliver 100 amps for 1 hour. More amp-hours can be delivered at a lower current than at a higher current. A well-charged 100-amp sailboat battery probably holds 85 amps once it is past its first blush of youth.

The fundamental relationship which links all this battery information to the reality of passagemaking lies between watts, volts and amps. The formula is simple: Watts = volts x amps

Put differently, this also means that Watts/volts = amps.

So, if a 24-watt light bulb is switched on in a 12-volt system it is drawing 24/12 amps or, over 60 minutes, 2 amp-hours.

Leave this bulb on for 40 hours and it will consume 80 amp-hours, which would effectively drain the battery we have been considering.

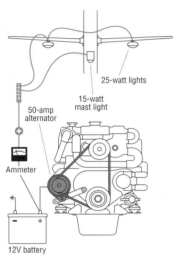

25-watt lights

15-watt mast light

50-amp alternator

Ammeter

12V battery

The light bulbs above are drawing a total of 65 watts which represents a draw of a little under 5.5 amps for a 12-volt battery. If they run for 8 hours, they will consume 44 amp-hours. To recharge, start the engine and watch the ammeter to see the rate at which the battery is recharging. Don't assume that a 50-amp alternator is delivering 50 amp-hours. Unless you have a specialized voltage regulator, the batteries will be recharged in about three hours, assuming a healthy system and the batteries were not flat to begin with.

While light bulbs, instruments, starter motors, radios and the rest draw upon a battery, the alternator charges it whenever the engine is running. A typical small boat alternator has a capacity of 600 watts and can delivers 50 amps at maximum output, which is how it is generally rated. At that rate, however, the battery would melt down, so the charger's output is controlled by a voltage regulator.

Most voltage regulators are automotive devices designed for a truck or fishing boat whose engine will be running for extended periods. Although they work well on a powerboat, they shut the charge down more abruptly than sailboat operators would prefer. Owners can solve this problem by fitting a "smart" regulator which allows their batteries to charge fully in a much shorter time.

Assuming you have a non-specialist regulator and an alternator whose theoretical output is at least 25 percent of the total battery capacity, you can expect to shove anything from 10 to 30 amps into your batteries in one hour, with the rate diminishing as the battery fills up. In a typical sailing night, you might use power as follows:

To replace this in a 180 amp-hour battery might take from two to three hours on a 50-amp alternator, depending on the state of the battery to start with. The larger the battery bank, however, the larger can be the alternator, so it can make sense for a serious cruising yacht with the space and the budget to run on 400 amp-hour batteries charged by a 100-amp alternator, thus reducing recharging time and easing the strain on the batteries.

Maintenance. Unless your boat is fitted with maintenance-free batteries, inspect the cells at least once a week to make sure they do not require topping off. If you can see the cell above the electrolyte, fill to cover the cell by at least 1/4 inch with distilled water. If one cell repeatedly dries out, it is dying and the rest of the battery will soon follow. The battery will need to be replaced.

Keep terminals tight and coated with petroleum jelly. This helps avoid electrolysis of the terminals.

Operation. Any passagemaker should have one battery dedicated to starting the engine. This is the first to be charged on any split-relay charging system, so it remains fully charged at all times. Should you encounter a starting problem from another source, your engine battery will therefore be capable of pumping out numerous starts before it dies. The same applies if your charging system fails.

Always take steps to ensure that this battery does not get mixed up with the domestic ("house") battery system. If you have a four-way combined battery switch that offers 1, 2, ALL (BOTH) and OFF, clearly label which number is for the engine battery. It must always be charging when the engine is running, and always isolated from use when the engine is at rest.

Troubleshooting. If batteries stop charging, first check that the drive belt for the alternator is intact and correctly tensioned. If this doesn't restore life, inspect all terminals both large and small on batteries, alternator, battery switches and the voltage regulator. Beyond this, there is little you can do on board without specialized knowledge.

Galley Propane. Because it is highly explosive, propane is to be taken very seriously indeed. Leaking propane is heavier than air, and so sinks into the bilge. If a spark ignites a substantial amount of accumulated gas, the boat can be destroyed.

Propane tanks must be stored in a sealed locker opening onto the deck or into a self-draining cockpit. The locker should have a vent low down that empties overboard. Piping must be of the approved grade and all fittings double-checked for tightness regularly. This is best done with a detergent-water mix whisked up into a bubbly state. The mix is applied liberally to all unions with a paint brush. Any leak will immediately show.

If you are specifying your own propane system, you can do no better than follow the ABYC (American Boat and Yacht Council) *Standards and Recommended Practices* guidelines to

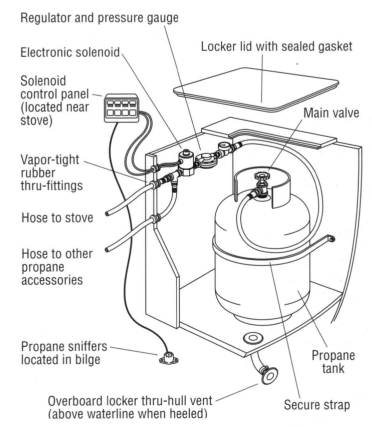

Propane safety systems

Regulator and pressure gauge

Electronic solenoid

Solenoid control panel (located near stove)

Locker lid with sealed gasket

Main valve

Vapor-tight rubber thru-fittings

Hose to stove

Hose to other propane accessories

Propane sniffers located in bilge

Propane tank

Overboard locker thru-hull vent (above waterline when heeled)

Secure strap

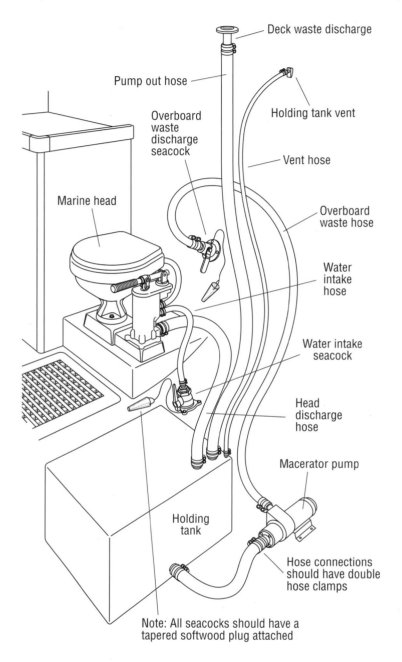

Deck waste discharge

Pump out hose

Overboard
waste
discharge
seacock

Holding tank vent

Marine head

Vent hose

Overboard
waste hose

Water
intake
hose

Water intake
seacock

Head
discharge
hose

Macerator pump

Holding
tank

Hose connections
should have double
hose clamps

Note: All seacocks should have a
tapered softwood plug attached

A typical head system

the letter. These recommend a solenoid-operated shut-off valve at the tank activated by a switch near the stove to keep the gas supply isolated at all times the stove is not burning.

All burners must have thermocouple devices which shut down the gas in the event of the flame blowing out. An electronic gas "sniffer" device must also be fitted in the bilge near to, but not directly below the stove and, if you want to go the whole hog, this also can be connected to the solenoid cut-off. As soon as a dangerous concentration of gas is detected in the bilge, the whole system shuts down automatically.

Black Water (Sewage). The last system that is considered vital enough to be mentioned here is the arrangement for pumping out holding tanks.

Most U.S. boats are now built so that sewage has no option but go into the holding tank. From there, it is either discharged at a "pumpout station," or pumped overboard by way of a macerator pump. A macerator (EPA Type I or II) is a Federally approved Marine Sanitation Device offering a viable alternative to the pump-out option. Macerating breaks up the effluent and treats it with a chlorination process involving electric current and seawater to lower the fecal coliform bacteria count to an acceptable level before discharge. However, several popular cruising areas have already legislated for "No Discharge" zones, including the Great Lakes. Many local harbors and bays are also designated, and more seem likely to push for "No Discharge" status. In such areas, effluent must be held aboard until the vessel is three miles offshore, or pumped out at a pumpout station.

Because the macerator discharge is generally protected by a seacock, it pays handsomely to open this before activating the macerator. Forgetting this crucial step can produce horrible results as the effluent breaches the weakest point in the system and discharges into the yacht.

Spares and Tools. Before venturing to sea on passage, a boat must be equipped with a tool kit that gives her people a chance of fixing most common eventualities. She must also carry spares organized on a priorities basis. Here is a minimum suggested list:

Tools

- ☐ Socket set
- ☐ Wrench set, appropriate for the jobs it may have to tackle
- ☐ Adjustable wrenches, large, small and tiny
- ☐ Vise grips and pipe wrench
- ☐ Hammers – medium and heavy
- ☐ Screwdrivers, large small and medium with various heads: slotted, Phillips-head, and square-drive head. Also include a set of cheap jeweler's screwdrivers for electrical work
- ☐ Hand drill or rechargeable electric, plus a set of sharp bits
- ☐ Hacksaws, large and small, with many spare blades
- ☐ Bolt Cutters and/or drift pins
- ☐ Wood tools for wooden boats, including basic saw and chisels
- ☐ Pliers: large, small and electrical
- ☐ Multi-purpose wire cutter, crimper and stripper
- ☐ Electrical multimeter
- ☐ Waxed twine, sail needles and palm
- ☐ Sharp knife

Spares

- ☐ Electrical connector terminals of all types and sizes. These cost very little
- ☐ Light bulbs, especially dedicated navigation light spares (make sure you have a spare compass light bulb – often overlooked)
- ☐ Electrical tape
- ☐ Duct tape
- ☐ Screws, wood and self-tapping, many and various
- ☐ A selection of odd bolts, nuts and washers, including copper washers
- ☐ Winch pawls and springs
- ☐ Electrical wire of various gauges
- ☐ Engine cooling water pump impeller
- ☐ Any belts used by the engine
- ☐ Gasket "goo"
- ☐ Grease, engine oil and freeing oil
- ☐ Caulking compound and gun
- ☐ Rope and small line, whipping twine
- ☐ Seizing wire
- ☐ Flashlights and batteries
- ☐ Various sandpapers and other abrasives
- ☐ Selection of hose clamps
- ☐ Any specialized spares for systems, such as "O"-rings, engine oil and fuel filters, and a rebuild kit for the head
- ☐ Shackles, clevis pins, cotter pins, a spare halyard and sheet, sail ties, self-adhesive sail repair tape, dacron cloth and contact adhesive

Coastal Seamanship

Seamanship can be taken to mean self-reliance, anticipating trouble and dealing with it before it develops. Seamanship is also about cure when prevention has failed.

Able skippers always seem to end up to windward of their objectives because they have been thinking in advance. They do not frighten people when maneuvering in tight marinas because they know which way their propellers will kick and they make early allowance for current and strong winds. Most important of all, they are constantly aware of lee shores encroaching on their sea room, both strategically on a passage and tactically when close inshore. Such skippers are also constantly concerned and caring for their crew. A good-humored reminder, "Do me a favor and don't fall over the side, old mate," as someone clips on to head up the foredeck on a dark night can kindly reinforce the use of harnesses.

Seamanship is the foundation of the premise that a boat's crew should be able to sort out her problems without assistance. Whether or not this proves to be the case, the cause will be aided by sailing a well-equipped vessel.

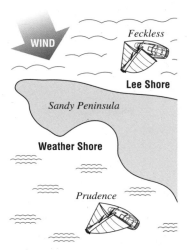

While the boats shown are the same distance from shore, *Prudence* is safe under the lee of a weather shore, while *Feckless* can be forced down onto a dangerous lee shore in heavy seas and strong winds. Learn this terminology! It can be confusing.

Equipment for Heavy Weather and Emergencies. Since it is the "sole and inescapable responsibility" of anyone in charge of a boat to ensure her safety and that of the crew, it is imperative that equipment does not let anyone down. While this holds for everything on board from engine and sails to seacocks, safety and emergency equipment are often regarded to form the front line. In reality it is the rearguard, as emergency equipment will only be used if something else (including, perhaps, the navigation) has failed. This does not, however, make it less important. The seaman hopes for the best and prepares for the worst. A regularly serviced "overboard" kit is therefore as much a part of a well-found boat as her keel bolts, while sensible personal gear such as harnesses and PFDs form a central part of emergency prevention. Practice drills for predictable emergencies such as fire and overboard are also a link in the chain.

Radar reflector. A small yacht in rough water makes a poor radar target, and a reflector is a cost-effective way of easing this situation. Many yachts have theirs permanently mounted, generally up the mast or on the wheelhouse. Others hoist it when needed in thick weather. Whichever your preference, equip yourself with one whose "equivalent echoing area" is 6 square meters. The old-fashioned octahedron which can be folded flat for stowing must be at least a foot across. Whatever type it is, to function properly its mounting must be at least 13 feet above water.

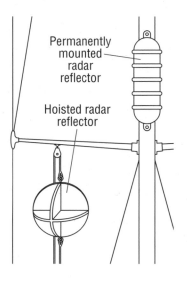

Permanently mounted radar reflector

Hoisted radar reflector

Firefighting and Extinguishers.
Firefighting is a specialized skill. Should an opportunity present itself to attend a weekend course in the off-season, grab it. Meanwhile, here are some helpful prevention tips:

Make sure all fuels are stored in properly vented tanks with shut-off valves that can be accessed away from likely sources of fire. All other combustibles, including solvents and even solvent-soaked rags, must be sensibly stowed. Many fires are started electrically, so if you have been working on wiring, watch out for electrical shorts.

The galley remains the main culprit for fire, at least in sailing yachts. Pay constant attention to this obvious source of fire risk.

Carry at least three "ABC" general-purpose fire extinguishers, one of which must be a heat-triggered device within the engine compartment. Site the others near exits from the boat and regularly inspect gauges indicating condition of the extinguisher. Replace and/or check extinguishers annually according to manufacturer's recommendations.

Every galley should have a fire blanket ready for instant action.

Action in the event of fire. The first crew to see a fire should call out "FIRE!" and move everyone on deck. Steer so as to lessen any apparent wind and keep smoke clear of crew. Since the situation may worsen rapidly and preclude going back below, make sure all hands are wearing their PFDs and that one of them is carrying the handheld VHF.

If the fire is burning on the surface of a combustible liquid, you may spread the fire. If you use a fire blanket, wrap one edge of it around your hands for protection before deploying it.

When using an extinguisher, sweep its discharge across the base of the fire and keep going until the extinguisher is empty. Watch the remnants for re-ignition.

If the situation seems at all serious, detail off one person to send a "PAN-PAN" or "MAYDAY" call as appropriate (see Chapter 7) and prepare to abandon ship.

Jacklines. These are lines running along the deck on both sides of the boat for the dedicated purpose of attaching crew safety harnesses. Jacklines should be positioned so that crew can clip on their tethers before leaving the cockpit and then traverse the deck from bow to stern without unclipping. The aft end should be positioned 4 to 6 feet from the stern so that if someone is washed off their feet and swept aft, they will not end up trailing astern. There should also be at least one pad eye in

Fire blanket in galley

Fire extinguisher near companionway

Automatic fire extinguisher

Fire extinguisher near forward hatch

Types of fires	Extinguishing methods
CLASS A: wood, paper, cloth, rubber, some plastics	1 Water, poured or hosed, on flames 2 Dry chemical extinguisher 3 Fire blanket for contained galley fires 4 FE-241, FM-200 automatic extinguishers (Halon replacements)
CLASS B: flammable liquids including diesel, oil, gasoline, alcohol	1 Dry chemical extinguisher 2 Carbon dioxide (CO_2) extinguisher 3 FE-241, FM-200 automatic extinguishers
CLASS C: live electrical fires	1 Carbon dioxide (CO_2) extinguisher 2 Dry chemical extinguisher 3 FE-241, FM-200 automatic extinguishers

A fire extinguisher mounted in the galley area should be positioned so that a crew member does not have to reach through flames from a stove fire for access.

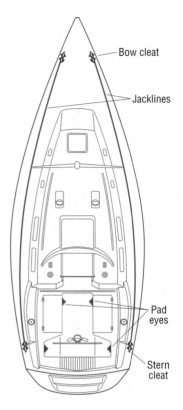

A sound jackline arrangement

the cockpit for the helmsman and another for crew exiting the companionway in rough weather.

Jacklines are sometimes made of ³⁄₁₆ in. (5mm) diameter stainless steel wire, but heavy nylon webbing with a minimum breaking strength of 4,500 lbs. is preferred. It is quieter down below as a tether slides along it, and it does not pose the hazard of rolling under the feet. Boots can, however, slip on it, and crew must be made aware of this. Spectra line, which has remarkably low stretch and high strength properties is also useful for jacklines, but be aware that Spectra and nylon webbing ultimately degrade in sunlight.

Because webbing stretches when it is wet, it is best to rig a jackline made of webbing with the material wet. Ends are typically secured to bolted or welded deck padeyes, deck cleats or through-bolted stanchion bases, with a strong lanyard on at least one end for tightening.

Overboard gear. Whether disabled by the incident or not, the position of overboard casualties must be marked with gear that can also help them survive. All coastal and offshore passagemakers are recommended to carry:

• A lifebuoy inscribed with the boat's name, carrying retro-reflective tape. Attached to this should be a self-igniting light, a drogue and an overboard pole with a flag (also called dan-buoy).

• A Lifesling, equipped with a self-igniting light, stowed so as to be ready for instant deployment. The Lifesling remains attached to the boat after deployment by means of a floating line used to recover the victim. NOTE: The stowage of the tether line in the pack should be checked to make sure it will run freely when deployed (usually new ones are not packed for deployment).

• A floating heaving line 50 to 75 feet long, ready for use near the cockpit. This should have a monkey's fist knot, or some sort of "victim-friendly" weighting device at one end. It should not be ballasted with metal. A rescue throw bag also works well.

A Man Overboard Module is a recent innovation being seen on more boats. They are often chosen because they are quicker to deploy than the overboard pole. The flipside is that there are inflatable parts which will require periodic professional inspection.

Flares and rockets. There is some discrepancy between the U.S. Coast Guard minimum requirements and the more comprehensive international SOLAS (Safety Of Life At Sea) Convention requirements.

For ocean and coastwise small passenger vessels under 100 gross tons the USCG requires six handheld red flares and six handheld orange smoke flares; however, some or all of these can be replaced with SOLAS rocket parachute flares. All must be carried in a watertight container. For commercial use a dedicated locker is required, but

Overboard Gear

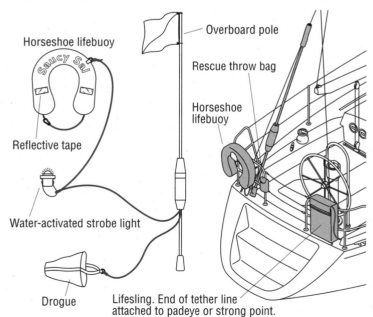

on a yacht "any sensible stowage" is appropriate.

There is no doubt that to initiate contact with distant rescuers, a parachute rocket flare is more effective than one held by hand at sea level. Historically, U.S. made parachute flares have required a launching device. SOLAS flares are self-propelled from within an integral tube.

The SOLAS recommendation for coastal passages more than 7 miles off the coast is four red parachute rockets firing to 1000 feet, four red handheld flares and two buoyant orange smoke signals for daylight.

"The more the merrier" should be your maxim.

When using rockets, fire one, wait two minutes, then fire the next. This gives anyone who thought they saw the first (but wasn't quite sure) time to reflect and get ready for another. Thereafter, fire at reasonable intervals.

Hand flares are primarily for pinpointing your position to rescuers who cannot yet see you, although you might have them in view.

In addition to these distress signals, it is worth carrying a number of white, non-distress flares. Hand whites signify "Here I am!" to anyone whose attention you want to catch — perhaps a ship converging with you in a calm when your engine has failed. White parachute rockets will illuminate an area and can be a lifesaver when trying to locate a crew overboard at night.

Liferaft. Liferaft procedure along the coast is the same as it is offshore, and this subject is covered comprehensively in Chapter 22. While a liferaft is recommended for coastal passagemaking, it is not essential. Whether you carry one or not, you should prepare a waterproof "grab bag" of abandon ship essentials. Along the coast, your wait in a raft or dinghy will probably be hours rather than days, so the coastal grab bag will contain more in the way of extra flares, a handheld VHF (charged regularly), a first aid kit, and high-energy candy bars than long-term survival equipment.

Personal Safety Gear. The PFD. The term PFD (personal flotation device) covers variations from a buoyancy aid such as a lightweight inflatable vest to a full collar life jacket. A Type 1 or Type 2 device must support an unconscious person in full clothing in such a way that the face is clear of the water. Nothing less will do for a passagemaker. Fortunately, today's inflatables, which derive buoyancy from air or compressed gas are easy to put on and can be worn in a deflated state. The most useful ones also incorporate a safety harness to which a tether can be snapped. Some auto-inflate when a victim hits the water, while others require users to pull on tabs or blow them up orally. There are tradeoffs to either method, so the choice is yours. Auto-inflating devices require regular service and you may not be pleased if it blows up accidentally and demands yet another fresh gas bottle. On the other hand, you'd be glad you're wearing one if you tumbled over the side in an unconscious or weaken condition.

US SAILING's publication *Safety Recommendations for Cruising Sailboats* recommends a minimum buoyancy of 35 lbs. for PFDs. Most Type 1 & 2 PFDs have 24, 22, or 15.5 lbs. of buoyancy. Although it may not matter as much for coastal conditions, a 35-lbs. life jacket or inflatable for offshore should be an important piece of safety equipment to have.

There will always be debate about whether a PFD must be used at all times afloat. Certain authorities suggest that it should be worn when foul-weather gear is donned. Perhaps the safest solution is to choose a life jacket

A self-contained SOLAS parachute rocket flare fires up to 1000 feet, so it is affected by wind. You will want it to start out overhead. Here's how: Fire the flare with your back to the breeze and angle the tube about 15 degrees away from vertical. As the rocket launches downwind it recurves to windward, breaking out its flare directly above you.

McMurdo Marine photos

The crew member above is wearing a Type V self-inflating life vest with built-in harness

Type 1 PFD

Chuck Place photo

that is really easy to wear, then in all but the sunniest weather you can slip it on just to be sure. It should certainly be worn in fog, not because you're more likely to go overboard, but because you won't want to be scratching round for it after a collision with another boat or a hidden rock.

Safety harnesses. Safety harnesses that meet the Offshore Racing Council's (ORC) minimum standard specifications (refer to US SAILING's *Safety Recommendations for Cruising Sailboats*) should be on board for each crew member. Numerous types of tethers are available for safety harnesses. Make sure you can operate yours with a single hand that is wet and cold. The ideal tether has a clip at either end, which allows you to detach yourself when you can't reach the end away from you. If the tethers on your boat are spliced to the harnesses, encourage crew to carry a sharp knife to cut themselves free if necessary (not a bad recommendation in any case, as a knife has more than one function on board).

Harnesses should be worn whenever one feels the need, and always at night. In daylight, clip on when leaving the cockpit if the boat is reefed, and when sailing in rough or cold water.

Crew Overboard. Short of losing the ship or one of your crew dying from injury or illness, this is the worst thing that can happen to you. Recovering a victim that has fallen overboard is a four-stage procedure:

Overboard Prevention

Stay on Board! A slip or loss of balance may be the difference of life and death.
- **Use footwear with good traction.**
- **Use safety harnesses with tethers and fittings that are in good condition.**
- **Use jacklines to reduce the need for having to clip and unclip as you move around on the deck (don't use the lifelines as a substitute!). A double tether will ensure you are always attached if you have to transfer the clip.**
- **When moving forward to mast or foredeck, it's safer to do it on the windward side.**
- **Lifelines work best if you keep your body low. They should be taut and for boats over 28 feet they should be double with the upper lifeline at least 24 inches above the deck. If light line is used to secure the ends of the lifelines, its breaking strength should at least equal the strength of the lifeline wire and it should be replaced routinely since it degrades with UV exposure and chafe.**
- **Any openings in the rails of the bow and stern pulpit should be securely closed while underway.**
- **When on deck at night, maintain your night vision by using flashlights with red lenses and keeping the light from below to a minimum.**
- **A frequent cause of falling overboard is using the "outdoor head." Either go below or attach your harness tether to the boat.**
- **As a big favor to your seasick shipmate, make sure his or her harness tether is always attached while on deck.**
- **Remember the maxim, "One hand for the boat and one hand for yourself."**
Note: US SAILING's publication, *Safety Recommendations for Cruising Sailboats*, contains guidelines for the construction and use of safety harnesses, lifelines and other safety equipment.

regaining physical contact, attaching to boat, getting back aboard and aftercare. Expertise in one without the others may prove deadly.

1) Regaining contact. As long as there are sailors there will be discussion about how best to regain contact with a victim, but a number of methods are broadly accepted. As with heavy weather survival (Chapter 23), the serious seaman should be aware of all the possibilities and which are appropriate for a particular situation. Practice each with your own boat and crew, and consider which can succeed with only one person on deck, perhaps someone less experienced than you. It might be you who goes overboard!

Spend at least a day practicing initially, then a couple of hours or more each season thereafter. Practice can be good fun! It increases your confidence and it could save a life should the unthinkable come to pass.

Before examining the options, several points are common to all:

• *Never lose sight of the casualty!* If this proves impossible, for instance at night, mark the position immediately. One crew member must immediately be designated "spotter" and concentrate on pointing at the casualty or overboard pole, no matter what. This vigilance must be continuous through tacks or jibes. If limited crew does not permit a dedicated watcher, the helmsman should take up the post, pointing whenever possible.

• With a conscious and uninjured overboard victim, it may prove better to lose the last of your way five yards or so to weather, then toss a line, rather than risk inflicting injury by direct contact in a seaway.

• So long as free-floating overboard gear (lifebuoys, overboard poles, lights, etc.) is fitted with drogues, it is not essential for the victim to take hold of it immediately. Except in the most extreme conditions, the gear will maintain station and there will be a good chance the victim can swim to a life ring. Since the main function of much of the equipment is to mark the casualty, a pole floating ten or fifteen yards away from the victim is doing its job. So is a floating light. You have only to return to its vicinity and you will spot the victim.

• The GPS "Overboard" button should be activated as soon as possible. Don't lose sight of your casualty on account of it, however, and be aware that in a current of only one knot, you and the casualty will have drifted a quarter mile from the fixed GPS position in 15 minutes. Put another way, in two knots of Gulf Stream you will move 300 yards in five minutes. Nonetheless, so long as you note the time as well, the original fix may give the Search and Rescue (SAR) people the essentials for an estimated position if you lose touch with the victim.

• If you have a full crew, send someone to radio the SAR as soon as you can. The U.S. Search and Rescue guidelines define a MAYDAY distress call as "when a craft or person is threatened by grave and imminent danger requiring immediate response to the distress scene." If the situation does not meet this definition, it would be a PAN-PAN call (Chapter 7). Shorthanded, however, the priority will probably be to make at least one good attempt, as this will save time if successful. As soon as you start to doubt your ability, and in any case after a maximum of five minutes or so, call for assistance. The timing of such a call is obviously more crucial in a gale on cold water than on a balmy subtropical evening in a shark-free area.

• Except in the case of methods specifically designed to use power,

Overboard Lights

• Small personal overboard lights are available for crew members to wear when on watch after dark. Wearing them could save a life. Typically they are either strobe or incandescent lights.

• Personal strobe lights work best for attention-getting and usually have greater naked-eye visibility than the steady white incandescent lights (an average of two miles compared to 1.5 miles), but bear in mind a strobe's lit period is measured in milliseconds so that it may not be on top of a wave when it sparks off. If that happens, it will be missed. In practice, with anything of a sea running, you will only see it occasionally from a boat, but it will be effective from a spotting aircraft.

• The blinding flash of a strobe adversely affects night vision and depth perception and can also be disorienting. The same applies to floating overboard strobe lights. On the other hand, the steady incandescent type of lights is best for distance ranging and close range recovery.

• Combination units with strobe and fixed incandescent lights, which allow the victim to switch on the appropriate light depending on the distance and circumstances, are expected to become prevalent as more manufacturers produce them. For more information, see the Overboard Light Study at US SAILING's website (http://www.ussailing.org).

overboard recovery maneuvers should be practiced and perfected under sail. Under circumstances such as insufficient wind, difficult seas, a limited ability to maneuver the boat or downwind overboards in strong winds, the engine may be used to close the distance with the victim or to slow the final approach (leaving it in neutral until needed). Before starting the engine, check each side to ensure that no lines may become fouled by the propeller. Great care must be taken to keep the victim clear of the area of the propeller, and the engine should be turned off when the victim can be brought alongside.

• Whether to make contact with the victim on your leeward or windward side depends on the conditions, the boat, the experience level, number of crew, and how things are shaping up as you make the approach. If there is only one chance to pick up the victim in heavy weather, approaching with the victim on your leeward side has a better chance of ensuring contact as the boat loses way a few yards to windward and slides to leeward toward the victim. In a less than ideal world, you may decide to take the risk of injuring the victim during pickup than to never make contact. Approaching with the victim on your windward side in rough conditions has the risk of the boat stalling and sliding off downwind too soon or too far for the heaving line to reach the victim. There is also the question of whether the condition of the victim allows him to catch and secure the line. In milder conditions you may prefer to pick the victim up on your weather side. In the end, if the recovery was successful and no one got hurt, whatever side you picked him up on was the right side. If the Lifesling recovery method is used, this all becomes a moot point. What's important is to practice the different recovery methods in different conditions because there are just too many variables for doing it only one way.

2) Attaching the victim to the boat. A weak link in overboard recoveries is what happens after contact has been made. Victims holding onto a line have been known to let it slip out of their grasp as they succumb to fatigue and hypothermia. Take immediate action to attach the victim to the boat by clipping a line to the victim's harness or using a sling. Once attached to the boat, the victim can be recovered on board without fear of losing him or her. If recovery has been made with a Lifesling, properly clipped around the chest, this eliminates the problem.

3) Getting back aboard. Except in calm conditions, lifting a victim aboard can be far from easy. It must be borne in mind that there will certainly be some degree of shock, an injury may have been sustained and hypothermia may be setting in.

Boarding by ladder. If the swim ladder is mounted over the stern, be careful lest the boat's pitching causes the ladder or hull to injure the victim. Consider other means if this possibility seems real. In the case of a simple trip over the rails on a calm afternoon, however, the stern ladder is your first and obvious way.

Lifting by sling. The over-riding advantage of the Lifesling is that the victim is ready for a lift when brought alongside. You have only to hook up a spare halyard, lead it to a winch (ideally via a tackle kept for this purpose) and heave away, keeping a spare crew member (if you have one) standing by to assist the casualty.

Unfortunately, this may well involve lifting the person vertically by the

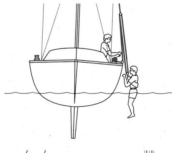

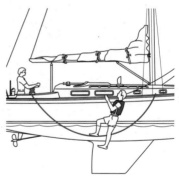

Make sure you try numerous methods of lifting overboard victims back on board, and see what else you can invent!

shoulders with the attendant dangers entailed. Try to raise the legs horizontally as soon as you can, and don't forget that if you cut your lifeline lanyards you have only to lift as far as the toe-rail. This method of lifting is also appropriate for use without a Lifesling, and some boats carry a simple under-arm "sling" for this purpose. Another system is to use the bosun's chair lowered into the water so that the casualty can work into it. There is a nasty moment in the early stages until the legs are out from under the boat, but thereafter the "bosun's lift" goes smoothly.

Other methods of getting the victim aboard. An injured overboard victim assisted by a swimmer on a safety line can be floated into a half-inflated dinghy, so long as the yacht is laid across the wind to supply a lee. From here, they may be maneuvered round to a "sugar-scoop" stern, or rolled in under the lifelines. If the victim has been hit by the boom, be aware of the possibility that there may be a neck or spine injury and take the necessary precautions to try to avoid paralysis.

When the person in the water is healthy, there is precedent for lowering a bight of jib sheet into the water on the lee side with one end secured to the boat and the other end led to a winch. This can be used as a foot support. A short second line is handed down so that the person in the water can heave upright. The slack of the sheet is snatched up on a winch as the boat rolls, raising the casualty steadily to a height from which it is possible to tumble aboard. Once again, being able to cut away the lifeline lanyards quickly can be a lifesaver. While this "elevator" method sounds easy, there can be a problem with the feet sliding under or jamming against the hull.

It cannot be over-stressed that the only way of achieving any degree of confidence that any of these systems will work, is to try them out. Practice with a wet-suited volunteer on a gentle day.

4) Aftercare. Take the greatest care of overboard victims who often succumb to hypothermia (refer to US SAILING's *Safety Recommendations for Cruising Sailboats* for further information on prevention, symptoms and treatment). Warm them gently with sleeping bags if cold, keep them lying down if the affair has been at all traumatic, and generally treat them like shock cases. If you are in any doubt at all or there is a suspicion of internal injuries, shock or water in the lungs, call up a "PAN-PAN medico" and ask for advice.

Outside Assistance. If you have a problem which prevents you getting back to shore, such as running out of fuel on a powerboat or on a sailboat in a prolonged calm, your first resource is a towboat rescue service. These operators are normally licensed by the USCG for towing and salvage, and work together with them in many circumstances.

If you are a member of one of these "help services," call their 800 number on

continued on page 79

A Lifesling can be modified with the addition of a thigh strap to provide more support for the lower body and legs. David C. Forbes photo

One of the primary advantages of the Lifesling system is its ability to raise the victim back on board with a built-in block and tackle once the victim has been recovered.

Lifesling is deployed.

Victim is attached.

Victim is hoisted on board.

Quick-Stop Recovery

The hallmark of the Quick-Stop recovery method is the immediate reduction of boat speed by turning to windward and thereafter maneuvering at modest speed, remaining near the victim. Many consider this method superior to the conventional procedure of reaching off, then either jibing or tacking and returning on a reciprocal course, since the victim is kept in sight throughout. The Quick-Stop requires a tack and a jibe; and jibing in heavy weather conditions may be difficult for some boats and crews. It is generally regarded as a good method for short-handed sailing. Here are the steps:

❶ Shout "Crew Overboard!" and provide immediate flotation for the victim. Throw buoyant objects such as cockpit cushions, life rings and so on as soon as possible. Even if these objects do not come to the aid of the victim, they will "litter the water" where he or she went overboard and help your spotter to keep the victim in view. Deployment of the overboard pole and flag (dan-buoy) requires too much time. The pole should be saved to "put on top" of the victim in case the initial maneuver is unsuccessful.

❷ Designate a crew member to spot and point to the victim in the water. The spotter should NEVER take his or her eyes off the victim.

❸ Bring the boat head-to-wind and beyond, leaving the headsail backed. If the overboard occurred off the wind, trim mainsail and headsail to close-hauled as the boat heads up. Keep turning with the headsail backed to further slow the boat until the wind is slightly abaft the beam. Do not release the sheets.

❹ Head on a beam-to-broad reach course (approximately 90 to 120 degrees off the wind) for two or three boat lengths, then change course to nearly dead downwind.

❺ Drop or furl the headsail (if possible) while keeping the mainsail centered (or nearly so). If the headsail is dropped, the headsail sheets should be kept tight to keep them and the sail inside the lifelines.

❻ Jibe when the victim is abeam or aft of abeam of the boat (timing of jibe depends on the boat's maneuverability and performance in existing wind and sea conditions).

❼ Approach the victim on a close reach course, adjusting speed with the mainsail; or glide up into the wind as you would when picking up a mooring. The approach will depend on your boat's maneuverability, position after your jibe, wind and sea conditions and helmsman's ability.

❽ Stop the boat alongside the victim and establish contact with a heaving line or other device. A rescue throw bag with 50 to 75 feet of light floating line can be thrown into the wind because the line is kept inside the bag and trails out as it sails to the victim.

❾ Attach the victim to the boat.

❿ Recover the victim on board.

Quick-Stop Recovery

WIND

Quick-Stop Recovery under Spinnaker

The quick-stop recovery procedure can be used when flying a spinnaker. As the boat comes head-to-wind and the spinnaker pole is eased to the headstay, the spinnaker halyard is lowered and the sail is gathered on the foredeck. The turn is continued through the tack and the approach phase commences. If after the spinnaker is lowered, the boat ends up too far to leeward of the victim preventing immediate rescue, it is advisable to turn on the engine to get upwind expeditiously.

Quick-Stop Recovery in Yawls and Ketches

Experiment with your mizzen sail. During sea trials, it was determined that the best procedure was to drop the mizzen as soon as it is convenient to do so during the early phases of Quick-Stop.

Powerboat Recoveries

A powerboat should experience little difficulty getting back alongside an overboard victim. Practice the approach from a position downwind of the victim. If your freeboard is too high to lift a fully clothed swimmer and you have no ladder capable of serving in rough water, rig a light, removable davit with a tackle led to a power source such as the windlass. This is a standard arrangement on many pilot craft, who are always at risk from overboard situations. A well-designed bracket allows the davit to be stowed flat when out of use. Another method is to use a five-part tackle with one end attached to a padeye on the side of the cabin (near an opening in the rail or bulwark) and the other end to the sling.

"Buttonhook" Recovery

This method (developed in the varying conditions of San Francisco Bay) is a modification of the Lifesling-type recovery and reduces the amount of time it takes to make contact with the victim.

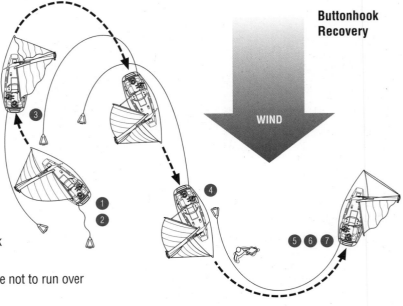

Buttonhook Recovery

WIND

❶ Shout "Crew Overboard!" as soon as a crew member falls overboard, throw buoyant objects and assign a spotter.

❷ Deploy the Lifesling and sail on a close reach as the line pays out. Double-check that the Lifesling is working properly.

❸ Tack onto a deep broad reach, taking care not to run over the trailing sling line.

❹ Approach with the victim on your windward side.

❺ Head up onto a close reach as you pass the victim.

❻ Ease sheets to slow and stop the boat as soon as you see the line has been taken.

❼ Drop or furl sails when the victim is in the sling. Pull or winch the victim alongside and then recover on board.

Lifesling-type Recovery

If there are few people on board, the Lifesling-type recovery method should be employed. The Lifesling is a floating harness that is deployed from the boat's stern with a long floating line attached. The end of the line is attached to the boat. Once the victim reaches the harness, he or she places the sling around his or her body, and is attached to the boat from that point on until being lifted out of the water. The success of this method depends on the victim grabbing the line and putting on the sling. It takes longer than the Quick-Stop and the other methods, but provides a means for a single crew member to effect a rescue of a victim in the water.

❶ As soon as a crew member falls overboard, throw a cushion or other buoyant objects to the victim and shout "Crew Overboard!" while the boat is brought IMMEDIATELY head-to-wind, slowed and stopped. The main is trimmed to centerline.

❷ The Lifesling is deployed by opening the bag that is hung on the stern pulpit and dropping the sling into the water. It will trail out astern and draw out the remaining line.

❸ Once the Lifesling is deployed, the boat is sailed in a wide circle around the victim with the line and sling trailing astern. The jib is not tended but allowed to back from the head-to-wind position, which increases the rate of turn.

❹ Contact is established with the victim by the line and sling being drawn inward by the boat's circling motion. The victim then places the sling over his or her head and under his or her arms.

❺ Upon contact, the boat is put head-to-wind again, the headsail is dropped to the deck or furled and the mainsail is doused.

❻ As the boat drifts, the crew begins pulling the sling and the victim to the boat. If necessary a cockpit winch can be used to assist in this phase, which should continue until the victim is alongside and pulled up tightly until he or she is suspended in the sling (so that the victim will not drop out and the torso is out of the water).

This system is effective if the line length is preadjusted to avoid running over the line, and if the method is practiced to achieve competence.

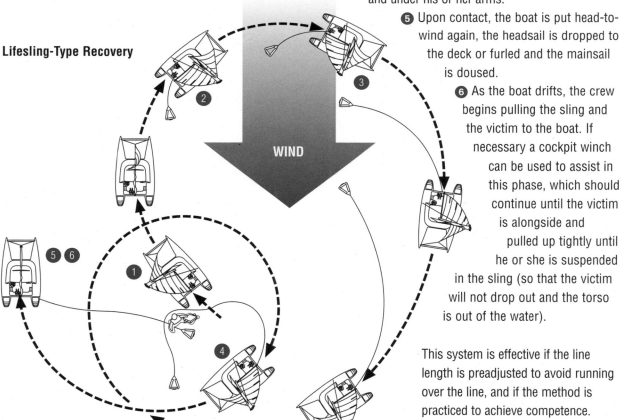

Lifesling-Type Recovery

WIND

The Heaving-to Recovery

❶ As soon as the victim goes overboard, turn the wheel hard over, regardless of your point of sailing. This will generally tack the boat. If possible, trim in the sheets as you come around. Leave the headsail sheet made fast so that jib and/or staysail can come aback.

❷ The yacht is now effectively hove-to. In a seaway this can be a messy maneuver, but in spite of ropes and sails flailing in disarray, the boat will often drift close enough to the victim to heave a line. If this doesn't happen, it may be worth trying to work across by juggling sheets and helm.

❸ If it looks as though you will not come close enough to effect a rescue, deploy your lifebuoy, pole and lights as appropriate, then make the big decision: to motor or to sail? Should you be unsure of your ability to lose all way alongside to the victim under sail alone, proceed as follows:

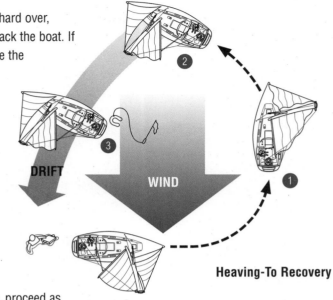

Heaving-To Recovery

Recovery under Power

❶ Keeping a constant eye on the victim, drop or roll away your headsail while still in the "hove-to" state, steering to stay on the same tack.

❷ Work downwind of the victim, checking as you go for any line that could possibly find its way into the propeller. Headsail sheets are a particular favorite.

❸ Start the engine out of gear.

❹ Make a second inspection for stray lines before putting the engine in gear.

❺ Tack or jibe if need be.

❻ Steer upwind for the victim. Trim in most of the slack on the main sheet to keep the sail quiet and keep the boat headed into the wind.

❼ The sail will now steady the boat as you move up to the victim from downwind, controlling your speed with the engine. It goes without saying that you will be more popular if you don't chop up the victim with your propeller, so make your approach with care.

❽ Approach just off head-to-wind with the victim on the boat's leeward shoulder (just forward of the shrouds). This keeps him clear of the propeller and also allows the boat to slide gently towards him while losing the last of her way. The engine should be turned off once the victim is at or aft of the shrouds.

Recovery Under Power

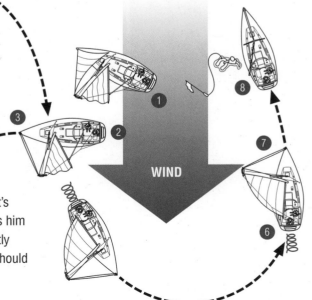

Quick-Turn Recovery

❶ After deploying your gear and reassuring the victim from the hove-to position, sail away for fifty yards or so on an apparent wind beam reach.

❷ As soon as you have the sea room for maneuver, either tack or jibe. Tacking will take you further upwind, but jibing may become difficult.

❸ The plan is to approach the victim on a close reach. This point of sail gives perfect speed control, using the main sheet as a "gas pedal," together with some space for altering direction. To determine whether you're in position for the close-reach approach, steer toward the victim and let off your sheets. If you are on a close reach, both sails will flog. If you are on a close-hauled course, sail up towards the victim, working a little to weather so you can crack off onto a close reach for the last few lengths.

❹ If your approach is too far upwind, the leech of the main will fill (on a fractional rig, release the main vang) and slowing down will be impossible. In this case, immediately run off almost dead downwind for a length or two.

❺ Then steer up for the victim again. In all probability this will position you properly for a close-reach approach. Should you still be too far upwind with a mainsail full of air, bear off hard a second time, etc. You sailed away from the victim to gain sea room to commit to these maneuvers and position yourself for that vital close reach. Do not squander your gains through indecision.

❻ On the final approach, control speed with the main sheet, which at very slow speed will also help you steer (the jib can be rolled away or left flogging in the early stages as appropriate).

❼ Stall the boat with the victim under the shrouds. The helm should be trying to steer the boat hard to weather at this point so that the yacht is drifting sideways. With the rudder hard over, the boat will remain stable while you move forward to make contact with the victim.

Quick-Turn Recovery

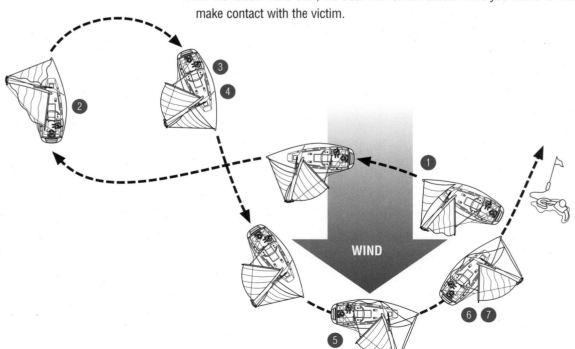

WIND

your cell phone. Otherwise, call VHF Channel 16 and ask for assistance. This is NOT a Mayday call.

A sensible hourly rate is levied for the towing service. Make sure that all concerned understand the arrangement, and if there is any suggestion that salvage may be involved, try to contact your insurer. If this fails, strike the best deal you can, but remember to agree with the towboat skipper about what you are signing up for.

The towboat operators' most common problem is locating a boat that provides vague or incorrect information. Unlike the USCG responding to a Mayday broadcast with a lat/long position, these people usually prefer a geographic location ("I am stuck under Low Bridge just south of Narrow Creek entrance"). If it is feasible, they then like you to anchor and await their arrival. When you see the boat coming, call up and talk them in.

Once alongside, be patient. Not all skippers have taken the trouble you have to get educated. The towboat captain doesn't know you, so if he seems to be asking annoyingly obvious questions, bear with him. To ensure your safety, he may assume your knowledge is minimal.

Distress. When you issue a Mayday, expect the USCG to respond. If they do not or cannot, some other responsible vessel with greater transmitting power than you may well relay your Mayday to them. (Refer to Chapter 7 for Mayday requirements radio procedure).

The Coast Guard will maintain radio contact with you as a rescue craft, whether it be helicopter or cutter, is on its way to you. The manner of your responses will tell a great deal about you and how you are coping. This in turn will help the rescue proceedings.

Tell the Coast Guard about your boat, your people, your problem, what you're doing about it, and politely what you would like them to do. If you announce calmly that you are holed and that the water is making against your pumps, despite having shoved a "nerf" ball into the hole, the rescuer will know that you are in charge of the situation and are in urgent need of rescue. If the cutter's throttle wasn't already against the firewall, it soon will be if you add that your engine has now failed and you expect the electric pumps to be losing power within fifteen minutes.

On the other hand, a rescuer will not know what to make of a panic-stricken voice that screams repeatedly,

"Help! We're sinking!"

As with a towboat, look out for the rescue craft. You will usually see them before they spot you. Talk them in until they have you in view, then do as you are told.

While help is on the way, you should prepare all hands for abandoning ship, making sure their PFDs and harnesses are properly worn. Have flares, orange smokes and the portable VHF ready for use. If you are giving your position in lat/long, tell the rescuers its source. A "Loran C" position may be adrift from the true location by virtue of a fixed error.

Rescuers can handle this because they will then use their own "Loran C" which will have exactly the same error. If you don't tell them your lat/long source, they'll assume it's GPS and may miss you if the weather is thick.

After dark, never aim a light at a rescue vehicle, although they may well shine one on you. Tell your crew not even to glance at a searchlight.

A cutter will have her own fenders which the captain may, or may not feel are appropriate for use. Don't bother with yours. Come to terms with the fact that there may be some structural damage as the vessels come together.

Rescue by Towing. If a tow seems likely, prepare your boat accordingly. Set lines from your bow cleats aft to the primary winches and heave these tight. This spreads the load away from the otherwise vulnerable cleats. Also look to chafing gear for a tow rope and, if appropriate, rig a very strong towing bridle from the bow. If lives are at stake and towing is the obvious way of saving them, the USCG will tow a vessel that is drifting. They will not tow a grounded craft into deep water, however.

Although a mechanism exists for the USCG to bill you for a tow, in practice they rarely charge a yacht.

Helicopter Rescue. Helicopters are heavy users of fuel, so when one is on its way to you there is not a moment to lose. You will probably know the direction from which it will come, so when you see it in the distance, call on VHF to indicate your relative position ("30 degrees on starboard bow," etc.). If it will help, show hand-held red or orange smoke flares, but never fire a rocket anywhere near a helicopter. Helicopters generate a huge racket, sometimes making it difficult to hear the pilot's VHF transmissions. Don't be afraid to ask him to repeat ("say again") his messages.

Not all rescuers want you to use pyrotechnics, especially if they can pinpoint you without them. If in doubt, inquire using the VHF.

Here are the steps for preparing for a helicopter rescue:

• The pilot sits on the helicopter's starboard seat, so he sees into your cockpit from the port quarter. This is where the "swimmer" will land when he comes aboard (if you are still able to control your speed and direction). You can help a great deal by clearing the aft deck of all projections such as antennae, ensign staffs and even toppinglifts. Make the boarding path as clear as you can.

• Tidy away any loose gear, especially lightweight items. These can be sucked up into the helicopter's air intakes and cause engine failure.

• Stand by to be briefed via VHF. If this is a medical evacuation, or some other emergency that has not disabled the boat, you may well be told to motor to windward at your best speed or, if you have no engine, to sail close-hauled on port tack. Be prepared for bright searchlights at night and stand by with your deck floodlights on. The helicopter may stand off surveying the scene for what seems a long time. The downdraft from the rotors may be heavy — enough to blow you overboard — but often it is less intense than you may fear. The noise, however, is awesome.

• Once given a course and speed, obey, no matter what. Choose a reliable helmsman and leave him or her to concentrate solely on steering until the job is complete or the time comes to rescue him or her as well. Warn the helmsman against looking back at the helicopter.

• If you are not able to control the yacht's speed and direction, you may be told to climb into the dinghy or liferaft for pickup. You may even have to enter the water. In less extreme wind and sea conditions, or in the case of a medical emergency, the pilot will probably opt for a trail-line transfer.

When under tow, spreading the load aft to big sheet winches with extra lines helps keep the cleats or bollards from being pulled out of the deck. Look out for chafe, and consider rigging a bridle if you have two cleats rather than a central forward securing point.

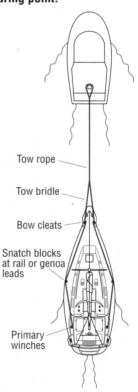

Tow rope

Tow bridle

Bow cleats

Snatch blocks at rail or genoa leads

Primary winches

Trail-line (tag-line) Transfer

The purpose of this method is to allow a rescue swimmer or an item of equipment to be lowered reliably into the boat's cockpit without the helicopter having to remain overhead for longer than absolutely necessary. First, a light line is lowered to the yacht. Its upper end is then attached to a rescue swimmer or a basket containing, say, a power pump, which is to be sent down on the cable, enabling the yacht's crew to pull it or him aboard. Here is the sequence of events:

1 The trail line is lowered towards you. Note that it carries a heavy weight on the end to stabilize it. In theory you should let the trail line touch the sea to dump static electricity, but this does not always happen.

2 When the line is in hand, take up the slack, flaking down the excess line. NEVER make it fast. If it should get tangled up with your gear, a "weak link" will break. Designate your strongest or fittest crew to hold the trail line.

3 The helicopter may now stand away for a better look. Keep working the slack on the line.

4 When the pilot is ready, the rescue swimmer or basket is lowered. Be sure to let a basket touch water or boat before you grab it, as the static potential can be high. Use the trail line to guide swimmer or basket, and be ready for a serious pull if required. Do not take anything below decks that is still attached to the helicopter. If a rescue swimmer comes aboard, he will take charge of the operation, perhaps evacuating injured personnel by means of a specialized stretcher know as a "Stokes Litter." If nobody comes down, do what is needed with the basket then signal the helicopter's crew to lift it with a vigorous "thumbs up."

5 Ease the trail line as the lift takes place, using it where appropriate to stop the basket from swinging.

6 Release the trail line when signaled to do so.

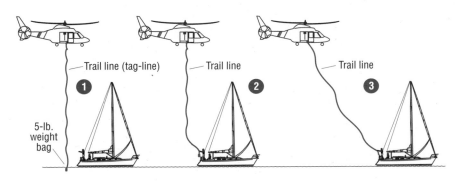

Trail-line (Tag Line) Transfer

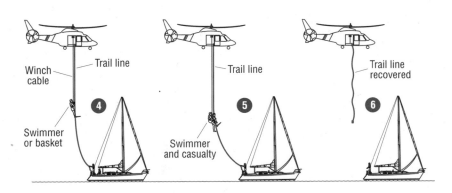

Coastal Heavy Weather

Heavy weather can be defined as conditions bad enough to confront the coastal passagemaker with the choice of either thrashing onward in extreme discomfort or considering a change of voyage plan, perhaps heading for shelter. This chapter considers the factors that may be involved in those decisions.

Wind and Wave. Apparent wind. Whether strong wind is a problem or not depends on how large and able a boat is and the wind's direction relative to her course. For a 30-foot sailboat with a big rig and light displacement, 25 knots "on the nose" in open water would certainly be classed as heavy weather, while a 40-footer with the same wind over her quarter would be enjoying a cracking sailing breeze. Apart from the discrepancy in boat size, the other important factor is "apparent wind."

The actual (apparent) wind you experience on deck is a combination of the true wind and the wind that is created by your boat's motion. In strong weather, the change in apparent wind becomes a serious safety issue. As you can see from the illustrations, a yacht running at 8 knots before a 40-knot blow will feel 32 knots of wind, a strong breeze, but not dangerous for most coastal passagemakers. Beating into it, however, you'll be coping with almost 46 knots of wind, a whole gale. When sailing a course across the wind, the apparent wind will be a composite in angle as well as speed.

Understanding apparent wind is vital to many decisions you will make on the water.

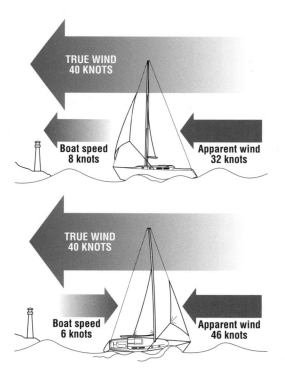

Wind pressure. A nasty shock awaits the mariner who imagines that 30 knots of wind will only be twice as strong as 15 knots. The graph (next page) shows wind pressure vs. wind velocity rising on a steepening curve. Fifteen knots delivers 0.8 lb. per square foot of pressure, while 30 punches a full 3.1 lb., almost four times as much. By the time the wind reaches 60 knots, its pressure is a whopping 12.3 lb. per square foot. Hopefully, on a coastal passage this example will remain academic.

Waves in theory. For the most part, it is not heavy wind alone that spoils our day, but the waves it kicks up. Waves can make us queasy and wet, cold and vulnerable. They make sleep difficult and cooking sometimes nearly impossible. A boat's motion in waves tests her gear sternly, occasionally to destruction.

Wave height is measured from the trough to the crest. At lower wind speeds, waves not aggravated by shoals or tidal effects are gentle in form, but as the wind velocity increases, they grow steeper. Ultimately, they break in open water, becoming highly dangerous.

The "fetch" of a sea and the length of time a given wind has been blowing are the two main modifying factors in theoretical wave height. A 40-knot wind is capable of generating seas up to 24 feet high, but it will take many hours before these heights are achieved. A fetch even as great as 50 miles will usually limit the height down to around 12 feet. Long swells from hundreds of miles away can influence local sea conditions even in calm weather. The speed of a wave is a function of the distance between crests, but in practice, given time to settle down, wave speeds often reach around 60% of the average wind speed.

The bottom line is that you should study your weather information to keep clear of major offshore horrors, such as 50-foot waves travelling at 40 knots and arriving at a rate of one every 18 seconds. Given an appreciation of the seasons and sensible use of weather forecasting, the worst wave you should see in a moderate onshore gale out in deep water is 10 to 12 feet high, travelling at around 20 knots. Even though it is only the crest that is tumbling at these wind speeds, the occasional wave can be a good bit worse, and the situation is one to be avoided at all sensible costs.

Waves in practice. Especially along the coast, waves do not travel in neat ranks like toy soldiers. Fluctuations in wind speed and direction produce waves that roll along from different bearings within a general pattern. When monsters meet coming from opposing directions, they can pile up to generate a steep, "pyramid wave," often much higher than the general average at the time.

Waves moving in the same direction as a current are usually not affected by it, but when they are driven against a current by a strong wind, they become considerably steeper and may be induced to break. A wind-against-current sea can always be detected by observation in a blow. The streaks of foam seem to travel down the backs of the waves faster than the wave is rolling. The phenomenon is unmistakable.

A classic example of a current running against the wind and generating dangerous seas is the Gulf Stream close to the Florida coast in a northerly gale. It's a place worth missing in such conditions, even if the wind is going your way. Many other locations can produce similar horrors.

Tide races and rips generate waves of their own, sometimes in otherwise calm weather. Many headlands produce a tidal eddy along the downstream side which meets the main stream a mile or so offshore in the form of a race. An area of uneven seabed can have a similar effect. Where two powerful currents meet, the conditions are best avoided on a pleasant day, and can be positively hazardous in an onshore gale.

As waves are blown into shoaling water they begin to pile up. When the water becomes so shallow that it can no longer sustain the wave height, the waves will break. Depths between breaking crests can then diminish quite suddenly to zero. Since this effect is exacerbated by a weather-driven current, little imagination is needed to picture a shallow sand bar at a river mouth with an outgoing tide ripping into a hard onshore blow. The bars of San Francisco and the Columbia River are two large-scale examples which are littered with wrecks. On a smaller, but equally lethal scale, many an East Coast inlet has seen small craft running for shelter, only to be rolled within sight of a secure harbor.

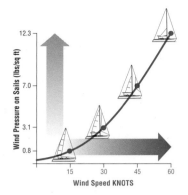

Wind pressure increases dramatically as wind speed rises.

Wave Height and Length

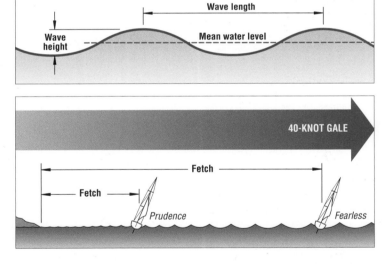

Fetch and Waves

Making Way in a Blow. **Powerboats.** A displacement powerboat's tactics when confronted with unexpected heavy weather will center on avoiding steep beam seas. Like a sailing craft, she can broach (be thrown round beam-on with the attendant risk of being rolled) when running with the seas, but this is only likely to happen in the sort of extreme circumstances that can usually be avoided on a coastal passage.

Common sense will soon show how fast you can power into a head sea. Waves coming in over the quarter or dead aft may prove more safely handled at speed than by slowing down, but it is impossible to generalize.

If you are left with no choice but to steam through a beam sea, put your best helmsman on and take each wave as it comes. Head either "up" or "down" for an ugly one, and if sea room is critical, make up in the smoother patches what you have given away to ride the steeper seas.

It goes without saying that fuel tanks and filters must be clean. If they aren't, the stirred-up sediment could cause your engines to fail, resulting in a possible life-threatening situation.

Sailboats. The limitation of a sailboat's capacity to work to weather in heavy going is the most critical factor in her safety along the coast. It is best, of course, to have a good suit of sails. But if you have only roller furling headsails, it may prove better to reef the main as deeply and as flat as possible, roll up the genoa altogether and motorsail. Don't attempt to bash straight into the waves. Crack off to 40 degrees or so off the wind (30 degrees apparent) and adjust your power to maintain speed a bit less than the boat can make to windward under sail on a nice day. If you sail slower than this your leeway will increase dramatically; go faster, and you'll shake yourself to pieces. Like a powerboat, there is little excuse for the sailing craft being caught out with dirty fuel tanks and no spare filters.

In less extreme circumstances, do all you can to flatten your sails and keep on sailing. Crank in plenty of tension on the halyard, vang and mainsail reef outhaul. Headsails should also be hauled up hard, with the sheet lead positioned to keep the sail flat and driving. This will generally mean sliding the genoa car aft a few notches in accordance with experiments already made in preparation for a rough night.

Crew Welfare. At sea in a blow, crew strength must not be taken for granted. Whatever the cost, offer everyone regular hot food. This doesn't merely sustain people, it reassures them in a quiet way that routine is not suffering and all is well. Skippers should watch their crews carefully, noting signs of sagging morale. They must always be ready with a reassuring word, a touch and, if need be, a firm insistence that a seasick sailor go off watch. Maintaining crew confidence and efficiency in this way is as important for their primary safety as a harness and PFD.

Keep watches rotating and make sure nobody stays too long at the helm. Care for those who chose to go to sea with you, but never forget that ultimately it is the skipper who makes the decisions, guides the ship to safety, and may at any time be needed for deckwork. The skipper

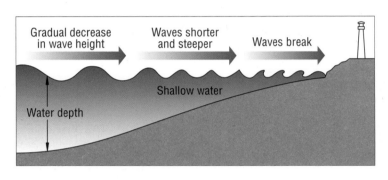

Gradual decrease in wave height → Waves shorter and steeper → Waves break →

Shallow water

Water depth

As waves approach shoaling water, they become shorter and steeper.

needs to be aware of his or her own fatigue, and pace themselves with suitably timed rest periods out of the wind and weather.

Tactics When Caught Out. We have said before that if you are in doubt about the weather for a coastal passage, it is prudent to wait until things are more settled. For all manner of reasons, both navigational and personal, this is not always possible. Even if you are the world's most careful sailor, sooner or later you're going to be caught out. Your tactics then depend on a number of key considerations.

Lee shores and other dangers. A coast onto which the wind is blowing is said to be a "lee shore." It is a potential ship wrecker, because any vessel close to a lee shore that does not have enough sail or engine power to claw back out to deep water will inevitably end up stranded on it. Sailors soon learn a healthy respect for lee shores, and it is this which forms the foundation of all coastal heavy weather tactics.

When caught along the shoreline by weather that makes you change your passage plan, you have two groups of options: either stay at sea or go for shelter. Staying at sea involves either "going for broke," turning up your collar and hanging on till you arrive at your destination, or resorting to survival tactics. Survival tactics are dealt with in Chapter 23, and are rarely relevant on a coastal passage. They are usually sea room dependent and are only employed in extreme conditions which sensible weather monitoring should manage to avoid along the shoreline.

In heavy weather, it is often best to "crack off" to 30-40 degrees apparent wind and sail at a moderate speed.

If you are intending to stick it out and press on to your destination, you must judge whether the entrance or approach will be viable in the sea and wind state you now expect upon arrival. It will be no haven if it has a shallow bar that the predictable ebb tide has turned into a lee-shore maelstrom. Even if the entrance looks good, check your cruising guide again to be sure that the berthing facilities will supply you with adequate shelter. If the answers to these questions are unsatisfactory, consider alternative destinations. If they are satisfactory, make all the ground you can by determined sailing and/or motoring before it really starts to blow.

Seeking shelter. Shelter will generally be available either to windward or to leeward. If there is a choice and you have the power to work your way up there, try to seek shelter to windward every time. As you approach the weather shore, you will benefit more and more from its lee. The seas will ease and the wind will seem to abate. Almost any harbor entrance that is deep enough for your boat is passable with the wind offshore.

If shelter lies only to leeward, you will at least arrive in the quickest possible time. The question is, what will you find when you get there? If the harbor has a bar, as noted earlier, the greatest care must be taken about timing your entrance. A haven whose entrance is formed by two extended piers may be too dangerous if the piers are close together. Protected water tucked in behind a headland on a lee shore, however, may be suitable, as long as you are confident of being able to head up as you make your turn back into the teeth of the wind.

A wide estuary leading to a winding river often provides desirable shelter. Further up, it may even have soft mud banks which you can run into without the world coming to an end.

The harbor you are really seeking, however, be it to weather or to leeward, is one from which you cannot see the sea. Open roadsteads can

Blownaway Billie finds himself with the classic dilemma. If he can work to windward in the big gale that's blowing, he can find shelter in Tidy Bight or Blanket River. Rolling Roads doesn't look too comfortable, but it's far better than the options to leeward, none of which is even a starter except Last Ditch Bight. There, so long as he can successfully negotiate that turn at the entrance, he'll be safe enough tucked up under the weather shore. The corner may prove dangerous, but if he can make ground to windward, it's his best chance. The walls at the entrance to Hell-Hole Harbor will be a death trap at the end of a 30-mile fetch, probably with breakers running up their whole length, with broaching as the only result for *Billie* if he tries his luck. Our hero should therefore attempt to hammer his way up into the north, perhaps under power with his main deep-reefed to help him along. Failing this, he must bite the bullet and run for Last Ditch Bight. Whatever his outcome, he's going to wish he'd listened to the weather forecast!

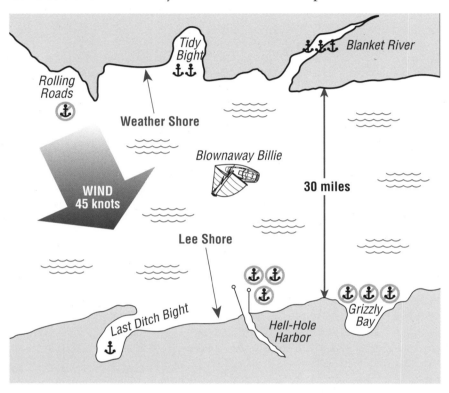

offer a romantic night at anchor as the gentle roll lulls you to sleep; but when it's blowing 45 and the water is streaked with foam and it's too rough to launch the dinghy, you'll long for a land-locked refuge and a secure night's sleep in your cozy bunk.

When a hard blow catches you at anchor, look around to make sure there is room to leeward and that other boats are not too close. Try to lay extra scope and double the anchor (see Chapter 12). Should you be secured to a dock or float that seems likely to become a lee shore, try to tie up with the dock between you and the wind if possible. When stuck in a berth that may turn ugly, double up fenders, and visualize your position if you heel considerably under the wind. Should things turn really nasty, consider taking a kedge anchor well to windward using the dinghy, then hauling your boat a yard or two off the wall. Tie a second line to the rode with a rolling hitch a couple of boat's lengths out. Lead the rode itself to the bow, the other line to the stern, then adjust from both ends, remaining parallel to the wall.

One final word. Never be afraid to leave a berth altogether for a mooring or anchorage. So long as you do not drag, you are safer well away from a brutal dock wall or even a float.

See Chapter 12 for more details on anchoring safely.

Anchoring

Typical anchoring skills and techniques are described in the US SAILING book, *Bareboat Cruising*, and deal primarily with anchoring under power. Passagemakers are likely to find themselves anchoring in more demanding circumstances than the bareboater, so this chapter is devoted to some of the finer points of the art.

The Basics. To recap, an anchor works primarily by digging into the bottom, not just with its weight. A number of designs have been developed to achieve this, each with its protagonists, but you can be confident that an all-purpose plow-type anchor will serve you well in most cases. If lost, or in extreme circumstances, this "bower," or "Number 1" anchor should be backed up with at least two others, one of which should be a "fisherman" of substantial size. So long as it is hefty enough, the fisherman, whether a "Yachtsman" or "Herreshoff" type, will bite into weedy bottoms where lighter, more modern types fail to penetrate. But whatever anchor you use, remember this sound advice, "Even a great anchor won't do well in poor holding ground."

Anchoring is not to be considered a hit-or-miss proposition, and conscientious cruisers pride themselves on setting a hook that will not drag. It's a matter of familiarity and technique. The basic concept is to gently pull the anchor horizontally along the seabed until it digs in and holds, and all methods of lowering are designed to expedite this. In *Bareboat Cruising*, it was explained that a minimum "scope" (ratio of length of anchor rode to depth) of 4:1 for chain and 7:1 for nylon rode was the key. This is a fair guiding principle. Under power, after the anchor is lowered, the boat backs down, working the flukes into the bottom with a gentle nudge astern after the required rode has been run out. Although this usually works, there are circumstances when the approach needs refinement.

When cruising to new areas, you may need to upgrade your anchors and rodes for greater depths and different bottom conditions. Also consider where you will stow and secure this equipment during the passage.

Chain versus Nylon. The overriding advantage of chain is weight. If you sail a light boat or multihull, you might move heaven and earth to minimize weight on board, especially at the ends. But there is nothing like sheer mass for making sure your anchor does its job. Chain hangs in a "catenary" (curve) whose form is similar to half of a suspension-bridge cable. Like the mid-bridge wires, the section of chain nearest the anchor is almost horizontal in any but the most severe winds (given reasonable scope). This minimizes upward pull on the anchor, and maintains its grip on the bottom. Even combined with a section of chain at its lower end, nylon rode cannot do this as well. Chain will not chafe in the bow fairlead or on the seabed as nylon can be prone to do. A chain's weight and consequent inertia also help the boat lie quietly on her tackle.

Anchored in rough water and high winds, chain can "snub" — producing shock loads — if it pulls tight, although with heavy enough

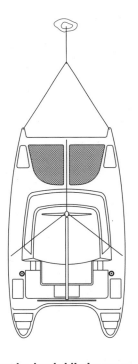

An anchoring bridle keeps a multihull headed into the wind, minimizing "sailing" while anchored.

tackle things must be pretty desperate for this to happen. If necessary, one can generally ease out more scope to improve the catenary. With a 10: 1 scope and 7/16 inch chain (G4 type weighs about 205 lbs. per 100 feet), a 40-foot boat with the right anchor will ride out virtually anything. Production boats rarely are equipped with chain of this size, however. Manufacturers typically opt for a gauge smaller. Chain also requires a windlass if the boat is over about 35 feet. This is a further cost factor, but on the night when your anchor has become your lifeline and security knows no price, size and quality are everything.

The scope of anchor rode is the ratio of the length deployed to the water depth + tidal range + boat's freeboard. Chain works well at 4:1. Nylon rode needs more scope in order to achieve the vital near-horizontal tug on the anchor.

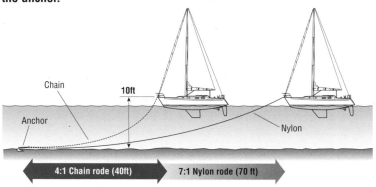

Nylon scores by virtue of its great elasticity and its lightness when stowed. Snubbing is not a problem with nylon, but scope can be. Because of its lack of catenary, you must let out considerably more scope than for chain. This can be inconvenient, but nylon rodes of adequate proportions have seen many an ocean sailor round the world and back.

A compromise favored by many is to anchor with chain rode, but to tie a short length of nylon (snubber line) hooked into the bight. The boat then lies to the line, with the intervening chain slacked away under the bow but properly secured aboard, lest the line should chafe through or let go. This reduces snubbing tendency and also relieves chain noise in the bow roller as the boat sheers (swings at an angle) to her anchor.

When anchoring under sail with no current, approach your drop location slowly, then drift downwind.

Anchoring under Sail. While techniques for anchoring under sail will vary somewhat between different boats, they are far more influenced by wind and current. Using a majority example, we shall consider a modern sloop.

Wind with no current. This is an easy call. Assuming your boat will maneuver under main alone, first stow your headsail to clear the foredeck. Next, maneuver so as to approach the anchoring point on a close reach. The reasons for this are the same as for the crew-overboard approach. The close reach allows full control of speed by using the mainsheet as a "gas pedal," while maintaining a degree of left-right maneuverability. When you are close to the drop location, luff off the last of your way, head-to-wind, and let go of the hook. You can now either shove the boom out square, backwind the main and steer backwards as the rode is paid out steadily, or you can let the boat drift back on her own. The former method is preferred, but if you

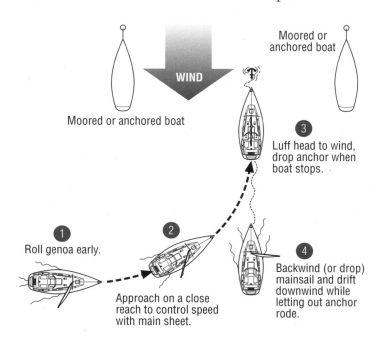

are shorthanded or in a large boat, it may be easier to drop or furl the main as you let go the anchor. You certainly must have a plan, because if you just hope for the best, the bow will blow off, the main will fill and the boat will begin sailing around when she ought to be dropping back. Some boats with a deep forefoot can sheet the main in hard when head-to-wind and then steer astern. A ketch or yawl can perform this to perfection using mizzen but no main. Whatever your boat, try it and see.

Wind with current. The technique here is the same as with no current, except that your approach needs adjusting so as not to be set downstream. This is achieved by watching natural ranges as you approach. Line up two shore objects, boats, mooring buoys etc., behind your chosen spot. If they stay in line, all is well. If they start sliding apart, adjust the heading accordingly.

Wind against current. This typically happens when anchoring in a tidal river. It sounds awkward but is in fact the easiest of all scenarios. The key factor is that the current will be the governing force, not the wind. You must therefore approach upstream. All well so far. That's what you'd do under power. Wait a moment, though! If you're headed upstream with the wind coming from behind, the mainsail cannot be spilled and you won't be able to stop. Having realized this, the rest is easy.

Drop the main a hundred or so yards away from your anchorage and approach heading upstream under genoa alone. Speed is controlled by playing the sheet and by rolling or partially dropping the sail as required. When you're ready to anchor, you should be stationary over the ground but still making way through the current. You then roll up the remainder of the headsail or drop it as the anchor is dropped and the proper scope is played out. The current now carries you downstream, but because of your residual way, it is no problem to stay head-up to it. When you snub the anchor line, the boat will drop back a few more yards before pulling up, unambiguously anchored.

Wind across current. This can be the tricky one, but it needn't be if you bear in mind the above principles.

Take a good look at the wind and current. How are other boats lying? Will your mainsail spill as you approach upstream? If the sail can luff, you have the option of leaving it set. If there is the slightest doubt, lower the main and proceed under genoa. The golden rule is, "When in doubt, drop the main!"

Am I Dragging? If the holding ground is good and you have laid plenty of scope, you shouldn't drag your anchor, but all manner of improbable contingencies can cause this to happen, including a beer-can stuck on the point of a plow!

It is often obvious that you're dragging, because the boat will swing off broadside to wind or current. If you are in any doubt, try feeling the rode with your hand or foot. If you feel vibration or chattering, the anchor is dragging.

Anchoring under sail with the wind against current is easier than it looks. Control is achieved by stemming the current under a quickly adjustable amount of sail.

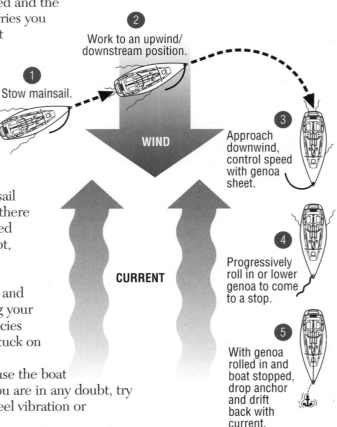

1 Stow mainsail.

2 Work to an upwind/downstream position.

WIND

3 Approach downwind, control speed with genoa sheet.

4 Progressively roll in or lower genoa to come to a stop.

CURRENT

5 With genoa rolled in and boat stopped, drop anchor and drift back with current.

A better way, and one which should be performed as a matter of course every time you anchor, is to decide which way you might drag if you were to do so, then look ashore at right angles to your projected route. Find two objects that line up to make a range:
- Are they staying put? Congratulations.
- Sliding away from each other? Let out more scope.
- Still sliding? Take steps to retrieve the hook and re-anchor.
- Some big-ship seamen prefer to take compass bearings on shore objects and note whether they change. This method is not as effective as a range for a small vessel, except at night when there is but a single shore light to be seen.

Anchor Watch. An anchor watch is scheduled to have a crew member awake to check that the anchor is not dragging and to avoid unforeseen collisions. While it may be routine on sail training vessels to set anchor watch, it is rarely required on a cruising yacht. However, you'll know when the time has come, and don't think that is only in strong winds. In practice, trouble can occur where the turn of a strong tide sets the stream into the teeth of a moderate breeze. With current and breeze neutralizing each other, sailing and power craft now begin a random and potentially dangerous dance. Collisions can occur (typically at 3:00 a.m.), with unkind recriminations hurled between pajama-clad owners. In Martha's Vineyard, old salts have dubbed this phenomenon "The Edgartown Waltz." Avoiding it may be a matter of setting an anchor watch.

Certain GPS sets offer a sentinel feature, sounding an alarm when the boat's position has shifted outside a given radius. This may be useful if the boat is fitted with DGPS and is not subject to a turning tide, but in general, traditional protocol is best. Make sure you are securely anchored, check for others encroaching into your swinging circle, then sleep easy.

Weighting the Rode. In circumstances when you cannot lay enough scope for comfort, such as a tight or crowded anchorage, the effectiveness of your anchor can be increased by sliding a heavy weight down the rode and suspending it halfway to the seabed. As the boat pulls back on her anchor, the rode will be held down by the weight just as it would be by the catenary of more scope.

This technique can also be used in a hard blow when you have laid out all the rode you have. If you carry a dedicated anchor weight it will surely

Lowering a weight halfway down the rode increases the catenary which produces a more horizontal pull on the anchor. It can be used in a really hard blow when all the rode has been let out, or to reduce scope in a crowded harbor.

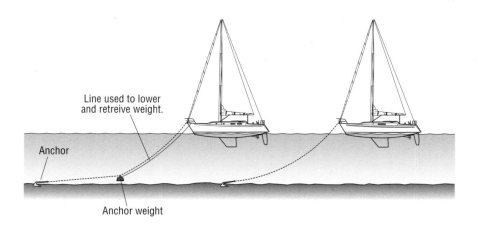

Line used to lower and retreive weight.

Anchor

Anchor weight

do more good down the rode than it will tucked away in its locker, so "when in doubt, rouse it out" and lie even more safely.

Fouled Anchors and the Trip Line. A trip line can prove valuable if you anchor on what may prove a littered bottom. Classic "litter" includes heavy communication cables and mooring chains. Drop a hook amongst these and you can expect problems.

A trip line must be heavy enough for a good pull, even using a winch, but it doesn't have to lift the vessel. Bend it securely to the crown of the anchor so it will capsize the hook and lift clear of its problems. Tie the top end to a fender and let it float free. Don't be tempted to bring the line back aboard, as successive swings may wrap it around the rode, progressively shortening the trip line and possibly lifting the anchor out of the seabed.

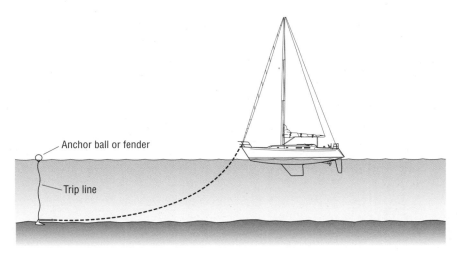

Anchor ball or fender

Trip line

The anchor has been retrieved by a trip line. Note how the anchor is upturned by the vertical pull of the line, allowing it to pull free from the snag on the bottom. Tom Cunliffe photo

To determine trip line length, figure the depth at high water, then add fifteen percent. You won't want to cut your tripping line to a different length every time, so learn how to use the buntline hitch, which will neatly bundle away the slack under the fender so other boats will not foul it with their propellers.

Showing You're Anchored. The Navigation Rules require that whenever you are anchored (unless in a "designated small-craft anchorage") you hoist an anchor ball in daytime and show an all-round white light between sunset and sunrise. The "ball" is usually two interlocking flat discs that come apart for easy stowage. These are painted matt black, and are easy to fabricate in an evening in the home workshop. Or you can buy a fine plastic equivalent.

Try to hoist your ball so that it doesn't pirouette like a ballerina between its halyard and downhaul. A third line led to the forestay will do the trick.

A good kerosene storm lantern can serve as an anchor light if you are concerned about saving electricity. Alternatively, use either a free-hoisted electric lantern or have one mounted at the masthead beneath a tricolor sailing light.

If you're feeling lazy about hoisting either ball or light, you might consider your legal position should someone accidentally run into you.

Dinghy Management

The dinghy is the wheelbarrow, the shopping cart, and the means of shuttling crew to the dock, the beach, or to other vessels in an anchorage. In harbor, if it is an inflatable powered by an outboard, you'd like it to be 15 feet long, fast and massively stable. Should it be rigid, the ideal is beautiful, capacious and capable of being rowed by up to two oarsmen for considerable distances. At sea, you simply want it to disappear. This is an eternal dilemma. The inevitable result is compromise.

Rigid or Inflatable? Most people would prefer a rigid dinghy with built-in buoyancy or a RIB (Rigid-bottomed Inflatable Boat), if for no other reason than they can come ashore with a dry seat to their pants. Such craft can also be effectively bailed, so dry feet are another bonus. Unfortunately, rigid dinghies and RIBs must be stowed on deck, and the modern yacht's topside layout usually precludes this option.

For a boat under 60 feet, stern davits are a realistic alternative to deck stowage, but in fair weather only. No seasoned passagemaker would head offshore with the ship's boat only feet above the briny. Classic yachts and workboats with more open deck space can generally stow a hard dinghy on deck, lashed down in chocks, either inverted or upright with a cover. The rest must settle for some type of inflatable. For passagemakers, it is helpful if the inflatable features at least a "roll-away" rigid floor. Since inflatables do not row well, a small outboard is indispensable for traveling any distance. For this reason, the dinghy should also have a rigid transom on which to clamp the outboard.

Stowage. The dinghy. Because the dinghy will be in use at most stops it must be easily accessible. This is not always convenient, but failure to give the matter consideration will add stress later on. Bringing the "dink" on deck and pumping it up should not be a frustrating chore.

Outboard. The favorite place for the outboard is clamped to a small board fastened to the stern pulpit. If this isn't practical, it is acceptable to stow it in a locker, so long as fuel cannot leak out of the tank or carburetor. To achieve this, turn off the fuel supply on your last approach to the boat, then run the motor until it stops. So long as the tap is off and the vent in the filler cap is screwed down firmly, the engine should remain fuel-tight laid on its side. Even in this neutralized state, however, an outboard remains a fire risk, as does any container of gasoline in a confined space.

Engines with remote tanks can be safely stowed below after the carburetor has been emptied as above.

Gas tanks. Together with propane

for the galley, outboard gasoline is the liveliest fire hazard on board. Cans should not be stowed below decks, but in a dedicated locker which vents overboard. Unless you have a large outboard or expect to be cruising an area where fuel is unobtainable, it is safe policy not to carry more than a gallon or so of extra gas.

Deployment of the outboard. Keep a lanyard attached to the outboard and make it fast to either the ship or the dinghy at all times. Dropping the motor into the water on a six-foot line is a major nuisance. Losing it in 15 fathoms may well be the end of its road. If the engine is heavy, it can often be lowered into place with a spare halyard. Some crews swing it out on a boom so that it can be eased down vertically onto the dinghy transom.

The dinghy as a liferaft. Because it lacks numerous survival features of a liferaft (see Chapter 22), no dinghy, unless purpose-designed like the Tinker Tramp, can be a fully adequate substitute offshore. The same is true on a coastal passage, but because the time generally elapsed before rescue is briefer and conditions often less severe, you could well endure successfully in a high-quality dinghy of sensible proportions.

Some coastal passagemakers opt not to incur the expense of buying or renting a liferaft. If this is your decision and your dinghy is an inflatable, consider finding a way of carrying it half-inflated lashed on deck. It can be deployed swiftly, but the pump must be readily available.

Dinghy Seamanship. On-board equipment. As with all seafaring, safe dinghy handling begins with the question, "What happens if...?"

However reliable your outboard, always carry a pair of paddles and the means to use them as oars, and choose a dinghy with a realistic arrangement for oarlocks.

It is a Federal requirement that you carry a PFD for every person on board. In heavy conditions, or in other unsafe situations, these should be worn. Some skippers insist quite sensibly on everyone in the dinghy wearing a PFD regardless of the circumstances. Do not fall into the trap of over-optimism. Dinghies are unstable and their motion can be surprisingly lively after time on the parent boat. This has surprised many an inexperienced operator.

In an area where help may not be immediately available should you lose your power, carrying a small anchor and rode is a safety measure.

When rowing or sailing a small dinghy after dark, your obligation is to show a white light to prevent collision. A flashlight is adequate. Under power, however, things are different.

The Navigation Rules make it clear that a power-driven vessel of under 7 meters (about 23 feet) not exceeding 7 knots must show an all-round white light. At over 7 knots, the boat is obliged in addition to exhibit port and starboard lights, which may be a bicolor. Theoretically, you should have a masthead and stern light like a larger power-driven vessel, but the rule states that under 12 meters length, (about 40 feet) these last two may be combined to an all-round white light.

The easy answer to staying legal is to show an all-round "white" and keep your speed below 7 knots. Today, many tenders are capable of planing at much higher speeds. If you do this in the dark, however, either rig up an additional bicolor or break international law.

Use a safety lanyard to keep the outboard attached to the dinghy at all times.

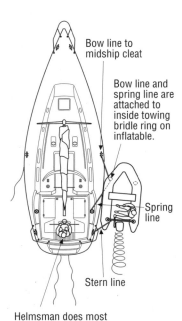

Bow line to midship cleat

Bow line and spring line are attached to inside towing bridle ring on inflatable.

Spring line

Stern line

Helmsman does most of the steering

Dinghy Equipment

☐ Anchor and rode
☐ Paddle and oars
☐ Bailer
☐ Lights
☐ Foot pump (for inflatables)
☐ Fuel tank and fuel line
☐ Dinghy registration
☐ Waterproofed chart

Wake. It is simple good manners to watch your wake as you power around an anchorage or river. Many anchorages and waterways enforce "no-wake" zones.

Towing the dinghy. The simple answer to the question of whether a dinghy should be towed on a coastal passage is, "No." Towing slows you down. If you doubt this, feel the drag on the painter when you're sailing at six knots. It also puts the dinghy at risk. Worrying about your dinghy when you're pondering a difficult harbor entrance is a needless diversion. Many a dinghy has been lost by tearing free of her painter, and on more than one occasion, the owner has pulled in the line after a tough passage to discover it still secured to the stem of the dinghy, but with no dinghy attached to the stem. A further nuisance is that a dinghy can pick up on a following sea and literally surf into the cockpit. An alarming arrival when you weren't expecting company.

Notwithstanding the previous comments, there will be times when a dinghy is towed between close-by anchorages, from the mooring to the dock, etc. When maneuvering under power with the dinghy in tow, always be aware of the dinghy's painter in relation to your propeller. The painter is one of the most popular sources of fouled propellers. Tow with a very short scope when coming up to anchor, or even move the tow point to amidships. Whatever you do, keep the painter short, even if it is made with floating rope.

Towing alongside. In the event of engine failure, or when cruising a yacht with no engine at all, the best way to power with your dinghy when any maneuvering will be involved is to lash it alongside. Set spring lines fore and aft, and have someone steering the yacht, because it has far more rudder area. Just remember you don't have much horsepower and bringing the show to a standstill may take longer than you imagined.

Laying out anchors. Often, the simplest way of laying out a second anchor (a "kedge") is by using the dinghy. This is especially true if the yacht is anchored on chain, in which case she won't want to execute any of those lovely textbook maneuvers for dropping the kedge.

If the kedge is to be set on chain, the trick is to load it all into the dinghy and dump it out in a line as you go. Do not try to drag it out behind you as someone feeds it over the bow if the boat. If you are using the outboard, flake the kedge rode into the dinghy and let it feed out as you power away to windward. Be careful that it doesn't tumble into the propeller, and have the anchor ready to drop quickly over the side — perhaps halfway over the gunwale already. If you're not prepared to drop, the tender can be blown halfway back to the ship before you wrestle the hook into the water. In a rising gale, hauling a 35-pound hook back up from deep water in a small dinghy and starting over again is not fun. Get it right the first time!

Sounding. From time to time you must transit a passage whose depths are unknown, either for want of a chart, or because of insufficient chart detail. The dinghy can now be pressed into service with a lead line to sound a safe route. Stand off or anchor outside while you launch the dinghy, and assign a reliable hand to the lead line. Note ranges for safe entry, then proceed. You won't have to re-launch the dinghy once inside, and you can take pride in surveying your own channel in the tradition of the great explorers. Name the channel after your boat, the saint whose day it is, or even after yourself, thus entering the ranks of the immortal!

Offshore Yacht Preparation

For coastal passagemaking, any well-found and well-prepared yacht working within its original design parameters can carry its crew to their destination successfully. Sailing offshore for protracted periods, a yacht must be prepared for everything mother nature might send her way. This demands a higher degree of preparation.

Sailing Performance. While the majority of passagemaking takes place in reasonable weather, the possibility of encountering a major storm is very real. The offshore vessel must be, first and foremost, heavy weather capable. This does not necessarily make her slow and ungainly. She should still be fun to sail and long-legged on passage.

For seasoned voyagers, the definition of sailing performance is different for an offshore passage than a trip along the coast. Close to land, windward pointing ability is a high priority, both for safety reasons and because to stay on schedule, you often have to sail with the wind "on the nose." On the ocean, you generally plan for a minimum of windward sailing. If you find the breeze heading you off below course, it's not a serious problem if you bear off and keep sailing at a comfortable 60 degrees to the apparent wind. You're bound to be lifted up again in due course.

Nobody but a masochist wants to sail close-hauled at more than 6 knots of hull speed in a boat less than 50 feet long. The motion is tough on crew and yacht. So, while the capacity to work to weather is a desirable feature, powerful reaching performance and an easy motion downwind are of equal value to offshore passagemakers.

With these issues in mind, the offshore yacht must be seakindly and strong beyond suspicion, yet deliver reasonable sailing performance even when loaded with stores for three months. It also doesn't hurt if she's sweet to the eye. If you are living aboard her for more than a few weeks, you'll spend a lot of time looking at her.

Equipping for light weather. A great deal of attention is focused on handling heavy weather offshore. Since failure to do so can be catastrophic, this is understandable, yet one more frequently encounters calms than storms at sea. Skippers must also know how to make the boat perform when the breeze is fitful.

While good light weather sails are important, a key decision for offshore skippers is how much fuel a boat should carry. The simple answer is, "more than you think you'll need."

The point is not to maintain a steady six knots of progress even when the wind drops. It is to combat the dreaded chafe and wear on a boat's gear and the crew's souls that usually occur in a calm. As a rule, a becalmed sailing vessel does not sit peacefully on a flat sea awaiting a building breeze to drive her onward. Instead, she wallows in a sloppy, left-over sea that threatens to shake the rig to pieces and drive her crew insane. If the asymmetric spinnaker cannot develop enough drive to settle the rig down, the next step is to furl the genoa, strap in the main and motor economically at four or five knots until you reach the next belt of breeze. To secure this happy option, large fuel tanks are a must. If you

On the ocean, you generally plan for a minimum of windward sailing. Sailing upwind for any extended period of time is tough on crew and yacht. While windward performance is a desirable feature, powerful reaching performance and an easy motion downwind are of real value to offshore passagemakers.

don't have them, make space on deck for cans of extra fuel.

Hull Profiles. Before considering the important issue of stability, we'll review some common yacht hull profiles. Understanding their sailing characteristics, as well as their capacity to resist capsize, is a key to storm survival.

Fin and spade monohull. This is the most modern of the basic monohull profiles and generally produces boats that have light displacement for their length. The hull usually features a relatively shallow "canoe" body combined with a narrow and deep (high aspect ratio) "fin" keel that is bolted on. A separate, free-standing "spade" rudder is supported by a strong shaft with bearings inside the hull.

This hull type features low wetted surface area and excellent performance when sailed without excessive heel. A fin keel is extremely efficient when moving through the water, but the hull itself has little inherent lateral resistance. Therefore, the boat sideslips easily when the keel stalls either due to low forward motion or excessive heel. Because

Light displacement cruiser/racers are potentially less stable than other types, particularly in a breaking sea.

the hull is shallow, the boat needs relatively high freeboard to gain accommodation space, particularly under 40 feet of length, but the broad sterns often associated with the form supply ample volume for aft cabins.

The flat "floor" of the canoe hull shape also means low bilge capacity, so if water finds its way in, gear in the lower lockers can have a damp ride. Shallow bilges are also difficult to pump out, because in the absence of a deep central sump, water gathers on the lee side. It also stands to reason that if a boat displaces only 12,000 lbs., 3,000 lbs. of gear, people, stores, water and fuel are going to have a noticeable effect on performance and stability.

Another tradeoff of the lightweight modern cruiser is that she sacrifices much the seakindliness that was axiomatic to boatmen through the ages. While the fin and spade type is quick on the helm, which can prove beneficial in a marina, it also requires far more attention on the helm at sea… watch after watch, day after day. An autopilot can alleviate this, but it remains reassuring if the helm can be left untended for long enough to go below and put the teakettle on.

On the plus side, fin and spade boats are easily driven (current racing yachts choose this type) and can thus carry a smaller, lighter rig than a heavier, deeper-bodied hull form. This makes them theoretically less expensive to build and less strenuous to sail. Many production builders favor this type, and you will find many such yachts out on the ocean.

Fin and skeg monohull. While superficially similar to the canoe-body type, the fin and skeg configuration is more of a natural development of the traditional working vessel. The lines of the keel, both fore-and-aft and athwartships, blend into the underbody of the hull smoothly. The keel itself is usually of a moderate aspect ratio with a longer fore-and-aft profile. The rudder, while separated from the keel and set far aft, is supported at its leading edge by a skeg.

Medium displacement fin and skeg cruisers are generally agreed to be a wholesome option for offshore work.

While the keel is not quite as efficient as a high-aspect-ratio fin, it provides improved lateral stability when the boat loses way, which is a benefit in survival conditions. Theoretically, a skeg-hung rudder is better supported than the spade rudder, and while the spade is more efficient at small steering angles, at large angles and in rough sea conditions it will stall more easily than the skeg-hung rudder.

Because the fin and skeg type displaces more than the flat-floored fin and spade type, it requires less freeboard and its motion is often easier. This makes it possibly wetter on deck, but also lowers the hull's center of gravity. Living space below is typically tighter than the fin and skeg type, and there may be less volume in the aft quarters.

Full or long-keeled monohull. The term "full keel" (or long keel) can be used to describe yachts from a traditional straight-stemmed cutter with a deep forefoot, deep draft and massive displacement to a yacht whose profile is cut away both fore and aft. For a full-keeler to deliver the benefits of her breed, however, she needs to maintain a reasonably deep forefoot and a sternpost that is not too steeply raked. A traditional long-keel cutter is easy to steer, moves with a comfortable motion and

Heavy displacement long-keeled cruisers can be very seaworthy indeed. Many sail well too.

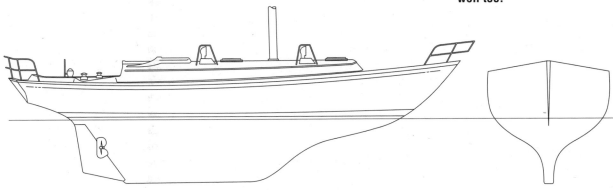

has enough displacement to load whatever stores and water her crew could reasonably want. Space below may not be very different from a fin and skeg boat of similar length, however, and because of the amount of material it takes to build her, she can prove more expensive than more modern displacement types. She will also require more sail if she is to perform reasonably and you may resort to engine use more frequently, but when you're weathering a heavy gale and no longer have the fortitude to go on deck, a boat like this will look after you with a minimum of assistance. While spade and skeg-hung rudders located near the after end of the boat deliver more effective steering control than a rudder attached to the keel, in rough conditions their location can make them more susceptible to loss of control.

Multihulls. Many of the desirable features of offshore monohulls are fulfilled by a catamaran or trimaran. Multihulls inherently deliver excellent reaching performance, minimal rolling and pitching motion off the wind (which helps minimize chafe), and like any light displacement boat perform well in light conditions unless overloaded. Multihulls possess high initial stability due to their wide beam, but their susceptibility to capsize if they roll beyond 70 or 80 degrees is a serious concern for an offshore vessel. With experience gained from offshore multihull passages has come improved techniques in preventing rollovers by large breaking waves, or broaching or pitchpoling while surfing down waves at high speed. These techniques

Multihulls offer excellent reaching performance and high initial stability but are susceptible to capsize if rolled in heavy seas.

are based on avoiding the attitude of the multihull lying broadside to the waves and reducing unwanted speed.

There are a wide variety of catamarans and trimarans ranging from fast, close winded performers with good tacking ability to sluggish performers with poor maneuverability. Underwater appendages vary widely, from deep, slender rudders and daggerboards to kick up versions that allow easy beaching. Above deck, configurations vary from full-wing deckhouses offering maximum accommodations to open superstructures that reduce weight as well as resistance to wind and waves. Typically multihull hull shapes feature low wetted surface area with shallow draft so relatively high freeboard is needed for accommodations.

Stability and Capsize Resistance. Recent research in this area has greatly advanced our understanding of the behavior of different hull types in extreme conditions. No ocean storm is the same, but certain hull forms have proven more seaworthy when the going gets tough. It's all in the physics.

Static stability. Yacht stability when subjected to a rolling force from either wind or waves stems from two different sources. One is "form stability," derived from a hull's buoyancy, resulting in upward force. Form stability increases as a yacht's beam increases. The second is the "center of gravity" of a yacht's weight (displacement), a downward force. Ballast in a keel lowers the center of gravity which increases stability.

When a yacht heels, the center of buoyancy moves outward from the amidships line toward the leeward side. As she heels more, the center of

continued on page 100

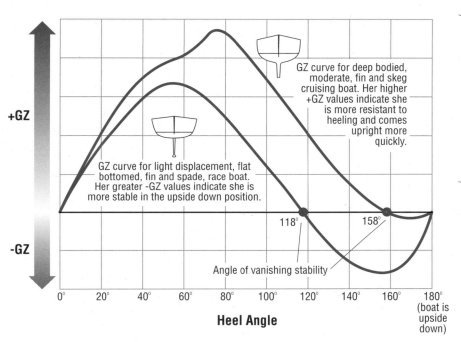

GZ curve for deep bodied, moderate, fin and skeg cruising boat. Her higher +GZ values indicate she is more resistant to heeling and comes upright more quickly.

GZ curve for light displacement, flat bottomed, fin and spade, race boat. Her greater -GZ values indicate she is more stable in the upside down position.

+GZ

-GZ

118°   158°

Angle of vanishing stability

0°   20°   40°   60°   80°   100°   120°   140°   160°   180°
(boat is upside down)

Heel Angle

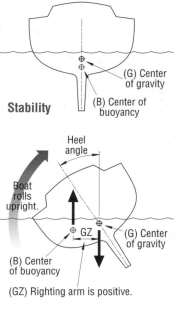

Stability

(G) Center of gravity

(B) Center of buoyancy

Heel angle

Boat rolls upright.

GZ

(B) Center of buoyancy

(G) Center of gravity

(GZ) Righting arm is positive.

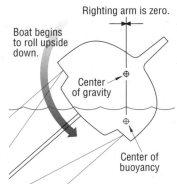

Vanishing Stability

Righting arm is zero.

Boat begins to roll upside down.

Center of gravity

Center of buoyancy

The two boats compared on the chart above are a moderate fin and skeg cruiser/racer and a flat-bottomed fin and spade racing yacht. Both are 32 ft. long. The racer has high freeboard and wide beam. The cruiser/racer has a more moderate shape, with less of both. The comparison of these hull forms for larger boats will have similar characteristics, although the numbers may vary. As heel angles rise, both boats display an increasing righting lever. The racer's peaks at about 55 degrees. The cruiser/racer develops maximum righting force when she is over at almost 80 degrees — reassuring if she takes a knockdown. At 118 degrees, the racer's righting lever disappears as her center of buoyancy moves under her center of gravity. This angle is called the "angle of vanishing stability." From here on in, not only is she upside down, she wants to stay that way. The fin-and-skeg yacht's angle of vanishing stability is 158 degrees. At this point, her negative stability is so low that the next wave will almost certainly right her once more. Another point shown by this graph is that the racer/cruiser's positive GZ values are always greater than those for the racer at comparative heel angles which mean she'll right herself more quickly.

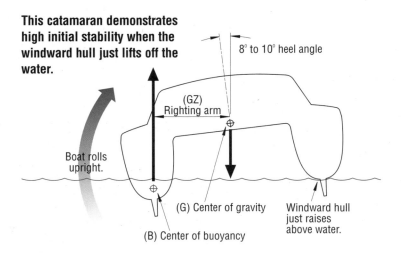

This catamaran demonstrates high initial stability when the windward hull just lifts off the water.

8° to 10° heel angle

(GZ) Righting arm

Boat rolls upright.

(G) Center of gravity

(B) Center of buoyancy

Windward hull just raises above water.

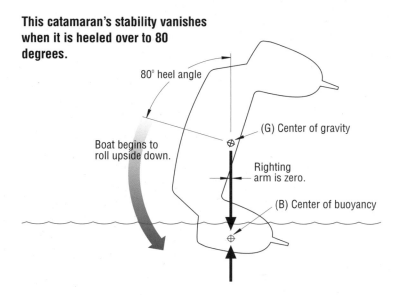

This catamaran's stability vanishes when it is heeled over to 80 degrees.

80° heel angle

Boat begins to roll upside down.

(G) Center of gravity

Righting arm is zero.

(B) Center of buoyancy

buoyancy moves further outboard as more of the lee side is pushed into the water.

While the wandering center of buoyancy bravely pushes upward to resist the heeling force, the center of gravity is pulling downward in its turn. So long as the hull is not half-flooded, the location of the center of gravity is largely unaffected by heeling. The two forces act together to generate a righting force (or moment). The strength of this force is affected by the distance between the center of buoyancy and the center of gravity. More distance makes for a longer righting lever (arm), and hence a greater force.

The horizontal distance between the center of buoyancy ("B") and the center of gravity ("G") is known in stability calculations as the righting arm or lever ("GZ"). When this value is plotted on a graph against progressive angles of heel, it shows a number of things.

Multihulls are very stable at low angles of heel due to their wide beam which produces a large righting lever (GZ). A catamaran develops her maximum righting lever just as her windward hull comes out of the water at about 5 degrees, whereas a trimaran peaks at around 15 to 20 degrees when her main hull lifts off. At low angles of heel, a multihull has greater stability than a similar-sized monohull.

A multihull's angle of vanishing stability occurs around 80 degrees when her righting lever disappears, just when our wholesome cruiser/racer is developing her maximum righting arm. As a multihull continues her roll-over, her negative stability increases. and she becomes stable in the inverted (upside down) position.

While generalizations can be dangerous, the conclusions drawn from the graph are hard to ignore. The GZ analysis, however, is not the end of the story. The actual righting moment is equal to the righting arm (GZ) times the boat's displacement, so a heavier displacement will increase capsize resistance for two otherwise equal boats. Capsize resistance is also higher in larger yachts because their righting arms and displacements are normally greater. Yachts whose submerged profiles are longer, such as fin and skeg and long-keeled types, will have better overall stability than fin-keel light displacement ones.

Dynamic effects. It would be convenient for designers, rule-makers and safety watch-dogs if the GZ curve and factors mentioned above were the end of the stability story, but they are not. It has been conclusively shown by authorities in Europe and the U.S. that in practice it is not wind, but the hammer blow of a wave that usually knocks a boat over.

A boat rolls around an imaginary axis running through it fore and aft. If you could lie along the center of roll, you would be rotated like a chicken on a spit. When a boat is hit by a wave, her initial resistance to capsize comes from inertia. Any weight (mass) which is far above or below the roll axis will have more inertia to resist motion than a comparable weight close to it because its lever arm is greater. The square of this lever (k) multiplied by the mass (m) is called the "roll moment of inertia" (I) or $I = mk^2$.

The illustration indicates that a rig on a monohull has a much greater lever arm than any other component of the boat. Increasing weight aloft therefore improves dynamic resistance to capsize even though it theoretically reduces stability. Where a rolling boat is ultimately pushed over on her beam ends, this increased weight is undesirable.

The desired effect, however, is to prevent capsize in the first place, so most experts maintain that weight in the rig is a plus in severe conditions. This suggests that rigs can be built more solidly than a strict adherence to "positive GZ" would otherwise dictate. When a boat is unfortunate enough to suffer a complete capsize, her rig is very much at risk. Additional strength where it counts can save the day.

For a multihull, the largest contributor to dynamic resistance to capsize comes from the hulls rather than the rig as shown in the illustration depicting roll moments of inertia for a catamaran. Since roll moment of inertia and GZ increase with beam, one would assume that increasing beam would continue to improve the stability of a multihull, but like many good things there is usually a limit. In this case, if the beam is increased too much, the multihull will become more susceptible to pitchpoling.

Since the late 1970s, much scientific analysis has been concentrated on the question of yacht capsize. As one might expect, the results follow seamanlike logic: heavier rather than lighter, longer if possible, don't scrimp on rig scantlings, but don't weight her up so much that a knockdown could be terminal. Moderation in all things is sound advice for life at sea as well as ashore.

Cockpits. All working sailing craft with cockpits placed them as far aft as possible, and the reasons are obvious once you are offshore. Motion is easier at the stern, so a watch will be less tiring. A cockpit that is lower in the boat is nearer to the vessel's roll center, which means less lurching, less seasickness and a safer ride. Placing the cockpit further aft puts more distance between you and the bow where the flying water originates. The only downside to an aft cockpit at sea is that if you are pooped you will be thoroughly soaked. But, as a sailor knows only too well, nothing in life is perfect. Cockpits should be watertight and self-bailing, and while a large cockpit may be acceptable in protected waters, offshore it becomes a liability if it fills with water and overwhelms the scuppers' ability to drain the water quickly.

Instruments should be located so they are readily visible in fair and foul weather, and when the autopilot is being used. Often this is at the forward end of the cockpit in the shelter of the dodger rather than on the steering pedestal.

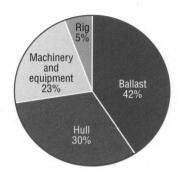

In terms of a typical monohull cruiser's weight distribution (above), the rig constitutes only 5% of the total. However, In terms of dynamic resistance to rolling capsize (below), the rig contributes 65% of the boat's initial resistance to capsize.

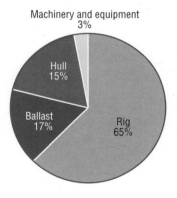

On a multihull (below) the windward hull is the most significant contributor to initial resistance to rolling or capsize.

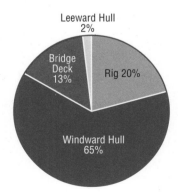

Ventilation. There is more to ventilating an offshore yacht than multiple hatches and an "airy" feel. Crew need fresh air in foul weather as well as fair, and noxious fumes must be vented out continually without seawater entering at the same time. All boats are different in this respect, and it is recommended that specialized research be done related to your specific yacht. However, several general points will be made here.

Companionway dodgers. A well-designed companionway dodger will do more than protect you from spray and rain. It can serve as a giant air scoop with the wind aft in pleasant conditions and as a major exhaust vent with the wind forward of the beam. Commission your dodger with this in mind.

Baffled vents. These allow air in and out while barring water. The classic and still largely unimproved favorite is the Dorade vent, named after the famous Olin Stephens-designed ocean racer of the 1930s. His brother Rod Stephens, one of the great practical seamen of all time, thought out the ventilators which still bear the boat's name. They have proliferated world-wide.

Typically, an offshore yacht might have two Dorades by her mast and a third well aft to vent the dead areas under the cockpit and engine space where fumes can gather. This vent can also promote an under-sole flow of air to keep the boat "sweet."

Mushroom vents, which screw down tight in the worst weather, are effective in easier going.

Other aids to ventilation. Louvered doors are helpful, particularly for lockers, where mold can grow in days if you give it a chance. It's a sad discovery to shake out the blazer for a club night at the end of an offshore passage, only to find it green with mildew. The wearer can only slink into the bar smelling like a cave dweller. Some cruising yachts pipe hot air from the engine or diesel heater into the wet locker to dry foul-weather gear.

While the forward hatch is particularly vulnerable at sea if water is flying, it can offer a massive boost to airflow. Try to arrange for it to hinge from the forward edge at sea and from aft in harbor. It can then vent air out or scoop it in as circumstances dictate.

Berths, and a Space for Everyone. Just as on a coastal passage, morale on an extended voyage is subject to all hands being able to sleep comfortably. But while the coastal crew of three or more might manage with one or two sea berths, offshore this is not acceptable. If a crew is to live cheek-by-jowl for weeks, each needs a space of their own. This doesn't mean a private cabin with shower, head and fancy lighting. All that is required is a place you lie down that is called yours. Here, within the bounds of consideration, you can leave the bedding out or roll it away to suit yourself. You can stick up a picture of your favorite film star, boat or pet (use blue painter's tape). You don't have to hot-bunk it, and there is no need to clamber out in the morning so that the rest of the team can sit down to breakfast.

If a crew member has a real sea berth, they are well on the way to contentment. Deprive them of this basic human dignity and you are sowing the seeds of discontent.

A bunk should provide:

The Dorade vent directs fresh air to the boat's interior while baffles in its base divert water and spray.

• Enough length to stretch

• Adequate width for a fetal posture. Often bunks are too narrow on the misguided fancy that the sleeper won't roll about. While huge doubles definitely do not work at sea, crew will wedge themselves into any sensible single by the way they are lying. Some extra space to thrash about is always welcome. For a six-footer, 22 inches of width is the absolute minimum, with 26 inches preferable.

• A solid leeboard that extends at least ten inches above the cushion. Failing this, a lower one or, if a wooden board cannot be arranged, a high canvas leecloth that is easy to rig and unrig.

• A decent reading light

• An ordinary vinyl or synthetic upholstery fabric cushion (4 inch foam is enough) is preferred over a more exotic fabric, so that when you turn in "all standing" on a filthy night you won't have to worry abut the upholsterer's bill. Consider loose covers for use in harbor.

Stowing for the Worst. The only policy for offshore stowage is to assume that the boat will suffer inversion at some point. Apart from the more obvious items listed below, many a sailor has been hurt by tools hurtling across the living space, and more than one of us has suffered a nasty black eye from the corner of the sight reduction tables book.

Batteries. These are one of the worst offenders for jumping their cradle, and the damage they wreak can be dreadful. All batteries must be strapped down firmly in a dedicated compartment that fits them well, and their straps must be attached to something strong with serious bolts. A battery is so heavy that once moving it leaves a certain path of destruction.

"Hatch" locker lids. These are found on most boats. They are cut out of the plywood that forms bunk tops and other surfaces. Even a liquor locker under the center of a saloon table has one. If you take a hard knockdown and these are not fastened down they will be thrown off, leaving the contents free to redistribute themselves around the cabin. Locker lids can be readily and inexpensively made safe with turnbuttons.

Floorboards. When these come adrift by roll-over or flooding, the crew must negotiate around gaping holes while assessing damage. Avoid potential trouble with some form of flush mounted positive latching system. While you're at it make sure you can access the entire hull below the waterline from the inside.

Companionway ladder. This is another large object that needs a positive latching arrangement to keep it in place in all conditions.

Books and other heavy items. There is no established method for securing everything in a yacht's cabin. Suffice it to say, once again, constantly prepare for the worst.

The stove. It makes sense to upgrade your stove for passagemaking (also see Chapter 4). Rig a stout "bum-strap" to lean back into when the galley is to windward, then make a thorough inspection of your stove's fiddle rail and pan clamps. If they look like something from a Toytown movie (many do), beef them up now before the soup makes a dive for your shirt on a rough night.

Make sure your stove is mounted so that it will stay in place if you suffer a knockdown or if the boat is rolled over.

On an offshore passage, each crew member needs a space to call their own.

Offshore Rigging and Sails

In this chapter, we shall investigate policies for helping sails and rigging endure long-term voyaging, and consider additional sails for gale conditions.

Most standing and running rigging on yachts built for serious offshore work require little additional strengthening, but some craft which "appear" ocean-worthy have inadequate rig scantlings. Bulking up the rig can be more complicated than it appears, however. It can be tempting in the light of findings about roll moment of inertia (Chapter 14) to increase the gauge of standing rigging by a factor of one or two, but this may not necessarily be an improvement on its own. A heavier gauge wire will require a greater load to achieve the same tension as a lighter one. This in turn increases strains on spars and fittings. Unless these two are also made heavier, beefing up the wires alone may be counter-productive.

Bringing the Rig Up to Ocean Standards. Few offshore passagemaking yachts carry enough fuel to motor to safety should they lose their rig in mid-ocean. The mast and all that holds it up is therefore the primary mode of propulsion and, second only to hull integrity, is to be treated as a top priority in the maintenance "pecking order." This subject has been covered in Chapter 2, but it cannot be overstressed that before heading offshore your rig must be above suspicion in every detail.

Unless you are a specialist on rig stresses, you will only have peace of mind in your first big gale if you've had a highly qualified expert survey your wires, terminals, fittings and spars before you leave. Choosing the right person for this job is not so easy. Plenty of riggers spend their working lives hoisting and lowering masts in boatyards, setting up shrouds and stays, and opening more cotter pins than most sailors will ever see. But when you find the truly knowledgeable rigger with hands-on ocean experience, you have discovered gold. Take this special person aside, share your plans, and commission a full rig survey. Also ask advice about spares for your particular needs and add them to those recommended here. Chapter 22 will consider jury rigging, together with the tools and spares to effect it, but an expert's advice based on the fittings on your boat is invaluable.

Boom vangs, goosenecks and their attachments to mast and boom are subjected to high loads and require close inspection before and during a passage. Check for signs of stress cracks, distortion, loose fastenings, and stressed welds. Be careful not to crank up the vang too much, which can cause damage to your boom, or in extreme conditions, cause your rig to fail. It's a good idea to design a weak link in your vang system, such as a shackle designed to break at a specific loading, so that it fails first before doing more serious damage.

You can generally survey sails yourself, because damage or tired cloth can be spotted. If in doubt, consult a sailmaker who will be happy to give an opinion and repair any defects.

Your sails and rig should be your pride as well as your lifeline. Choose them wisely, treat them with respect and let them speak well of you.

Sail Repair Kit

- ☐ Sticky-back tape
- ☐ Ripstop
- ☐ Sticky-back sail cloth
- ☐ Spare sailcloth
- ☐ Contact adhesive
- ☐ Waxed sail twine
- ☐ Thimbles
- ☐ Boltrope for traditional sails
- ☐ Selection of needles
- ☐ Palm
- ☐ Chafe protection material
- ☐ Spare batten material
- ☐ Slides
- ☐ Batten cars

Chafe Protection. Sails take a far worse beating on offshore passages than in any other form of boating outside racing. This is largely because of chafe — the bane of the long-distance voyager. Traditional rigs, with their extra spars, lack of vanging and multiple purchases used to suffer horribly as boats rolled down the tradewinds, making the fight against this creeping destruction a daily chore. While today's rigs are easier to deal with, the problem is still not defeated.

Fighting mainsail chafe. Chafe is worse when sailing off the wind. The boat rolls more, apparent wind speeds are lower so sails are not always pressed full, and there is a greater degree of movement on eased sheets. Sails and lines can rub against standing rigging, stanchions, spreaders and anything else they can find, day after day. A squared-out mainsail that presses against cap shrouds, lowers and spreaders, can be chewed up in short order if movement is left unchecked. The answer is not, as you might imagine, to oversheet the sail to keep it clear. This may help the chafe situation, but it will also slow the boat down and increase weather helm. It is far better to vang the boom down and, if necessary, rig a preventer (see Chapter 2).

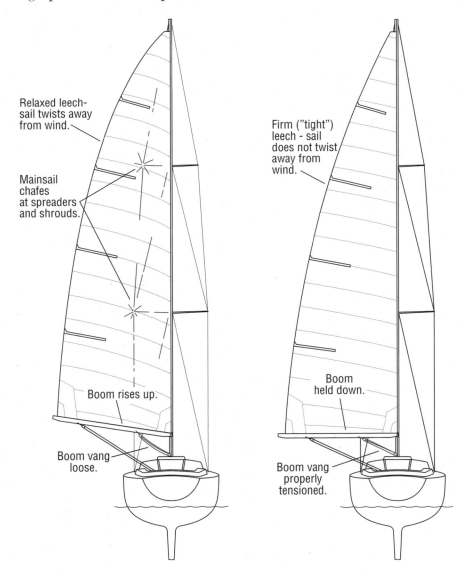

Relaxed leech-sail twists away from wind.

Mainsail chafes at spreaders and shrouds.

Firm ("tight") leech - sail does not twist away from wind.

Boom rises up.

Boom held down.

Boom vang loose.

Boom vang properly tensioned.

The boom vang is an important key to minimizing mainsail chafe.

Vanging the boom stops it from pumping with each roll, which holds the sail rigid and prevents it from rubbing against the rig. If it's not moving, it's not chafing. The sail may develop dark marks where it meets the rigging, but these are honorable stains.

It is especially important to address this issue when a rig uses swept-back spreaders. Such rigs are particularly prone to mainsail wear. In extreme cases, having the sailmaker stitch a sacrificial strip of cloth on both sides of the sail at key chafe points is well worth the effort. Other remedies include sliding plastic tubing over the aft lower shrouds before the terminals are locked in place and installing anti-chafe spreader end covers.

Headsail and sheet chafe. Since it sets forward of the mast and shrouds, a headsail should in theory be chafe-free. On a long reach, however, headsails rub against the pulpit and the sheet can suffer interference from the lifelines. To re-lead the sheet, use a spare length of line (a "change sheet") and bend it onto the clew. Lead it, still unloaded, outside the lifelines, then load it onto a spare winch and slack away its predecessor. The sail itself should not suffer more than the typical dark marks from smooth metal of the pulpit, as long as lifeline cotter pins have been neutralized with tape or silicone. These are the most important cotters on the boat when preparing against chafe. They will cost you dearly if left unguarded.

Keep a close eye on all working lines, both on deck and aloft (routinely inspect using binoculars). On long passages adjust halyards and end-for-end sheets. Windvane tiller lines are another favorite target for chafe, as well as jib-furling lines. If your jib-furling line is partly frayed through friction, it will surely part in a gale. The results are horrible to contemplate.

Storm Sails. The size of your storm sails is critical. All too often they are designed to serve double duty as a #3 or #4 headsail and a #3 reef — a foolish waste of money and lack of sensible seamanship. In storm conditions, the proper amount of sail area is critical to keeping your boat under control. Don't assume your storm sails are the right size. As a guide, US SAILING's *Safety Recommendations for Cruising Sailboats* specifies that storm jib area should not be greater than 5 percent of the foretriangle height squared with a maximum luff of 65 percent of the foretriangle height. Storm trysail area should not be greater than 17.5 percent of the mainsail luff times its foot. Offshore authority Rod Stephens recommended even more conservative guidelines for storm sails: 2.5 percent of the foretriangle height squared for a storm jib, and 5 percent of the mainsail luff squared for a storm trysail.

A dedicated track for a trysail is highly recommended, but if you

Headsail sheet chafe can be virtually eliminated by carefully re-leading the sheet.

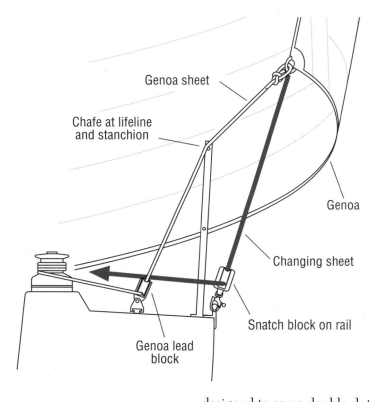

Genoa sheet

Chafe at lifeline and stanchion

Genoa

Changing sheet

Snatch block on rail

Genoa lead block

intend to set a trysail without one, you may have to modify the location of the gate on the main track. In order to bend on the trysail at sea, it will be necessary for all the mainsail slides to fall below the gate with the sail in the stowed position. If they do not, you are in for a bad time.

Before setting off on your passage, practice rigging the storm sails in light conditions to make sure you've got all the pieces, the slides and gates work and the sheets can be led properly. It also makes sense to have dedicated sheets for the storm sails permanently attached to them.

Storm jibs. For serious offshore work, any boat with a roller reefing headsail must have a provision for bending on a proper storm jib. The exception is a yacht with a cutter rig, where the jib is on a roller and the staysail is rigged conventionally. If small and strong enough, or reefable, the staysail may serve instead.

It is possible to set a storm jib "flying," attached only at the tack, head and clew. It is not hanked on to any stay and the straightness of its luff is maintained purely with halyard tension. Such a system can work well, but the sail will require a wire or Spectra luff and a powerful halyard winch. It also needs some form of direct backstaying where the halyard meets the mast to support the increased luff tension. A more popular arrangement for a single-headsail foretriangle is to have an additional inner forestay that is easily rigged when needed. This "storm forestay" can be tensioned in various ways, including a forestay release lever, a "Highfield" lever or a short tackle with its tail brought aft to a winch. The tackle could be replaced by a Spectra line led through a single turning block at the base of the stay and back to a winch.

A true storm jib is generally used in winds over 35 knots, so it should be made of heavy material and well reinforced at the corners. Attention should be paid to its sheet lead, and often a tack pennant is needed to raise the clew above the waves. It is a sound plan to have storm jib and trysail made from high-visibility orange material.

Trysails. A trysail is bent on the mast in place of the mainsail in extreme conditions. Smaller in area than a deep-reefed main, it has two further advantages. First, it is sheeted independently of the boom so if this or the gooseneck has been damaged, it is still usable. Secondly, because it is rarely used, it remains in good condition, often for the life of a boat. Just make sure to inspect it now and again.

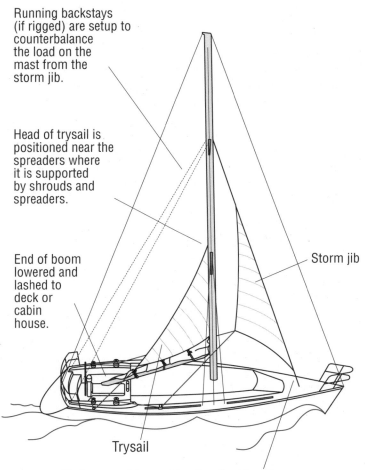

Shown is a typical trysail and storm jib setup for heavy weather.

Running backstays (if rigged) are setup to counterbalance the load on the mast from the storm jib.

Head of trysail is positioned near the spreaders where it is supported by shrouds and spreaders.

End of boom lowered and lashed to deck or cabin house.

Storm jib

Trysail

Tack pennant is used to align the jib with the trysail and raise the foot above the waves.

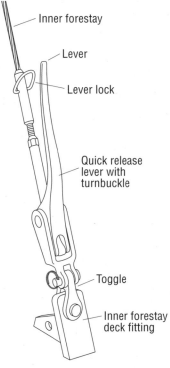

Inner forestay

Lever

Lever lock

Quick release lever with turnbuckle

Toggle

Inner forestay deck fitting

A Highfield lever allows inner forestay tension to be adjusted, and the stay to be conveniently removed when not needed.

Anatomy of a Trysail

Main halyard

Head

Double metal sliders at head.

Storm trysail

Mast

Trysail track

Tack

Track gate

Tack pennant fastened to gooseneck.

Sheets led to blocks then to secondary winches.

Tack of trysail clears mainsail stowed on boom.

Clew

End of boom is lowered and secured to deck.

Setting the trysail:

• Drop mainsail and stow it tightly. Use additional sail ties if necessary. If the boat has no boom gallows, lower and lash the boom end to the deck rather than leaving it on its toppinglift or rod vang.

• Remove the main halyard from the head of the mainsail and attach it carefully at deck level. Actively remind yourself and your crew, "DO NOT LOSE IT ALOFT!"

• If the boat has a dedicated trysail track, the sail will probably already be bent on, stowed in its bag ready for deployment. If not, the sail must be bagged with its tack and luff extending from the bag. Open the gate on the mast and, keeping the body of the sail in its bag out of the wind, secure the trysail tack pennant at the deck or gooseneck. Work the slides into the groove, starting from the top or bottom depending on how much spare track you have, then close the gate.

• The sheets are recommended to be left on the sail in the bag. Extract them from the bag and lead them to their winches, usually via turning blocks on the yacht's aft quarters. Note that the tack pennant must be pre-measured to ensure the sail hoists to the correct height for its sheets. This might place its tack ten feet above the boom.

• Attach the halyard and hoist away. You do not need to be head to wind to do this, but if the wind is aft of the beam and the canvas is blowing forward of the mast, crank on a little sheet to keep it under control. Remember it's howling and there will be action 'aplenty as soon as the wind sees the sailcloth.

• Sheet in on the lee side, then put the kettle on.

Running Backstays. It has justifiably been said that if you install running backstays on a cruising mast you make it vulnerable. This is because an all-standing jibe onto a tensioned runner can bring the mast down or bend the boom. An ideal cruising rig is unlikely to depend on runners for its day-to-day operation, and the less they are used, the lower is the possibility of a mishap. However, some boats are rigged with runners whose job is only to supply extra support on a long reach or run. Set up against an inner forestay, they will stop a mast from "pumping." With a boom preventer in place, any chance of jibing onto the wire by mistake disappears, and the arrangement may one day save the mast. It will certainly prolong its life by lessening metal fatigue. For offshore passages, carefully conceived running backstays used judiciously should at least be considered, especially for rigs relying on swept-back spreaders.

Offshore Passage Planning

The most important determining factor in ocean passage planning is weather. No sane person, for example, would cross the North Atlantic to England in February for pleasure, or consider rounding Cape Horn in July, the southern winter. These examples are obvious and no specialized reference works are needed. For the most part, however, determining when to sail and what route to take can be a surprisingly intricate process. The seasonal effects of ocean weather will be covered in Chapter 18. Here, we shall discover where to find the information you require.

Once you have filtered through "macro-issues" such as winter, or tropical storm seasons, you then must consider fair and foul winds, currents, temperatures of sea and air, fog and ice. In addition to these, there is also advanced planning involved with visiting foreign ports and awareness of potential piracy and its dangers.

Meteorological Considerations – The Pilot Chart. The likelihood of specific conditions of wind, wave, current and fog has been predicted since the nineteenth century when U.S. Navy Lieutenant Matthew Fontaine Maury began collating passage data submitted by hundreds of merchant and navy ships. The material was collated into statistical probabilities of wind strength, directions, etc., for a specified ovean area in a given month and presented in the form known today as the "pilot chart."

A monthly pilot chart for a particular ocean is by far the most significant passage planning aid the world has ever seen. It provides all the information you could possibly need, such as wind, currents, sea

Each square on the pilot chart has a "wind rose" which predicts the statistical probability of wind strength and direction in a given month. It is a valuable tool in offshore passage planning.

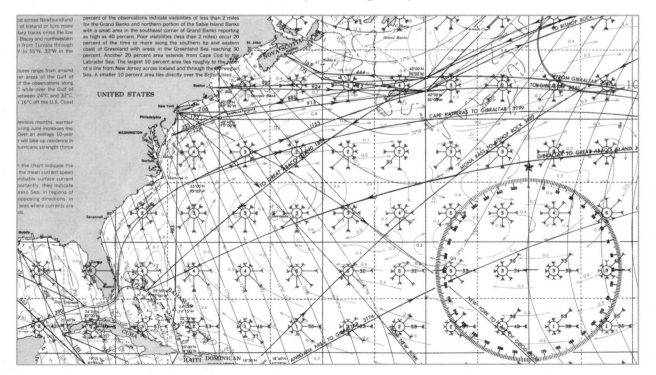

The length of the arrows on a wind rose indicates the percentage of probability of wind from that direction. The number of barbs indicates the force of the wind (two barbs indicate Force 2). The large number in the middle circle indicates the percentage of calms or light winds.

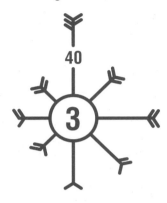

WIND ROSE INFORMATION

Direction	Percentage	Strength
N	40%	Force 5
NE	8%	Force 4
E	14%	Force 4
SE	8%	Force 3
S	10%	Force 2
SW	5%	Force 3
W	7%	Force 3
NW	5%	Force 4

Light green arrows (shown light grey here) represent ocean current directions, numbers indicate current speed in knots.

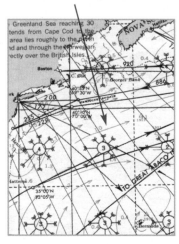

conditions, fog, shipping routes, and gale probabilities.

Once you have decided where you are bound and when, lay out the pilot chart and the best route is generally an obvious decision. Planning a passage without consulting a pilot chart would be anathema to a seasoned ocean mariner.

The nature of the wind roses makes trends easy to read at a glance, with trade-wind zones and areas of predominantly westerly weather standing out clearly. The eight arrows, which fly with the wind, are arranged around central circles. Each one gives the average force experienced from its own direction. By comparing the arrows attached to an individual circle it is easy to determine your chances of breeze from a particular quadrant and to form a useful idea of its likely strength. Critically, the charts show selected tropical storm tracks, forecast their probabilities and also describe typical depression routes.

Currents are more important on a long passage than you might imagine. A mere half-knot current will move a boat twelve miles per day. For a day's run of 120 miles, a half knot of fair current would mean 132 made good. With a foul current, it would be only 108. Even if the difference is between fair stream and no stream, 12 "free" miles a day could shave two days off a 20-day passage. Step onto the South Equatorial Current running west along the north coast of South America and you're in for a 2-knot sleigh-ride! The "rivers of the ocean" are to be taken seriously. Choose the chart for the month you expect to sail, but take a hard look at the months either side so as to gain a feel for developing trends. This helps you cope if the pattern you expect is early or late arriving, which is not uncommon.

Lines indicating probable incidence of fog are useful, as even with radar, nobody wants to cruise along at six knots day after day into 50 yards visibility. Ice is often associated with fog in higher latitude sailing, and one does not have to be navigating Arctic waters to encounter this menace. Anyone crossing from Newfoundland to northern Europe will traverse the Grand Banks where, in the midsummer months icebergs and growlers are rumbling in numbers with the Labrador current running down from Greenland. It is not unusual to meet one as low as 45 degrees latitude. If you were making the same trip from Cape Cod, you would be well advised to divert from the direct route across the Grand Banks. A prudent course would be to steer due east until beyond the shoals, then join the great circle (see Chapter 19), weather permitting, and let the Gulf Steam begin working its magic. All the information required for such decisions is on the pilot charts.

One surprisingly helpful feature of a modern pilot chart is the great circle courses which loop across its oceans, each inscribed with distance from its point of departure to its destination. The routes themselves are of interest, but more important to the sailing vessel which rarely is able to follow a predetermined tack for long is the hint they deliver as to likely shipping densities. Areas where ships concentrate are well worth a wide berth.

Ocean Pilots. *Ocean Passages for the World:* This remarkable volume comes complete with ocean climate charts, current distribution charts and world sailing-ship charts. These repeat the pilot chart information in somewhat less detail, but they enable you to split it up for an easier digestion. The sailing-ship routes recommended on the charts and in the text have seen little adjustment since the days when the four-masted barks ploughed south from the North Atlantic to load up on Chilean nitrates, and emigrants hung on grimly as madmen drove their clippers round the Horn to San Francisco. With modern yachts out-pointing such vessels by anything up to 30 degrees, the advice given seems extraordinarily conservative for weathering the great capes, yet the reality of long-distance sailing is that nobody wants

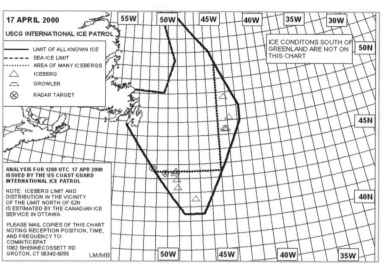

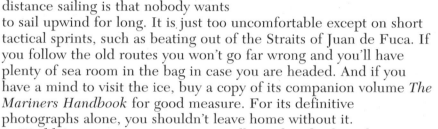

Ice flow charts are an important tool for planning passages in higher Northern and Southern latitudes. The above chart was obtained online at *www.uscg.mil*.

to sail upwind for long. It is just too uncomfortable except on short tactical sprints, such as beating out of the Straits of Juan de Fuca. If you follow the old routes you won't go far wrong and you'll have plenty of sea room in the bag in case you are headed. And if you have a mind to visit the ice, buy a copy of its companion volume *The Mariners Handbook* for good measure. For its definitive photographs alone, you shouldn't leave home without it.

World Cruising Routes, a commercially produced volume by Jimmy Cornell, is worked up from up-to-date reports and information and is specifically aimed at today's ocean passagemaker. It contains advice for over 500 ocean routes, including Spitzbergen and Antarctica.

Further reference: The U.S. Coast Pilots are far more useful than their dry appearance would suggest. They contain all manner of material about the ocean you are sailing, its currents, weather, habits and even snippets about its history. When it comes to landfalls, these "official" pilot books are second to none for their descriptions of the coast, forming the perfect companion to pilot charts. Other specialized guides such as Hammick's *The Atlantic Crossing Guide* are useful for the information they offer on political situations, bureaucracy, etc. *Cornell's World Cruising Handbook* is packed with intelligence about customs procedures and the like, but perhaps the best source of all, particularly when it comes to such delicate and changeable matters as piracy, is good old dockside "scuttlebutt." Keep your ears open, talk with reliable people who have been before you, and take along every official piece of paper you can find "just in case," whether it concerns you, your crew or the ship. And never be slow to visit the consulate to have a question answered.

The Crew and Their Needs. Compatibility. Perhaps the most important factor in bringing together a compatible crew is your own self-knowledge. Taking the wrong person often stems from wanting to like somebody. Perhaps it's a relative, or a workmate, a drinking buddy or even someone who sails with you at home. Any of these might seem great shipmates, but just because you get on with them in safe, controlled circumstances doesn't mean they will hold up under the stresses of bad weather and discomfort at sea. Each crew member should be interviewed as if they were a stranger. Explain the objectives for the passage, then ask why they want to come, what they expect, and what they want out of the trip. If this all seems to concur, inquire last what they will be contributing.

The answer to this question doesn't have be, "Twenty years at sea, three round-the-world races and a medical degree." It may be better if they say, "I know how to set a sail, I can steer a compass course and cook in rough weather; plus I'm a thoughtful and pleasant person." If you really believe it, this is the sailor for you. It doesn't matter if they can't work out a seven-star fix or steer at 15 knots under spinnaker.

The self-knowledge factor comes into play at judgement time. You know that you're a likeable sort of character and that you don't enjoy letting people down. This guy wants to come, he's taken the trouble to ask, and he means it. Crew never seem to offer their services when you want them, and he seems a decent guy.

This is where you must trust your animal instincts. If your gut is muttering, "I'm not so sure…," just say no. It can be tough to do, but if you shrink from it now, you'll probably live to regret it. And regrets at sea have a high cost.

Medical. The essential difference between a medical occurrence offshore and on a coastal passage is that far from land you must deal with problems from within your own resources. You might establish a radio or internet connection with a doctor who can give advice and help you use drugs in your medicine chest, but a medical professional cannot prescribe something you don't have.

The best course of action during the planning stage is to talk to a doctor who has been offshore and knows what you ought to be carrying for your crew and your trip. Failing a seasoned offshore doctor, talk to your family GP. He or she should be able to advise sensibly on which drugs and other stores you should acquire, and help you to do so. For a little extra cost, some pharmacies will "blister-pack" pills to keep out air and moisture and extending shelf life. You will also carry an instruction list describing each package, what it is, what it does and what you use it for. This forms an essential core of information which you can complement by reference to *The Ship's Captain's Medical Guide*, or some other maritime medical bible. They contain information from how hard to heave up a bandage to what size the national ensign should be to cover up a victim prior to burial at sea.

Make sure you ask each crew member for a medical history. For their privacy, it may be given in a sealed envelope until emergency arises.

Keep a "self-help" First Aid kit easily accessible and a "serious" medical kit in a dry, cool, secure place. Typically, extra medical stores for offshore work will include:

• Antibiotics. These vary in grade and type, perhaps including one for respiratory complaints, another for a tooth abscess, and a third that might keep a grumbling appendix under control until you can reach help. Such drugs are not bulky or prohibitively expensive. Carry them as your medial advisor recommends.

• Antibiotic wound ointment for dressing cuts and abrasions, especially those sustained in coral seas.

• Additional bandages, sterile wound dressings, antiseptic wipes, surgical tape, eye pads, finger splints, etc.

• Medicated burn dressings.

• Heavy-duty painkillers for dire cases. If these are morphine-based they may require declaration with customs officials on arrival.

• Butterfly bandages for deep cuts. As an alternative, use duct tape on either side of an open wound, after cleaning, then suture duct tape together.

Finally, check over your medicine chest at the end of each passage, and top up as necessary. After the initial commitment, such matters tend to be "out of sight, out of mind," and it is all too easy to forget.

Choose crew so that, even if there are only two of you, one can cope alone in an extreme emergency. This may mean limping slowly but safely along under reduced sail, but it is unseamanlike to sail offshore in circumstances where one person is indispensable.

Food and stores. The same principles hold offshore and coastwise. Make up daily menus of meals you can cook under varying conditions and stock accordingly, and don't assume the freezer will work for the entire passage. Ask crew for their general preferences. Buy plenty of basic needs, store them, and then buy special treats. Allow a 50 percent time contingency so that should you be dismasted and lose radio contact, starvation won't be one of your worries. The contingency food should keep well and be quick to prepare if stove fuel is low. It can be unexciting and inexpensive because hopefully you won't be using it.

If you haven't had the experience previously, expect several trips to the supermarket on stock-up day, unless you have hired a small truck. Don't be horrified at the checkout bill. It's surprising, but feeding an equivalent number of people at sea and ashore is roughly the same.

Pets. Sadly, foreign quarantine regulations often require pets to be shut away expensively and for months on end. If you cheat and are discovered, Fido will be disposed of in a way that will do little to improve international relations, and he will have no right to trial by jury. Best leave him with family or neighbors.

Firearms. Regardless of your views about whether a cruising yacht should carry firearms for protection, the following facts must be considered. If you carry anything at all, from a small revolver to a small arsenal, you may be called upon to declare every item, including ammunition, at any foreign port of entry. When you declare your arms, one of three things will usually happen. If you are lucky, they will be sealed aboard. Alternatively they are either confiscated or kept ashore by the authorities until you leave. If the latter, they are unlikely to be well cared for, and you will have to return to the port of entry before departure.

Firearms aboard are a problem. If you take them, you may not have lawful access to them except outside territorial waters. Leave them back home and you won't even have them at sea. Should you opt not to declare your guns and they are subsequently discovered, the penalties in some countries are dire. You may be jailed and your boat confiscated. Even if you declare your firearms, the bureaucratic process that follows can be extraordinary. Consider alternative solutions such as mace, pepper spray, etc. Whatever you choose, investigate the laws in the countries you plan to visit before departing.

When stocking food supplies, allow a 50 percent time contingency. Contingency food should be quick to prepare in case fuel is low.

17 Life Aboard an Offshore Passagemaker

Today most people cross oceans by air, arriving at the other side in a matter of hours, having expended little significant effort other than using a credit card. On a sailboat, the process requires genuine personal commitment. In Scandinavian sea towns, votive ships are hung from church rafters not in thanks for heavenly services rendered, but to remind the faithful that life, like an ocean voyage, is a long journey.

Ocean Life. The length of an ocean passage is significant. It is not a sprint between ports, to be accomplished as quickly and efficiently as possible, but a measurable sector of life's total experience. We have discussed how to make a boat truly habitable at sea. We will now see the importance of this. The ship is our world for however long we are out there, so she must be designed in every respect to be in harmony with that environment.

Similar criteria apply to our state of mind. It is sad to hear someone say that they find life on passage boring. The sea itself and the sky are always different, the boat and her navigation must receive ongoing attention, there is marine life to observe, weather to contemplate, meals to plan and enjoy. Above all, there is time to do the things shore life never seems to allow.

Coping with distance. It is hard to contemplate 3,000 ocean miles. Even if you are enjoying the trip, you will still be looking toward the end, and it can seem a long, long way if all you do is watch daily runs crawl across a huge ocean chart. It is better by far to set up a series of achievable objectives, then cross them off one by one.

For the first half of a passage, sailors tend to look back to where they have come from, to life in that country and problems left behind. Somewhere in mid-ocean, the mind undergoes a mysterious transformation and one's mental energy is taken up with planning ahead, wondering what the landfall will bring, what new people will be met and what culinary treats await the hungry seafarer. Crews appreciate a celebration at times like this — the half-way point of a passage, the first thousand miles, the Date Line, some unmarked milestone in the ocean — indeed, any excuse for a party. If you are not running a dry ship, award all hands an extra beer. If you don't touch the stuff, bake them a cake, but do something physical to mark the occasion.

In the days of celestial navigation, noon was special because the ship's daily position was entered on the chart. The whole 24-hour cycle revolved around this ceremony. Now that we have GPS, the significance of noon has disappeared. This is bad for the rhythm of on-board life as it removes the suspense of awaiting the day's run. Ration the troops to one position per day, and make it noon. The news that you've made yet another 120 miles is cheering, but if they perceive progress a mile or two every half-hour, they start to think they'll never get there!

As mentioned earlier in Chapter 4, communication and thoughtfulness are important factors in maintaining a happy ship while at sea. Periodic ship's meetings and rotating chores can defuse potential strife and maintain a positive on-board atmosphere. And remember, everyone needs some "private space" to allow time to themselves.

Nature. Let your shelves contain charts and books for recognizing sea life. Outside the tropics, birds are an endless delight in mid-ocean. In lower latitudes, they can be spectacular as land is approached. Don't miss the opportunity to learn about them. Where have they come from? What are they doing out here? And how do they survive? The bored sailor might not ask these questions, but anyone with a soul should want to know.

Whales are regularly seen from yachts. To meet a solitary bull sperm as he voyages from one hemisphere to the other is a philosophical sight. He has been living at sea longer than you have been on the planet. What is he thinking? What has he seen? What does he know? Read about him, and you might begin to hazard a guess.

Scratch the surface of an ocean sailor and you'll find a stargazer. Night after blazing night the stars wheel overhead. New constellations rise and set as latitudes change. Steer south, and stunning Scorpio sails higher each night. Go east and, when the solar system sets the orbits up for you, watch Venus come up before the sun, so bright you can't believe it. Follow Orion, the great hunter, as he marches west with the morning, and stare in wonder into the throat of infinity as you gaze into the Pleiades through your binoculars. Star charts will give you the names, and even if you don't use the Nautical Almanac to plot your position from Aldebaran, Arcturus and Antares, get to know them like old friends on the long middle watch. It's one thing to line up a moving star against the spreader to take your eyes from the compass. It's another altogether to know that your guide is bright blue Sirius, the Dog Star, so close to Earth that his light has reached us in the blink of your own lifetime.

Fishing. In tropic seas particularly, fishing is more than a hobby for many. It is certainly a sure-fire method for producing fresh protein. You can fish successfully with as little gear as a

At sea, routine is vital, but so are periodic celebrations of goals met, skills mastered and distance covered.

strong line, a coil of wire trace, a few stout hooks, a length of auto inner tube in the bight to absorb shock when a big one hits. Some old can lids and red bunting will make a lure, or you can spend thousands on rods, variable drag reels and all the other wonders in the tackle shop. Whichever route you take, it is rude not to fish when surrounded by nature's bounty.

Music. Many crews develop a "theme song" from tapes or CDs that either started life among their collection or were given to the ship by a fellow-rover in some far-flung port. Music needs careful handling, because what one person loves can drive another nuts. The best advice is to use earphones to climb into that challenging symphony there's never been time to listen to. Then at least you can enjoy your favorite numbers, both on and off watch, without disturbing your shipmates.

Hobbies. Ancient artifacts leave no doubt that sailors have indulged their hobbies from the beginning. Scrimshaw on whalebone is illegal now, but there is no law against fancy ropework, weaving, sewing or any other creative pastime. One ocean sailor of the 1980s even made commercial-quality fiddles in his fo'c'sle. Life at sea is also a good opportunity to learn new skills whether they be celestial navigation, cooking, or even varnishing.

Reading. For most busy people, an offshore passage is a perfect opportunity to catch up on some quality reading — solid food for thought. Try a classic novel. *War and Peace* is a much easier read than you'd imagine. Time is required to sort out the characters, but at sea you have it.

How long has it been since you read *Hamlet* or *Macbeth*? You won't believe how many of the lines you'll still remember. Or how about one of the popular books on astrophysics. "Not my scene!" But did you ever try? If all else fails, rip into a stack of good thrillers. At least you'll forget your troubles.

Ocean Plimsoll Lines. There are a good many ocean sailors who choose not to venture north or south of the 30th parallels. These "Plimsoll Lines" keep them within reach of the tropics, away from the clutches of depressions, fog, dismal misty weather and, so long as they work the storm seasons right, gale force winds. Tropical sailing is a different experience from navigating in temperate or high latitudes. In warm weather, you spend far more time on deck, while the generally easier conditions permit greater freedom to enjoy the delights mentioned previously.

In the higher latitudes the going gets tougher. Life on board often settles into a watch routine with only the helm or lookout on deck. More of the day is spent in the bunk than at any other period of your life, saving illness. Reading is therefore even more important, unless you like studying the overhead for the remains of last summer's mosquitoes or wandering leaks.

Make sure you're prepared for what your chosen latitudes will bring. If you're sailing to a coconut island, consider learning a (quiet) musical instrument, taking up fancy ropework, or discovering whether or not you can sketch. On passage to the Aleutians, make sure you have Gibbon's *Decline and Fall of the Roman Empire* beside your bunk – all ten volumes!

Ocean Weather

Ocean Winds and Pressures. Weather on the oceans divides itself into a number of definable "belts" (see illustration). With regional variations brought about by the location of land masses, these belts are largely dependent on latitude and season. In the northern hemisphere, one can see the polar high pressure zone with easterlies spilling off to the southward, meeting the westerlies of the northern oceans at the polar front (Chapter 5). The depressions roam in the forties, fifties and low sixties, picking up their initial circulation from the prevailing tendencies on their northern and southern edges.

Next comes the mid-oceanic "high," typified by the "Azores High" of the North Atlantic and the "Pacific High" in the northern Pacific. Its circulation is the enormous, slow-turning engine which powers up the westerlies and, on the sector nearer the Equator, the easterly trade winds. These easterly trades, the most reliable winds of all, blow from the northeast in the northern hemisphere and southeast in the southern, although in practice they tend to follow the isobars (circulation wind) of the highs, causing the northeasterlies to veer and the southeasterlies to back.

Winds in the central zones of the oceanic highs are variable and often light — bad news for sailors. In the Age of Discovery, when a caravel or galleon blundered into these regions, often with a foul bottom that further hindered progress, she sat for weeks, using up drinking water. The horses consumed more than the men, so when things became critical the unfortunate beasts were thrown overboard. Their memory lives on in the term "Horse Latitudes."

Between the trade-wind belts, wandering north and south with the sun, lies the "Inter-Tropical Convergence Zone" (ITCZ). Here, in a band of low pressure of varying width, lie the unstable "doldrums" with their calms and squalls (see illustrations on next page).

Global Pressure and Wind Distribution

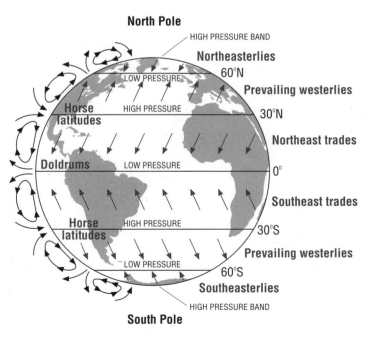

North Pole

HIGH PRESSURE BAND

Northeasterlies
60°N
LOW PRESSURE

Prevailing westerlies
HIGH PRESSURE
30°N

Horse latitudes
HIGH PRESSURE

Northeast trades

Doldrums
LOW PRESSURE
0°

Southeast trades

Horse latitudes
HIGH PRESSURE
30°S

Prevailing westerlies
LOW PRESSURE
60°S

Southeasterlies

HIGH PRESSURE BAND

South Pole

Winds and Weather of the Tropics.

Not everyone enjoys the heat of the tropics, but a sailor is yet to be born who does not love tropical trade winds. The trick is to be in the right place when they are blowing, because the trades do not caress the coral isles incessantly. Like most stable systems, they move north and south with the seasons, and are often at their best during the local winter months. Trade winds coincide with less extreme temperatures, and so great joy is to be had. Even in their season, however, the trades do not always blow with the balmy regularity. At Christmas in the Caribbean, for example, it is not unknown for them to hammer across the Windward Islands at 35 knots for two

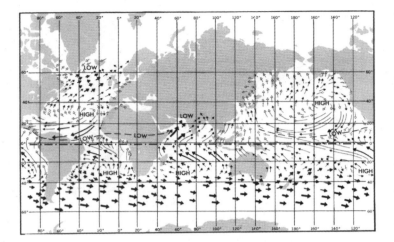

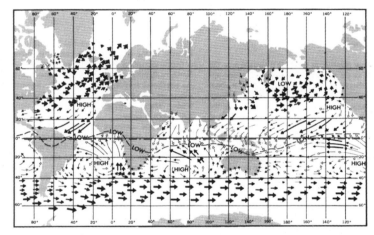

The average velocity and constancy of direction for surface winds are shown in these illustrations for July-August (top) and January-February (bottom). The dashed line wandering near the Equator (shown in blue) indicates the band of low pressure or Inter-Topical Convergence Zone (ITCZ). Note how it varies depending on the time of year.

The American Practical Navigator (1995), © United States Government. Reprinted with permission.

weeks or more.

Squalls are a feature of the trades. It is impossible not to spot these in daylight, and on all but the darkest nights you can generally see them coming.

Not all squalls produce rain, but you can assess its likelihood by observing the horizon under the cloud. If it is blotted out, grab the foul-weather gear or strip off and soap up for a free shower. Some squalls generate high winds, others pass with little comment. It is almost impossible to tell which will be which but, in general, if the cloud has a full "skirt" of precipitation running down to the sea, watch out! If it's too much trouble to reef for a squall that hits with the breeze forward of the beam, don't be shy about bearing away to decrease the apparent wind speed. You won't lose a lot of ground and you can make it up when the flying fish come out to play again in half an hour.

Monsoons. These are predictable tropical and sub-tropical winds which reverse with the seasons. They occur on a grand scale as a result of pressure differences between continental land masses and oceans.

The best-known example is caused by low pressure over northwest India in the sultry summer months of May through September. The continental low sucks the Southeast Trades of the Indian Ocean northward to cross the Equator. As they join the monsoon circulation they veer southwesterly, subduing any residual Northeast Trades locally and even as far away as the western North Pacific.

This Southwest Monsoon brings bad weather to the Bay of Bengal, with high winds and torrential rains. It also creates the threat of cyclones, the vicious local version of the tropical revolving storm. Further east, in the China Sea, the monsoon is generally more tame with less west in it, often swinging round to blow from east of south. But despite its more benevolent character, it can still give birth to a cyclone. The monsoon reverses in winter under the influence of an enormous anticyclone that develops seasonally over Siberia. The resulting dry, pleasant northeasterly provides lovely sailing in the Indian Ocean. In the Bay of Bengal, although a tropical storm can occur at either change of monsoon, they cause most damage in the typical northern hemisphere "watch" months of July through October.

As the northeasterly monsoon crosses the Equator, it backs northwesterly, eventually reaching Northern Australia as the Northwest Monsoon. By the time it arrives in China and Indochina, the wind has picked up moisture from the ocean and become stronger, carrying with it overcast, dismal conditions.

Less extensive monsoon conditions are experienced in other parts of the globe. A monsoon-like condition occurs in the Gulf of Mexico, while in mid to late summer the Gulf of Guinea in West Africa generates its own southwest monsoon that can be felt far out into the South Atlantic.

The Tropical Revolving Storm. Nobody in North America needs to be told what a hurricane is. The power of these Tropical Revolving Storms (TRS) is household knowledge. For an offshore sailor, however, it is not enough merely to know that they exist and will almost certainly be forecast. It is important to understand their nature, how they begin, and what is their likely behavior should one be coming your way.

A TRS cannot survive within the belt formed by latitudes 5 degrees North and South, because it relies on Coriolis force to power up its "spin." There is no Coriolis at the Equator (it's maximum at the poles), so any disturbance in these ultra-low latitudes is doomed to fizzle out. This is not a seasonal effect, it is caused by the physics of the sphere. A TRS also demands a critical sea temperature of around 80 degrees Fahrenheit (26 degrees Celsius) for the reserves of warm, moist air upon which it feeds. Such requirements are found in the tropical latitudes of the oceans in late summer and autumn.

An area of low pressure is formed by moist air rising. If this embryonic system becomes sufficiently significant, Coriolis force kicks it into circular motion. At this early stage, it is called a "tropical depression," with winds of up to 35 knots, but its potential for villainy has been created.

As moisture "rains" out of the rising central air mass at higher altitudes, latent heat is released. This fuels the rising air even more until it finally spins out at the top at an altitude of approximately eight miles. This dry air is thrown centrifugally to the outer limits of the system, where it is drawn back down toward sea level to replace air streaming in toward the low pressure center. When it reaches the water, it becomes saturated once more and spirals inward toward the center, where it is hurled upward to repeat the cycle at increasingly higher velocities.

By this time, the center of the storm forms a distinct "eye," clearly visible from above. Winds near it will be anywhere from 35 to 55 knots. When 60 knots is exceeded, a full hurricane, cyclone or typhoon is born. In 1988, Hurricane Gilbert hit 139 knots, and whilst even higher velocities have been recorded, a typical North Atlantic hurricane brings a mean windspeed of around 90 knots. This wind and the resulting seas are far more than any small vessel can presume to survive.

While atmospheric pressure in a TRS may not be any lower than a deep winter depression (around 955 millibars, though Gilbert's fell to a stunning 888), it is the gradient that is extraordinary. In a TRS, a drop of 10 millibars within 50 miles of the eye is expected. A typical TRS has an active diameter of 150 to 200 miles, but 1000 miles is not unknown.

"Storm surges" are frequently associated with TRS activity, and it is these as much as the wind which cause damage ashore. If you are anchored and

This satellite view of a classic hurricane (TRS) shows a well formed eye. NOS/NOAA photo

Hurricane Cross Section

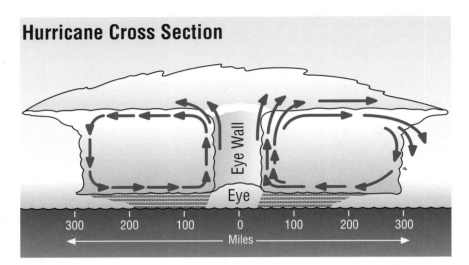

sheltered, it is essential to remain aware of this possibility. The waves fanning out in front of an approaching storm can run the water level up to 20 feet above normal when combined with a high tide, low pressure and a deluge of rain gushing seaward in flooded rivers.

The mariner's view of the eye of a TRS is remarkable. The torrential rain stops, the winds are light, and the armies of mountainous seas now tumble in disarray under a clearing sky. Circling on all sides are the mighty cloud walls of the hurricane, striding forward to ultimately envelop the sailor once more in violent winds.

Movement of a TRS. A Tropical Revolving Storm can be born anywhere its needs are fulfilled and is able to progress in most directions but, with notable exceptions, those in the Atlantic and Pacific generally become identifiable toward the west side of the ocean. Their travel is usually northwest or occasionally west. They begin slowly and accelerate as they approach 20 degrees latitude, by which time they may be moving at around 12 knots. At some point in this vicinity, they often "recurve" away from the Equator, and take a turn to the right (left in the southern hemisphere) and accelerate towards higher latitudes, sometimes following the isobars of the oceanic high. The question of how much a TRS will recurve, and when, is crucial to whether or not it comes ashore, and forecasting this particular phenomenon is notoriously difficult. Sometimes a TRS does not recurve at all, and occasionally it can "loop the loop" before continuing close to its original path of destruction.

When a TRS makes a landfall, it is deprived of the warm water vapor that is the source of its power, and usually spirals down. Occasionally, however, particularly where the land is narrow, it can hang onto life long enough to rebound out over the ocean to start all over again. This kind of rebound recently wreaked havoc in Central America, while in India, cyclones have rampaged clear across the sub-continent to kick-start themselves once more over the Arabian Sea.

Even if a TRS does not come ashore, once it deserts the warmer seas that gave it life, it either moderates to become a temperate depression or gets absorbed into an existing system. All sailors should beware that dangerous and sometimes unpredictable possibilities exist whenever a hurricane is decaying to the south of their position. A depression supercharged by the remnants of a TRS can be ugly.

Typical Worldwide TRS Tracks

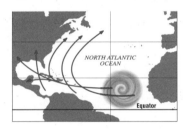

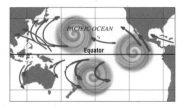

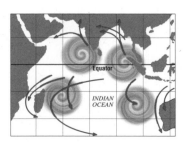

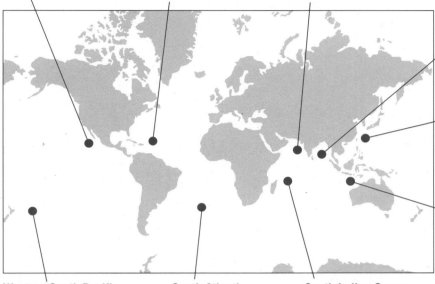

Eastern North Pacific
Hurricanes: June to November
Worst months: August and
September

North Atlantic
Hurricanes: June to November
Worst months: August to October

Arabian Sea
Cyclones: April to July and
September to January
Worst months: change of monsoon:
May and June, October and November

Bay of Bengal
Cyclones: April to December
(have been recorded all months)
Worst months: June and July,
October and November

**Western North Pacific
and China Sea**
Typhoons: July to November
(have been recorded all months)
Worst months: July to November

Northwest Australia
Cyclones: December to April
Worst months: January and
February

Western South Pacific
Hurricanes: December to April
Worst months: February and March

South Atlantic
No tropical cyclones have
ever been reported.

South Indian Ocean
Cyclones: November to April
Worst months: January and
February

Generally, Tropical Revolving Storms (TRS) occur on the western side of an ocean (except Australia's "willy-willys" and the eastern North Pacific ocean) during the summer and fall of their area. They usually travel in a westerly direction and at some point "recurve" away from the Equator.

Predicting a TRS with a barometer. Sailing in tropical latitudes, the barometer is generally steady for weeks, except for a rhythmic pulsing of pressure of between 1 and 1.6 millibars either side of the normal known as "diurnal variation." As its name implies, this subtle pressure cycle occurs twice daily. Highs peak around 1000 and 2200 local mean time, lows at 0400 and 1600. The mean pressure is found an hour or so after noon and midnight. If pressure should climb up a notch, beware. There may be a TRS between 500 and 1000 miles off. Should it begin to fall, start logging the readings, because 3 millibars or more below the mean is also a bad sign. A 5-millibar drop means you might be within 200 miles of a TRS.

Clouds and sky. Watch out for outrageously colored morning and evening skies generated by developing high clouds. Any "chevrons" could be pointing toward a far-off vortex. Air quality may become unusually clear as a TRS approaches, and if the storm is typical, cirrus clouds will first be seen 300 to 600 miles away from the storm's eye. At this time you will begin to notice a rising swell. By the time you realize "you're in for it" you'll see a lowering cloud base and rain-soaked black scud.

Sea state. A steepening swell moving unusually rapidly is frequently the first sign of a TRS, coupled with cirrus clouds. The swell moves quicker than the storm itself and may often be seen a day or more before the barometer begins its plunge. Wave direction is no indication of the storm's axis of movement. The seas around the edge of a storm don't necessarily line up with the isobars, and the advance may have changed direction in any case.

Wind. In the northern hemisphere, winds spiral counterclockwise around a TRS, clockwise in the southern. If the wind were blowing straight along the isobars, you could find the storm center by the method described in Chapter 5 for a depression, turning your back to the breeze and looking down your left arm outstretched sideways. With a TRS, however, there may be as much as 45 degrees of inward draft across the isobars 200 miles from the center. As the vortex is approached this draft falls to almost nothing as the enormous centrifugal force knocks out the air's desire to blow straight in. In the early stages, therefore, you can expect the center to be, say, 35 degrees forward of your arm.

Knowing where the center of a TRS lies in relation to your position is a crucial starting point in avoiding its worst effects.

TRS avoidance strategies. The yearly timing of hurricanes and other TRS variants is not an exact science, and being somewhere else during hurricane season does not guarantee you will never see one. It does, however, improve your chances greatly, which is all you can reasonably ask. Use ocean pilot books, pilot charts and all other sources to determine which are the best months to be in a given area.

However, this ideal state of affairs is not always feasible. An example of a passage where perfect timing is difficult would be from Maine to Bermuda in mid-October. Perhaps you have chosen to leave no later than this to avoid cold weather in November, arranging to lay up the boat in Bermuda and return in early December to complete the trip to Antigua. By then, the hurricane season has officially closed.

This could prove a reasonable plan so long as full use is made of weather forecasting, particularly for the more dangerous first leg. Even though hurricanes are known to form in October and to recurve over Bermuda, you could expect to fetch the island with a fair wind so long as the day you leave calls for neither existing storms nor decaying remnants. Remain aware, however, that there is always a small possibility that you may be put to the ultimate test. Keep monitoring the weather.

Tactical management of a TRS. Outrunning a TRS in a small sailing yacht is rarely a realistic proposition, although a large, fast yacht might manage it, or a powerboat with adequate fuel range. If you can make an informed guess about where the storm center lies, however, and which way it is travelling, you should have a chance of sidestepping its worst effects. Within range of forecasting services, your odds improve, with the proviso that a forecast can be wrong. Even far from help, you can improve your odds if you keep a cool head.

Dangerous and navigable semi-circles. Before deciding a course of action, you must first divide the approaching TRS into "quadrants" or "semi-circles" for tactical purposes. The illustration shows how these are determined. For reasons of clarity, all comments in this chapter relate to northern hemisphere storms. For tactics in the southern hemisphere,

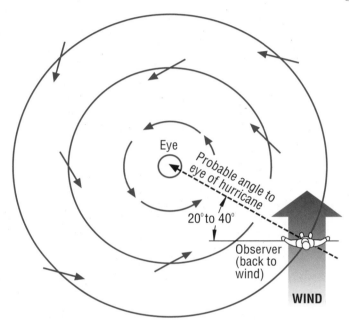

Locate the center of a northern hemisphere TRS by standing with your back to the wind and pointing left. The storm center should be 20-40 degrees forward of your left arm.

everything is to be treated as a mirror image, with winds circulating clockwise, recurvings bending left, and dangerous quadrants on the left-hand side of advancing weather systems.

It is important to realize when planning storm avoidance tactics that any TRS can veer up to 100 miles to either side of its predicted track within a 24-hour period. It may not divert from its forecast track at all, of course, but as with all weather matters, the mariner is well advised to hope for the best but prepare for the worst. If it is feasible, try to work on the basis of the worst-case scenario.

Apparent wind created by the storm's forward motion modifies its (counterclockwise) gradient air circulation.

If the system is moving westward, the easterlies in its upper-right-hand quadrant will be accelerated and the westerlies on its lower-left-hand quadrant eased, creating an overall difference in windspeed of up to 30 knots. Furthermore, because the storm will probably recurve (if it has not already done so) to the right, a boat in this "dangerous sector" may be in for double treatment if her luck runs out.

To escape the eye, a yacht in the path of the leading quadrant of the dangerous sector is faced with little choice but to sail close-hauled on the starboard tack as fast and as far as possible. You have only to attempt this in 45 knots, however, to realize it's a hopeless cause in 70 knots. Yet if you lie a-hull doing nothing, you will inexorably be carried toward the eye. Your best hope is most likely to make what ground you can to the north, probably motorsailing on starboard tack. If this ceases to be feasible, you can only heave-to on starboard, trust your storm canvas, double-bolt the companionway and strap yourself in. Even when the worst has passed, the wind will continue to batter you towards the vortex. But unless the storm recurves onto you, it is at least on its way out of your life.

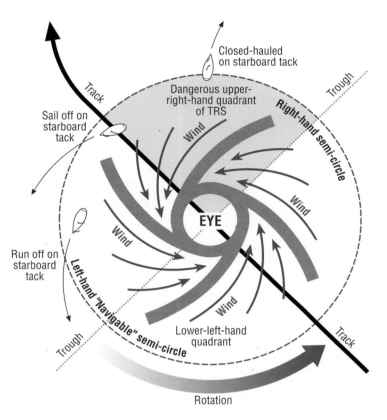

Northern hemisphere TRS Dangerous and Navigable Semi-circles

The dangerous quadrant is therefore to be avoided at all costs. If an approaching storm seems likely to place you in its path, you must make a decision and make it promptly. One option is to make progress to the north while you can, as far beyond the storm's path as possible, and hope you don't take a recurvature "hit." Alternatively, you can try to sail across into the track of the less dangerous, so-called "navigable semi-circle." With early warning and a successful assessment of your likely position relative to the vortex both now and in a day or so, the second choice may prove more feasible.

A hurricane 300 to 400 hundred miles away moving at 8 knots could leave you with winds that could help you for 24 hours. Even if it's doing 12 knots you might have 15 hours to make headway in directions other than before the wind. This translates to 90 to 150 miles in the bag. If your pre-decision situation would have left you 50 miles north of the eye as it passed, your efforts will now have placed you at least that far from it on the navigable side; a huge return for your trouble. As a bonus, you can now continue running clear of its path, and you would be unlucky indeed if the storm were to recurve your way, because you are between it and the Equator, where it normally has no wish to go.

While preferable to the dangerous quadrant, life in the navigable semicircle is far from pleasant. But least there is no discussion about what you should do. So long as you are confident the eye will pass north of you, you must make the best way you can with the wind over the starboard quarter. Even if this means running under bare poles, don't hesitate to keep moving. The more ground you put between you and the path of the eye, the better. This is true even after the vortex has passed and you seem to be heading in toward the center. By then, the storm is trundling away faster than you are closing in, so conditions can only improve.

To remain proactive and thinking clearly under the threat of a hurricane demands the Right Stuff in large doses. But if you keep your head and remember these rules, if your boat is sound, and if the day brings the luck you deserve, you'll be a member of a very exclusive club to which there is no joining fee save that you survived.

Weather Predicting Tips

- **A barometer falling** at a rate of 1 mb (0.03 inch) per hour in 12 or 24 hours indicates an imminent storm, or worse (this assumes it's not a diurnal variation that occurs in the lower latitudes). It's also an indicator of a Rapidly Intensifying Low (RIL, sometimes referred to as a "bomb"). Another rule of thumb is a falling rate of 10 mb in 3 hours forebodes force 8 (gale) conditions.

- **When using Buys Ballot's law** to determine the location of a depression, if the direction remains constant, expect the center to pass over you (not reliable for TRSs since the inward draft of wind across the isobars can vary as much as 45 degrees).

- **Using isobars to predict wind strength.** Generally, isobars spaced closer together indicate greater pressure gradients which generate stronger winds. Winds at sharp bends in isobars increase by 20% in highs and decrease by 20% in lows. With the same isobar spacing, winds in a high pressure will be stronger than those in a low pressure, and winds at lower latitudes (tropics) will be stronger than those at higher latitudes (polar). Geostrophic wind scales, sometimes shown on weatherfax charts, can be used to convert isobar spacing to wind strength for a given latitude on that chart (don't attempt to transfer a scale from one chart to another).

- **The movement of lows**, whose formation has been influenced by upper-level troughs, usually parallel the jet stream flow (the 5,640-meter contour line on the upper-air 500-mb chart) and move at 30 to 50% of the speed of the 500-mb winds.

- **Estimating wave heights based on fetch.** Fetch is the unobstructed distance over which wind and waves traverse before reaching a specific location. In gale conditions, wave height (feet) can be estimated as 1.5 times the square root of fetch (nautical miles). It also seems to work for fetches of 200 miles or less in open sea. In some regions, weatherfax is also a source for sea state forecasts (see next page).

- **There is a high risk of fog** when dew point and air temperature are within 2° Fahrenheit of each other or there is a 10° difference and the air is cooling rapidly.

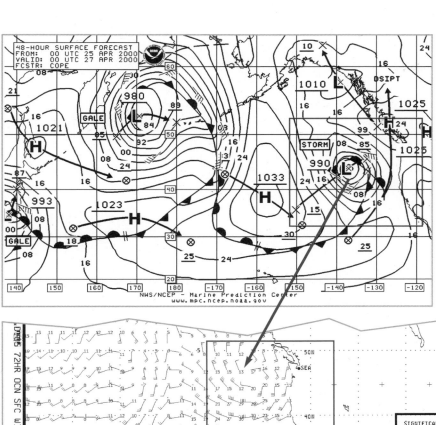

On April 25, the National Weather Service issued a 48-hour surface forecast chart valid for 00 UTC April 27, 2000 that showed a storm in the North Pacific Ocean to the west of Seattle (approx. 44° N and 137° W) with 50-knot northwest winds to the west of the depression, 40-knot southwest winds to the south and 40-knot easterly winds to the northeast.

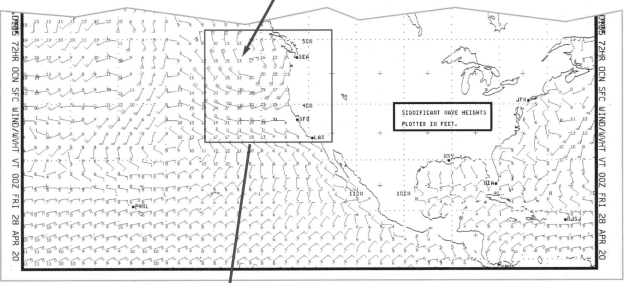

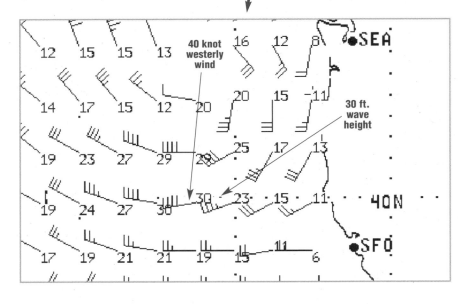

On the same day, the National Weather Service issued a 72-hour forecast chart for surface winds and significant wave heights valid for 00 Z April 28 that depicted 40-knot wind to the south of the storm with significant wave heights ranging from 23 to 30 feet! If your original course was going to take you through this area, this 72-hour forecast should give you fair warning to change course to avoid the worst of it.

Offshore Navigation

As the centuries have passed, there has been an ongoing march of major breakthroughs in the art and science of navigation. Perhaps the first of these was the compass, which began seeing use by western sailors in medieval times. Yet even before then, the Phoenicians traded with societies far beyond the Pillars of Hercules and the Vikings crossed the North Atlantic without the aid of charts. The thought fills us with amazement.

Next came the concept of latitude deduced from celestial bodies, followed in the mid-18th century by the accurate measurement of time at sea, which opened the door to accurately calculating longitude by even modestly educated navigators.

Each milestone has left sailors wondering how they ever managed before. At the end of the second millennium, GPS enabled us to instantly obtain an accurate fix at any hour, day or night, anywhere in the world at the push of a button. While this is merely the latest station on the long road of development, it has finally removed the greatest hurdle that the ocean navigator had to leap. It is no longer necessary for an offshore yacht to carry a master of celestial navigation. Even with a master on board, it is unlikely that the sextant will ever be taken from its box, unless there is a desire to practice for old time's sake, or to make sure both it and its operator can still function in an emergency.

GPS in Perspective. Those of us who can pilot by the stars may lament the redundancy of our expertise. We may continue the established "day's work" of the navigator, but with GPS installed we would really only do so for fun — given that the device keeps on delivering positions on demand. It cannot be overstressed, however, that even its manufacturers advise that GPS is not a stand-alone system. It must be said that hundreds of miles offshore where the meat of the navigator's job has always been to determine the ship's position, it becomes the first source of data as long as it works.

It is significant that while the U.S. Naval Academy has abandoned in-depth education in celestial navigation, it still insists that midshipmen remain capable of shooting the sun and feeding the results into a calculator which will reduce the sight for them. Naval officers, however, work on large ships with multiple layers of backup on every conceivable system. Small boat sailors don't, and so must take basic celestial even much more seriously.

In the days when the sextant was the only way to fix a yacht's position, navigators took pride in deducing their whereabouts from more than just the sun. Stars, planets, even the moon were pressed into the service of the creative pilot. There were no exclusive skills for taking these sights, although finding the heavenly bodies and handling the subsequent calculations demanded effort. These arts remain available and supporting information base continues to be published in nautical almanacs. The satisfaction gained from developing your celestial talents are enormous, but if all you need is a GPS backup, you can manage with sun sights alone.

In an age of push-button electronic navigation, taking sun and celestial sights with a sextant remains a vital skill.

Observe the sun at noon for latitude and run a morning sight up to the line to give a fix. This process has formed the backbone of celestial navigation from the time of Captain Cook and will stand you in good stead. Use a computer for the sight reduction process if you must, but it is recommended that you master the basic written proformas. The sums required can be handled by a 10-year-old. There is no need for spherical trigonometry, and if electric power and all batteries are lost except the one on your wrist watch, you can still fix your position to within two miles. Until the advent of electronics, this degree of accuracy has been as good as anyone dared hope.

Great Circle Sailing. Along the coast, questions of distance and direction are largely unaffected by the fact that the earth is a sphere. The Mercator projection on which most coastal charts are based distorts the earth's surface in order to have a true course depicted as a straight line. If you plot a course from home base to an island 30 miles away, this will not only hold good until you arrive, it will also represent the shortest route.

Unfortunately, this convenient convention only works on a coastal passage scale, where one can ignore the distortion generated by drawing naturally converging meridians of longitude as parallel. The problem increases in higher latitudes, but even on passages of 200 miles or more, the effects remain practically negligible. On an oceanic scale, however, the picture changes radically. On a Mercator projection, a direct course between two continents will not be a straight line.

The shortest distance between two points on a sphere is a "great circle." This is the line defined on a sphere's surface by a flat plate which passes through the sphere's center. To use a more familiar example, if you were to cut an orange in half, no matter whether you sliced through its "poles" or not, the cut line visible on the surface when you then pressed the two halves together again would be a great circle. If you slice the orange so that cut failed to pass through the center, it would not be. On

Meridians are all great circles, but only the Equator makes the grade from the latitude parallels.

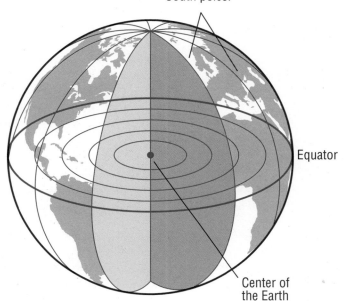

Meridians of longitude run through North and South poles.

Equator

Center of the Earth

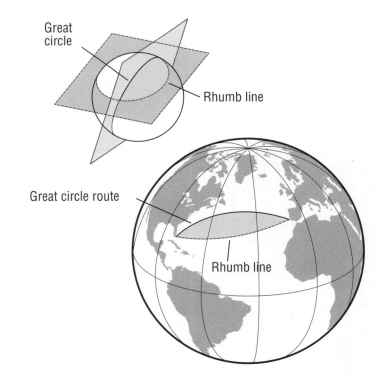

Great circle

Rhumb line

Great circle route

Rhumb line

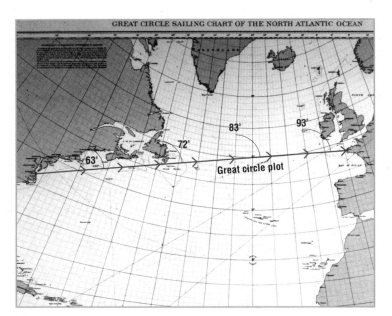

GREAT CIRCLE SAILING CHART OF THE NORTH ATLANTIC OCEAN

63° 72° 83° 93°

Great circle plot

Above, a great circle course is plotted on a gnomonic chart. Note changing course measured off at various meridians along the route.

Below, a great circle and its corresponding rhumb line are plotted on a Mercator Chart

a global scale, the only parallel of latitude that is a great circle is the Equator. However, every meridian fulfills the definition.

If you are travelling due north or south, you will by definition be sailing on a great circle. Steering east-west, however, the only latitude that qualifies is the Equator. The further from the Equator you move, the greater will be additional miles sailed by sailing on the parallel. At a latitude of 50 degrees north, the difference in distance sailed between a rhumb line course and a great circle can be several hundred miles. As the heading swings to approach north-south, the discrepancy is reduced.

Many ocean passages are more east-west than north-south, and in such cases it pays handsomely to use the great circle in latitudes north or south of 30 degrees or so. The route must, nevertheless, be studied in respect of ice limits, weather and any other limiting factors.

Plotting a great circle. Before GPS, the easiest way to plot a great circle was to use a "gnomonic" chart, which is projected in such a way that a straight line across it corresponds to the great circle course you are seeking. The illustration above shows clearly that this course crosses the meridians at varying angles. If you take a plotted course from a gnomonic chart and re-plot in onto a Mercator chart, the straight line will now look like a parabola which bulges towards the pole. In reality, this apparently

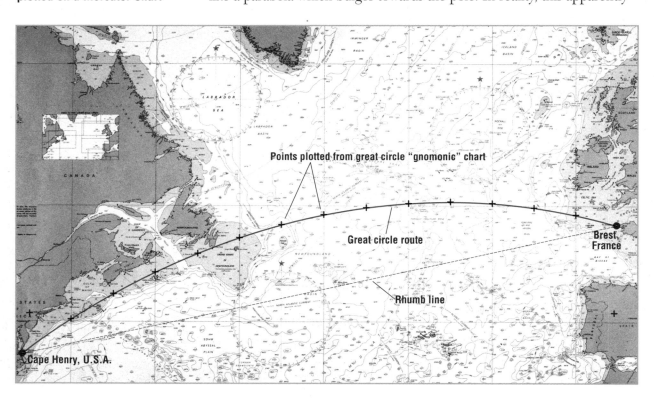

Points plotted from great circle "gnomonic" chart

Great circle route

Brest, France

Rhumb line

Cape Henry, U.S.A.

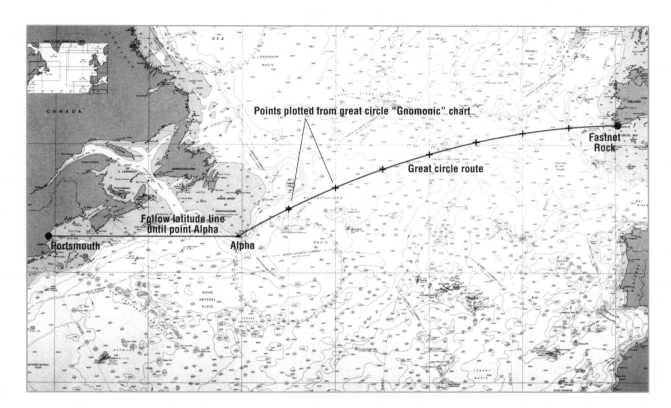

eccentric line is the shortest distance between you and your destination.
To stay on it, you must alter course every few degrees of longitude.
Ultimately, you arrive at your destination sailing a totally different
heading than when you started.

Composite great circles. Because of their tendency to bow towards
a pole, great circle courses sometimes take you closer to areas of ice, high
winds or other hazards that you might normally prefer to avoid. A typical
situation is described in Chapter 16 where a boat on passage from Cape
Cod to the English Channel stays south of the great circle until she is
clear of the Grand Banks. In the Southern Ocean, a long leg can carry a
vessel into the Antarctic ice and heavy gales. The classic method of
compromise is to sail the great circle until you reach a predetermined
"safe latitude," run along this parallel
until the great circle re-crosses it, then
follow the circle route to the destination.

The great circle in practice.
Sailing a pure great circle course is only
marginally feasible for sailing vessels.
This is because sailing yachts often
follow the best apparent wind angle,
strategically and tactically, and often will
vary from the navigator's ideal course on
a daily basis. If the great circle course
places her on a dead run, for example,
the yacht might head up 15 degrees or
more onto a reach. In a steady wind, she
might maintain this heading for several
days, taking her further and further

**Above is a composite great
circle course.**

**A modern GPS will read out a
great circle course, doing away
with the need for careful
plotting on a gnomonic chart.
Such a chart is nonetheless
useful on board as a visual
backup.**

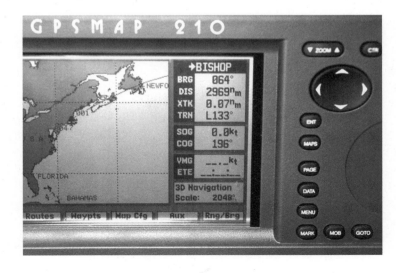

from the direct track. At some stage, whether or not the wind shifts, the pilot will have to determine a fresh great circle course from the current position. If she has only deviated from the original course by 100 miles, the odd degree or two might not warrant a fresh course. For these reasons, many used to feel that great circle courses were irrelevant for the small cruising yacht.

With GPS, the question is moot. Most GPS sets either read out a great circle as the default course, or offer a choice between rhumb line or great circle. Once you've made your choice, all you need for instant, ongoing access to a great circle course is an "arrival waypoint" at your destination. Each day when you plot the noon position, hit "Go To," or whatever button delivers the goods. You will be given a distance to run and, more important, a great circle course. If you cannot steer it and are wondering which tack to choose, lay off along the tack that will bring you closest to a great circle track. By noting the desired GPS course and comparing it to your close-hauled heading, you can work out at a glance when the moment comes to tack.

Staying as close as possible to a great circle, even if it is a series of new ones, can save a day or more on a typical mid-latitude ocean crossing.

The ship's log and the distance log. On a private yacht, there is no need to make hourly ship's log entries when far offshore, unless observations and barometer trends demand a regular recording of atmospheric pressure. When this is not the case, such as periods of extended fair weather, most people will be content to restrict entries to important events, such as sail changes, weather observations and, of course, the noon position. At this time, the total distance run must be noted for a number of prudent reasons. An entry at every change of watch leaves a useful record, and if crew write down comments as well as the hard navigational facts, the ship's log can provide lively reading in years to come. Remarks about the skipper's personal habits, the excellence of the cook's duff, the return of a fulmar who seems to be following the whole trip, a whale visit or the first sight of a land-based bird from the far side of the ocean are all worth noting. Sketches make a log memorable, as do pasted-in photos, so encourage the artists and leave space for illustrations.

If you are following a full celestial navigation regimen, you will also note distance log readings at each observation in order to relate them to previous and subsequent ones. Electronic logs make this a great deal easier than using an old-fashioned "taffrail" log. To reduce mechanical wear in taffrail models, the log can be streamed when taking a forenoon sight until noon for the running fix. The log could then be brought aboard once more until next morning. If evening stars are shot, the distance run since noon is guessed for purposes of the vital DR position. Using the heightened sensitivity which non-electronic sailors enjoy, this is usually accurate enough to serve.

As the destination coast approaches, the need for detail in the ship's log increases. By the time you are expecting landfall, you should be back into the coastal navigation routine of plotting and logging regularly. A GPS can fail at the end of a long trip just as easily as two hours out from home, and many a sailor has encountered trouble after failing to clock back into "Coastal mode" with its attendant demands for accuracy and regular position checks.

Offshore Communications

Offshore communications fall into three categories: distress, weather forecasting and recreation. Today, any of these can be accomplished via the Internet, but the cost and complexity of doing so makes voice communications the standard for yachts in the foreseeable future.

In these times of technological change, many of the world's long-range coast radio stations are closing their link facilities and shifting their listening watch to GMDSS (see below), so it's probable that HF/SSB will ultimately be used primarily for inter-yacht communication and for staying in touch with the shore via Ham operators. SSB, however, remains the primary source of weather information.

Satcoms will steadily take over long-range distress calling as well as links to the shore-based phone net. It is anticipated that global satellite telephone will be the future of communications.

Distress. If you do not have access to a satellite telephone, your options in distress when outside of VHF range are as follows:
- Call the U.S. Coast Guard on 2182 kHz on SSB radio.
- Call in a distress message to a Ham station to pass on.
- Broadcast via GMDSS.
- Activate a 406 EPIRB.

U.S. Coast Guard via coast radio station. This is the simplest option. By talking with the Coast Guard you know you're dealing with professionals who will understand the best action to take. You also gain direct access to the planet's most developed search and rescue operation. A broadcast on 2182 (or VHF Channel 16) will also be picked up and

relayed by any vessel operating near the U.S. coastline. Unfortunately, much of the rest of the world has moved on from 2182 distress calling. Since February 1999 it is no longer required for ships or coast radio stations outside the U.S. to monitor this frequency. This is due to the rise of GMDSS (Global Maritime Distress and Safety System).

Ham operators. There is no reason not to send a distress message via a Ham operator, as long as you are aware of the obvious limitations compared with the official services. See "weather forecasting" below for further information.

GMDSS. The Global Maritime Distress and Safety System was instituted in 1979 by the International Maritime Organization (IMO). The system is now required on commercial vessels over 300 tons, but remains

Many of the world's long-range coast radio stations are closing their link facilities and shifting their listening watch to GMDSS, so it's probable that High Frequency SSB (above) will ultimately be used primarily for inter-yacht communication and for shore links via Ham operators. SSB, however, remains the primary source of weather information.

optional for recreational craft. In addition to the recommended 406 EPIRB, the system relies on radio communication via Digital Selective Calling (DSC), which sends out an identification code to the distress network that is dedicated to your boat. The distress message includes an accurate position, as long as the set is hooked up to a GPS. This eliminates the need to maintain a listening watch on 2182kHz or VHF Channel 16.

As long as your radio is on line with a DSC "add-on" box, all you do in a Mayday situation is press a button. Offshore, within 150 miles of at least one MF coast station, a MF transceiver is needed plus a DSC box capable of transmitting on 2187.5 kHz. Further offshore, there are two options: either Inmarsat capability, or an SSB transceiver with a DSC box.

As of 2000, no FCC approved DSC SSB radios were legal for sale in the U.S. that would fit on a typical cruiser. However, where coastal radio stations (such as those of the U.S.) still monitor the traditional distress frequencies, you effectively activate GMDSS when you call them.

GMDSS and selective calling will ultimately phase out any "voice" listening service. From then on, unless you can rely on a global satellite telephone or a Ham link-up, you will require DSC or at least a 406 EPIRB to make contact with rescue services.

Inmarsat. Many would argue that a sensible option for small cruisers at the start of the new millennium is a DSC VHF radio, and Inmarsat-C. "Sat-C" is a data-only apparatus that is part of the GMDSS system. Weather bulletins, Notices to Mariners, etc., are automatically received in text form for a defined navigational area at no cost. The system can also be used to send and receive Internet e-mail. A typical unit also has two buttons that activate a distress call with GPS information (usually from an internal GPS) that is then routed to all vessels in the area.

The radio is about the size of a large VHF, with similar power requirements, and the typical dome-shaped antenna is approximately six inches high with a seven inch diameter. To process weather information, the set must be hooked into a terminal — usually a PC — but the basic emergency function is stand-alone.

The 406 EPIRB. This is the ultimate piece of survival gear for offshore yachts. Even if you failed to broadcast your Mayday, or it went unheard, a 406 EPIRB is highly likely

EPIRB Rescue System is activated as a last resort.

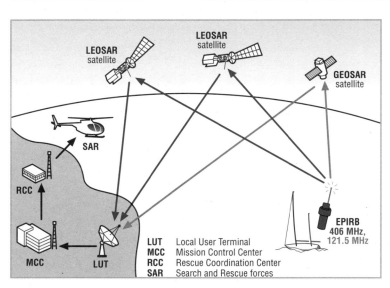

to attract attention (see Chapter 7 for more detail). An EPIRB is not to be activated until all else has failed. False alarms are not taken lightly.

Weather Forecasts Offshore. In addition to weatherfax information (see Chapter 8) and Inmarsat C, modern communications open the door to a selection of "voice" weather forecasts. The essential guide to SSB, VHF, Weatherfax and Navtex forecasts is to be found in the Admiralty List of Radio Signals, Volume III, Radio Weather Services, but a number of excellent Ham operators cover many popular cruising routes. An example has been the Canadian, "Herb" Hilgenberg, call sign VAX498, who has advised crews in the North Atlantic on conditions and strategies along their passages.

Even if you do not have transmitting capability, it is worth listening in to someone like Herb. His advice to others adds to the big picture. Beyond weather information they supply, some Ham operators have been officially recognized for relaying distress messages. Such people are an important part of the maritime safety net and should be taken seriously.

Official data on weather systems within reach of the U.S., their movements and associated wave patterns is delivered by the U.S. Coast Guard in the form of a robot voice affectionately known as "Perfect Paul," or "Iron Mickey." These forecasts can be picked up by anyone with a list of signals and a receive-only SSB set, available at modest price from any general electronics store. They will carry you well-informed across most of the well-traveled oceans.

Weatherfax offshore. In addition to the essential surface pressure chart, weatherfax (and the Internet) also offers data on the upper air movement which can be extremely useful offshore, particularly when downloaded charts are your only source of weather information. High in the atmosphere, ribbons of moving air known as jet streams circle the earth at velocities in excess of 200 knots, although 50 to 150 knots is more typical. These upper air streams tend to "steer" weather systems such as depressions, so that in the absence of a full forecast, an upper air chart can give a preview of where a given system is likely to move. To an experienced eye, the charts can also indicate possible formation points of lows.

The most useful chart for the mariner is the "500 millibar chart," which plots the isobars at around 18,000 feet, the point at which the atmosphere breaks clear from surface friction effects. This level is about halfway up through the earth's atmosphere. Winds blow directly along these upper isobars, so the charts are easy to read.

To make the most of this information, it is recommended that the student consult a specialized reference book. If time does not permit this, information from the upper air will help to expand the information of a surface pressure chart.

Recreational Radio. Inter-yacht "nets" criss-cross the globe, some local, others long-range. It is worth the effort to research these nets. Not only is the happy hour conversation a welcome diversion for many people, such nets can also be a gold mine of real-time weather data, information on local port entry requirements, and useful gossip about where to go or what destinations to avoid. They are also a prime source for up-to-date reports on piracy, port information and other incidents often ignored by officialdom.

Below is a typical modern navigation area.

Systems Aboard an Offshore Passagemaker

Readers of this book will notice that Chapter 9: Systems Aboard a Coastal Passagemaker concentrated on such top priorities as the engine and its associated technology. Continuing this theme of prioritizing, the critical items offshore are 1) a truly comprehensive tool collection, without which nothing can be done for any ailing system, and 2) a full kit of spares. The boat must also have a creatively collected "maybe box" of odd bits and pieces which could be made to fulfill a variety of unexpected functions. Assuming a sound hull, steering, rig, engine and drive train, the following priorities are 3) fresh water and, for short-handed crews, 4) the autopilot or windvane. In this chapter we shall consider these in order.

Tools. Short of a major engine rebuild or casting new metal fittings, there should be nothing on board the yacht that cannot be at least stripped and rebuilt using your own resources. Think hard about tools in relation to the systems you have chosen, working from the assumption that they will surely fail in mid-ocean. In addition to the coastal cruiser's requirements, she must therefore carry at least the following:

• An extra-large adjustable wrench for huge nuts you didn't know even existed on board.

• A length of galvanized steel pipe, usually stowed in the central bilge where its weight will do most good. This may turn out to have a number of surprising uses, but its main function is to slip over the handle of your "industrial grade" tools to achieve increased leverage.

• A lump hammer, or one-handed sledge, for moving the immovable.

• Two cold chisels, medium and very large, both kept sharp. Like many of your tools, these will be required only once in a number of years, but on their day, nothing else will serve. They cost little to buy.

• Three or four hardwood wedges. Driven home with the sledge hammer, these will literally lift the boat. They may also find other uses. Never go to sea without them.

• A steel wedge. Nothing can resist its capacity for destruction or for forcing things apart.

• A small, sharp hatchet.

• A set of bolt cutters for removing damaged rigging. There is no substitute for these. You may imagine that you'll be able to disconnect clevises and the rest to free broken spars if you have to, but to attempt it when the rig is hanging from them can be dangerous and time-consuming when the latter commodity may be in short supply. Before departure, try using them on a length of scrap wire or rod rigging so you know what sort of performance to expect. Add a drift pin to help knock out clevis pins. And for times when all else fails, include a hacksaw with several spare blades.

• A pin punch and ball peen hammer for replacing broken links on steering chain.

• A portable bench vice and somewhere to set it up. If you aren't lucky enough to have a tiny workshop on board, perhaps it will clamp to a cockpit coaming, or an extra-strong galley fiddle.

• A wrecking bar. This will be more useful than you imagine, and for a quick result when things go wrong, it takes some beating.

• Extra socket wrench extensions. Some day when you have to get at that third starter motor bolt that's impossible to reach, you'll thank your lucky stars you've got just the right extension to fit the job.

• A magnet that you can use with a stick to fish that starter motor bolt out of the bilge, and a grabber device to reach it when the magnet doesn't work.

Spares. Make up your spares kit assuming that whatever can go wrong will do so, and do it far from help. If a system is axiomatic to your happiness or safety, consider calling the manufacturers before deciding what to take. In addition to the "coastal" spares and any standard replacement items such as filter elements, or "specials" relating to non-essential systems, here are the basics of a long-passage spares list:

• At least one diesel injector, plus a set of copper washer seals
• A fuel lift pump rebuild kit
• Fuel filter glass bowl (if appropriate)
• Cylinder head and rocker box gaskets. Even if you do not consider yourself competent to lift the head, a mechanic may have to. He'll need the new gaskets and it may be a long wait for them to be flown in.

• A torque wrench for tightening down the cylinder head, etc. Check the manual for torque settings before you leave. If they aren't listed, get a more comprehensive edition.

• Assorted copper and fiber washers for filters, sump plugs, etc. Also, as many "O" rings as you can possibly require.

• Stern gland and head pump packing material
• For extended cruises to inaccessible places, a spare starter motor and alternator carefully packed against moisture can keep the engine going. If you decide against the complete item, talk to your local mechanic about what spares you should carry for them. At minimum, take a set of brushes for the starter, and the same for the electric windlass if you have one. Consider a spare voltage regulator, particularly if your boat has a tendency to generate rust on unprotected engine parts. These can fail suddenly from moisture-induced decay.

• Two or three long lengths of marine quality electric cable of varying gauge. You may believe your electrical system is perfect, but sooner or later it will come up short.

• Spare antenna for SSB radio
• Spare winch handles
• Spare toggles, eyes, cable clamps and cable
• Fiberglass repair kit, touch-up paint, varnish, teak cleaner/oil, solvents and thinners, patching compound, sealant, preparation materials and brushes

The "Maybe" Box. One of the tradeoffs of fiberglass hulls and mass-production parts is the heightened challenge of cobbling up repairs. There was almost nothing on a wooden yacht with hand-made fittings that could not be repaired with "bits and pieces" adapted on board to suit the situation. Owners of production craft, however, should not despair. Keep a large box with old hunks of machinery, plumbing fittings, large bolts, broken turnbuckles and anything else that takes your fancy. The

Watermaker System

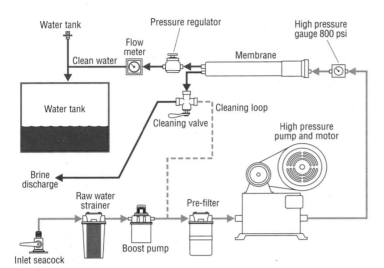

On-board watermakers provide an independent water supply that can eliminate the need to dock at undesirable or unsanitary locations.

Water filler caps placed outboard near the rail can serve as rain collectors when scuppers are plugged.

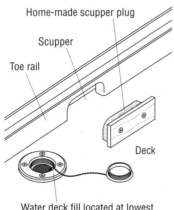

Water deck fill located at lowest point and outboard as far as possible

only proviso is that nothing in this "maybe one day…" box should cost a single cent. Such trivia are universally available from dumpsters, boatyard pathways, and your own junk. If you are setting forth on the ocean, don't throw anything away that might conceivably be fashioned into something else in an emergency. Inaugurate your collection today with a couple of wire coat hangers.

Fresh Water. Many offshore yachts rely on watermakers to maintain their own independent water supply. Apart from health safety benefits, it eliminates the need to dock in undesirable tropical venues. In trade-wind zones, the engine sees so little use that watering up is a far bigger issue than refueling, yet docks are often dirty and insect-ridden. It is infuriating to score a cockroach infestation after docking to fill your water tanks.

If you have a watermaker, but are in an area where topping off your tanks is clean and convenient, you might be tempted to give the system a rest and fill from the hose instead. However, many watermakers thrive on use. Refer to the manual for advice.

A lower-tech method of self-watering is to have the boat built so that her deck filler caps are well outboard at the lowest point of the sheer. In a vigorous downpour, give the deluge a few minutes to wash the salt away, then plug up the scuppers and watch the tanks fill themselves with pure rainwater. It's easy, cheap and hassle-free. It's remarkable how many gallons wash in during a healthy squall. At sea it's also possible to collect rain off the mainsail at the gooseneck. Keep a bucket ready. If you're rationing water, it's great to have a deck bath for free.

At sea, it is best not to use pressure water, except for an occasional treat at shower time. And do not forget to turn off the water pressurizer when not in use. The best practice is to use only hand or foot pumps to conserve water. The savings are considerable.

Try not to stock all your water in one tank. A large reserve or two separate tanks are both judicious safety requirements. In either case, also carry spare water in cans or bottles. If you ever are forced to abandon ship, it's easier to take some with you.

Autopilots and Wind Vanes. On a boat with only a couple as crew, these are of paramount importance. Many short-handers swear that they would rather go to sea without a stove than without the wind vane. If you choose an electronic autopilot instead, take at least one spare motor with you. These are known to burn out. Replacing the motor is usually not too difficult or expensive, but try the job before departing to make sure you can manage.

Autopilots are excellent when motoring, but do not generally cope as well as a wind vane under sail at normal sailing speeds. A powerful, servo-pendulum wind vane is often preferred for a boat that takes muscle to steer, but some very satisfactory auxiliary rudder types are also available.

A wind vane can take time to set up. Don't expect it to work perfectly "fresh out of the bag." Practice with it on all points of sailing before you need it for real, and try to find some waves to give it a challenge. Study the manual, and do not be disheartened if it takes several days to sort things out. Downwind, particularly in light airs when the apparent wind falls to almost zero, vane gears are notoriously tricky, but the dividends for perseverance are ample. Wind-vane boats have low power drain at sea and operate without the constant roar of a wind generator disturbing the peace. A well made, well adjusted wind vane will steer its owners around the world and back again at no cost to the batteries, demanding no more than new tiller lines every so often and maybe a set of bearings after the second circumnavigation. Many wind vanes are given names and a respected place of honor among the crew.

On a wind vane system, a small ram-type electronic autopilot can be rigged to the servo paddle in place of the vane. However, these units are not powerful enough to steer

Scanmar International photo

the boat's own rudder for long or operate in heavy weather. This system is used primarily in light air, under power, and on high-speed multihulls where apparent wind shift on acceleration makes it extremely difficult to set a wind vane to a compass course.

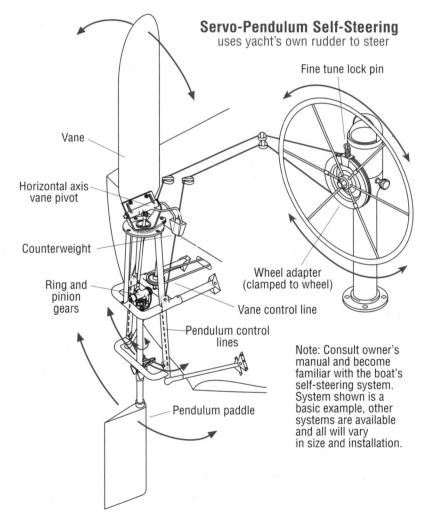

Servo-Pendulum Self-Steering
uses yacht's own rudder to steer

- Vane
- Fine tune lock pin
- Horizontal axis vane pivot
- Counterweight
- Ring and pinion gears
- Pendulum control lines
- Wheel adapter (clamped to wheel)
- Vane control line
- Pendulum paddle

Note: Consult owner's manual and become familiar with the boat's self-steering system. System shown is a basic example, other systems are available and all will vary in size and installation.

Auxiliary Rudder/TrimTab Self-Steering
uses auxiliary rudder to steer

Vane is at full power in vertical position and de-powered in horizontal position.

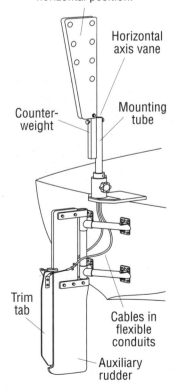

- Horizontal axis vane
- Counterweight
- Mounting tube
- Trim tab
- Cables in flexible conduits
- Auxiliary rudder

Head Discharge System. If your head discharge system is set up for holding tank operation, don't expect pumpout facilities outside of the U.S. Consider adding a Y-valve between the head and the holding tank, so while passage making at sea you can bypass the tank and pump the effluent directly overboard.

Handling Emergencies Offshore

When, despite all efforts to the contrary, things on board go badly wrong, the priorities for an offshore sailor must always be self-help first and foremost, coupled with an emphasis on strong, calm, leadership. This section deals with some of the more common emergencies that may occur on an ocean passage, and concludes with the final option of abandoning the yacht in favor of the liferaft.

Crew Overboard. For all practical purposes, the difference between having a crew go overboard offshore and one on a coastal passage is that in mid-ocean, no outside help can reasonably be expected. This does not affect the rescue techniques listed in Chapter 10, but should you lose contact with the casualty, the option of calling for assistance is gone. You are on your own.

If contact with the victim is lost. While remaining aware of the effects of current, activate the GPS "Man Overboard" function. Even if you cannot see your shipmate, at least this will give you a datum point for your search. In daylight, site a lookout as high up as is safe. If it is dark and it is not blowing so hard as to obscure all extraneous noises, stop the boat, call out, then be silent and listen. Send up a white parachute rocket, after first preparing all hands to look at the sea, NOT at the flare which will blind them temporarily.

If none of the above finds the victim, you will be obliged to institute a search pattern on the basis of a sensible "distance unit" within which you are confident of spotting someone in the water. Suppose conditions are not too stormy and 25 yards seems a dead certainty. Your unit length will be double this, say 50 yards. Drop sails and motor for fifty yards either due north or dead to windward if you don't want to use the compass. If your log does not measure distance to 0.025 miles (50 yards), simply timing the run can be easier to execute. At 5 knots, the boat will cover 50 yards in 18 seconds, which you can round to 20 seconds. When you have been steaming north for 20 seconds, turn sharply east, and repeat the process, looking out on both sides continually. After 20 seconds, turn to starboard again, heading south (or downwind), but this time continue for two units (0.05 miles or 40 seconds) before swinging hard to the west for a further two units. Back on north, the next leg will be three units long, and so on. Just remember the units come in "twos." Two at "1", 2 at "2", 2 at "3", 2 at "4", until you either find the victim or feel you have searched the full area of possibility. In which case, return to your GPS MOB position (duly adjusted for current if appropriate) and start again. By working this system strictly, the boat is bound to pass within 25 yards of her overboard crew member if he or she is still afloat.

Unfortunately, by the time you resort to a pattern search, the chances of recovering your shipmate will not be good. In such dire circumstances it is not uncommon for even well-balanced individuals to become hysterical. Be prepared for this and maintain discipline at all costs. Holding your leadership against these odds is now the only hope for the person in the water. While guarding against any tendency to "freeze,"

1 search unit = 50 yards or 20 seconds

25 yards

25 yards

Hit MOB on GPS as soon as person has fallen overboard

In your search pattern you will want to sail a course schedule as shown below...

two 1 units,
two 2 units,
two 3 units,
two 4 units,
two 5 units,
and so on...

remind yourself constantly to remain calm and in total command. If you surrender your grip, the battle is lost and so is the victim.

Rudder Loss. Yachts have been abandoned for no other reason than that their steering has failed, yet there is often plenty that can be done to deal with this emergency. First, it is important to realize that if the rudder has fallen off, the boat will be less directionally stable than she was with it on. All rudderless sailing drills should therefore be carried out with the understanding that coping with the rudder gone will be even more of a challenge.

Steering with the sails. Nearly all yachts will round up into the wind if left alone with no rudder. How vigorous the tendency depends on rig type, hull balance, and how much sail is set. The essential principle of rudderless sailing is that sail set forward of the center of lateral resistance (usually somewhere in the keel) will make the boat bear away from the wind, while anything drawing from aft of the CLR will head her up toward the wind. If you ease your genoa out and trim in the main, the boat should head up. If you ease the main sheet out and haul in the genoa, your boat will fall off. If this does not happen, reef the main to reduce its area or roll in the genoa a bit. Keep trying different combinations until you find one that balances consistently for the prevailing wind and sea conditions — and practice so that you'll be able to cope when faced with the loss of a rudder at sea. Balanced sails are also less of a strain on the autopilot.

If the boat is a ketch or yawl, the option of dropping the main and steering with "jib and jigger (mizzen)" is attractive. Not only does this shorten sail and thus make the task easier by keeping the boat more upright, it also moves the lever arm of the aft component further from the center of lateral resistance, making it more effective.

Steering upwind or on a reach with your sails is relatively easy compared to when the breeze hauls far aft. With the wind behind, sail-only steering is labor intensive and can become almost impossible. In these circumstances you should consider a jury rudder. Keep in mind that you should expect to complete your passage at half the boat's usual speed when steering with sails.

Jury rudders. The most convenient jury rudder is the auxiliary rudder of a wind-vane gear (if you are sailing with one). Often these will steer the boat adequately under short canvas, across an ocean if need be. Although smaller, the paddle of a servo-pendulum vane system locked in the up-and-down position can also be used to trim a boat struggling to steer with sails alone. There is also an emergency rudder conversion kit available for the servo-pendulum system which includes a larger paddle. If you do not have either of these, consider rigging a jury rudder using a spinnaker pole lashed to the stern pulpit or a spare spinnaker car mounted on the transom with a dinghy paddle on the outboard end. This can work successfully, although heaving the pole from side to side requires muscle or creative seamanship. The main problem is that the paddle tends to float up. Lashing an anchor to it can help, but does little for its hydrodynamics. A preferred solution is to contrive some form of lashing system to hold it down and help articulate the jury rudder. On multihulls, their wide beam makes steering with a drogue and bridle another alternative. The bridle is led through a block on the stern of each

Practice steering with sails. It will not only teach you about balancing the helm, it will allow you to maneuver your boat if your rudder fails.

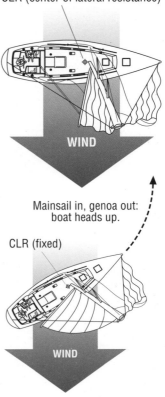

CLR (center of lateral resistance)

WIND

Mainsail in, genoa out: boat heads up.

CLR (fixed)

WIND

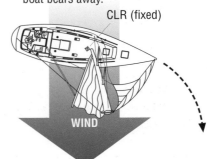

Mainsail out, genoa in: boat bears away.

CLR (fixed)

WIND

Broken Spreader

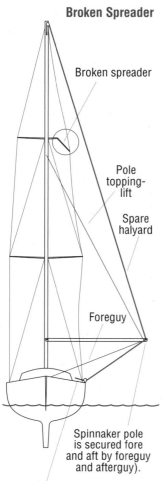

Broken spreader

Pole topping-lift

Spare halyard

Foreguy

Spinnaker pole is secured fore and aft by foreguy and afterguy).

Spectra line led through block at chainplate to winch tightens spare halyard.

hull (or outrigger) to winches and can be adjusted to change the angle of the pull of the drogue (see Chapter 23 for more details on rigging a drogue).

It is important that you have a clear idea of your options in the event of rudder loss, and have practiced beforehand. Like other emergencies, the effect of the real thing can be so alarming that it is difficult to think clearly.

Rig Damage or Loss. Rig damage does not always happen in gales and storms, or to components under heavy strain. The "slack" side of a rig is vulnerable to shaking loose on a long reach, particularly in a heavy sea, so always check before you tack. We have already noted the importance of keeping the rig regularly surveyed, even at sea. Watch for wire strands starting to part near terminals. If you have any doubts, take action to back up dubious elements. If it is a lower shroud, a prudent solution would be to attach a length of Spectra at the hounds, setting it up at the deck with a spare turnbuckle.

When a rig component gives way under load, the boat must immediately be maneuvered to relieve the strain. If a weather shroud breaks, switch to the other tack. If the forestay goes, head downwind, and so on. Once the situation is temporarily stabilized, ponder the possible effects of any action you may take. Some solutions can create new problems.

Dismasting. When a yacht has been dismasted she is in immediate danger of further damage from spars and rigging floating alongside or rolling around the deck. The motion of the boat will be extreme without the inertia of the rig to dampen it. Before contemplating long-term solutions to your unfortunate situation, however, certain priorities must be addressed.

Rigging Emergency Spares Suggestions

☐ Cotter pins

☐ Clevises

☐ One or two general-purpose turnbuckles

☐ Spare terminals and the tools needed for using them

☐ Shackles

☐ Thimbles

☐ Cable clamps for instant splices in wire

☐ A 10-foot length of rigging wire with a terminal of the type used on board already installed on one end. This can then be clamped to a damaged wire.

☐ A length of rigging wire at least as long as the longest stay, or…

☐ A coil of Spectra rope – lighter than wire, equally strong, even lower stretch coefficient and far easier to use in an emergency. The only drawback is its tendency to chafe.

☐ An emergency radio antenna

☐ A sound bosun's chair that works well at sea, plus the means of hoisting a competent person aloft. This may be a winch, but consider the anchor windlass with the halyard led through a snatch block. If it is electric and above the smallest size, it will be plenty powerful enough.

Priorities when dismasted:

• DO NOT start the engine. A dismasted yacht is surrounded by a veritable dragnet of gear, all of it hungry for the propeller.

• Make sure all crew are safe and still on board. Injuries are surprisingly rare in dismastings, but if you have any, send them below and administer first aid before attending to damage on deck.

• Take a thorough look at your state of affairs. If the rig is alongside, the knee-jerk reaction is to chop it away as quickly as possible, but this may not be the best option. If the mast butt is not secured to the mast step, the below-deck section may come adrift and flail about dangerously in the cabin.

• Protect the yacht's watertight integrity first and foremost, but save whatever you can bring aboard from the wreck to give your crew a fighting chance of contriving a jury rig substitute. If the mast is largely intact and you can see no way of re-erecting it, jettisoning it may be the only sensible course of action if there is a big sea running. Try to save its gear, however, and make absolutely sure you retain booms, spinnaker poles or sections of mast that can be dragged onto the deck. They and your coil of spectra line are the building blocks of the jury rig.

• Only when you are certain that all lines, sails and wires are secure should you consider starting the engine. Remember, there could be gear down there which will do worse than just wrap the propeller up. A rogue forestay could rip the shaft out of the boat. Losing your power can transform what is currently no more than an expensive inconvenience into a life-threatening situation.

• Read accounts of passages successfully completed under jury rigs. There can be no text book for this subject. It is rather a matter of

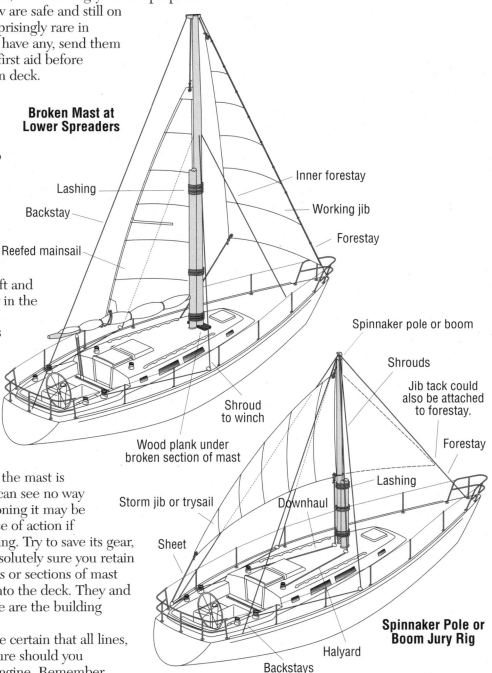

Broken Mast at Lower Spreaders

Lashing
Backstay
Reefed mainsail
Inner forestay
Working jib
Forestay
Shroud to winch
Wood plank under broken section of mast

Spinnaker pole or boom
Shrouds
Jib tack could also be attached to forestay.
Forestay
Lashing
Storm jib or trysail
Downhaul
Sheet
Halyard
Backstays

Spinnaker Pole or Boom Jury Rig

personal and team ingenuity, but the more you have studied other successes, the better chance you have of dreaming up an arrangement that will bring your ship safely home.

Once you have dealt with your urgent priorities, you can go about constructing your jury rig and rigging your spare antenna.

Flooding. The ultimate emergency at sea is having the boat sink under you. This can happen following a traumatic collision with a floating object, perhaps unseen at night, or it may result from a failure of the vessel herself. Whatever the cause, the symptom is the same: bilge water rising rapidly.

Little cranks up on board stress levels like water sloshing around above the cabin sole, so a drill is necessary to combat the natural tendency of crew members to "freeze." Immediate action follows the maxim, "reduce, locate & stop the flow." An action plan might go like this:

1. Start pumping. A modern yacht will probably have electric or power pumps, so this task should not employ all hands in hard manual labor. At best, however, the pumps may do no better than reduce the rate of flooding. A five-square-inch hole, one foot below the waterline, allows approximately 300 gallons to enter the boat every minute. The same hole 4 feet below the waterline will flood at almost 1000 gallons per minute. A typical bilge pump rated at 60 gallons per minute is unlikely to achieve better than half its rating in an average installation. If you have suffered damage of this magnitude, your chances of pumping your way out of it are nil. Mercifully, leaks other than those caused by collision are generally more manageable.

2. Locate the source of the leak. This can be a challenge, but you must keep a clear head and try to identify likely ingress points. Other than leaks in the structure of a wooden boat or collision damage, these are likely to be:

• An open basin drain below the waterline allowing water to pour into the boat when heeled to the point that the basin's "plug-hole" moves below the waterline. The same thing can sometimes happen to a toilet. Close the seacock!

• A leaking stern tube (see Chapter 1 for details of how these glands function). These leaks are most common to older boats with packing glands where, tightening the gland, greasing, or inserting extra packing will bring leaking under control. It is not unheard of for a propeller to become entangled with a floating net, resulting in the shaft being ripped out of the boat. The resulting hole requires immediate plugging, a dedicated wooden plug being favored. Fortunately, losing the stern gear is likely to be accompanied by a noticeable commotion, so the problem is unlikely to sneak up on you.

• Failed hoses. Hoses below the waterline should be double clamped, but even these can fail. Older hoses may crack, creating a slow leak which progressively becomes worse. Chafe can cause sudden hose failure, a prime example being steering cables rubbing against cockpit drain hoses.

• Worn steering tube/rudder stock. A common source of leaks on older boats is a worn rudder stock tube. Many boats "squat" when under power, which can lower the gland below the waterline and result in leaking.

• Failed through-hull fittings. Occasionally a through-hull fitting itself will fail. Soft wood plugs (attached or mounted adjacent to each through-hull fitting) hammered in, a t-shirt or even a potato forced into the hole will supply a short-term fix. Know the location of all through-hulls (a location diagram is a useful reference for crew members) and make sure they are accessible.

3. Raise the hole. Bringing a hole nearer to the surface can substantially reduce the rate of flooding. If you are close-hauled and the leak is on the leeward side, heave-to or tack. If you are motoring at hull speed, slow down. If on a run, try heading up. Whatever technique works, raising the hole is your first priority after finding the leak. Doing so can buy you time to deal with the problem.

4. Mend the leaks. This is where the ability to improvise can literally save your life, but to have a chance, you need the right gear at hand.

Clearly, a good supply of spare hose, duct tape, plumbing fittings, gland packing and hose clamps is essential. However, striking a submerged object remains a horror lurking in the back of the offshore mind. Collision often results in a jagged gash or rip in the hull, rather than a neat, round hole. Gashes and rips are generally patched from the inside, a solution that is rarely ideal.

Stuff anything into the hole as a temporary measure, such as spare life jackets or a nerf ball, but even bedding has saved the day. Emergency patching materials should include a strong, pliable material such as thin marine grade plywood, rubber sheeting, or a mat of some sort. Serious quantities of sealant are a prerequisite.

Sealants. There are numerous sealants appropriate for on board repair, but each has its limits.

Epoxy resin. It should be noted that most epoxy will not "cure" under water. At best, it will harden slowly, perhaps taking a few hours. The effect can be partly avoided by mixing a "hot" batch with extra hardener. This reduces the strength of the epoxy, but you may be less concerned about this than in achieving a fast result. If this method is your choice, you should experiment prior to leaving shore.

Underwater epoxies, sometimes supplied in two-pack putty form, can be a lifesaver. Kits are available commercially. Buy two! One to practice with prior to leaving.

3M 5200. This extra strong sealant is a one-tube application which cures under water, forming a remarkable strong bond. It is relatively inexpensive and easy to apply. Unfortunately, 5200 resists adhering to wet surfaces. Again, experiment before departure.

Capsize. When monohulls of sound construction and sensible design for cruising capsize into an inverted (upside down) position, they will roll up again either as a result of momentum or the motion of the next wave. However, capsize can become a reality if the keel breaks off and/or the hull form has too much negative (inverted) stability. (For more information on stability and hull forms, see Chapter 14.)

Multihulls have hull forms that make them very stable once in the inverted position, but unless their hulls have broken up, they can remain afloat for days until rescue arrives. In fact, the inverted multihull is often the best "liferaft" for survivors. Offshore passages should include planning to deal with this situation. Here are some points to consider:

• Minimize water ingress and reduce the water level in the living space. For information on watertight bulkheads, refer to the US SAILING's *Recommendations for Offshore Sailing including ORC Special Regulations.*

• Minimize contamination of the inverted "living space" from diesel oil, battery acid, etc.

• Ensure the availability of fresh water, food, medical supplies, handheld VHF, EPIRB, flares, strobe light, tools, survival suits, etc.

• Pre-plan areas adaptable for inverted "bunks" that will be high enough to remain dry.

• Make provision for an emergency escape hatch that won't flood when in use and can allow ventilation (refer to *Recommendations for Offshore Sailing including ORC Special Regulations*).

Abandoning Ship. It has been shown time and again that abandoning a yacht prematurely is more likely to lead to loss of life than staying with her until she sinks under you. Boarding a raft in heavy seas can be dangerous. So can the process of being rescued out if it. Even if all hands make the transfer successfully, the raft is an uncomfortable, cold, damp environment in which to survive. Rations will inevitably be short and maintaining morale can be a severe test even for a trained professional. If the command structure breaks down in a raft, disaster can result. Furthermore, a raft is harder for an aircraft or a ship to spot floating among waves than a yacht. Do not consider it an option until fire or imminent sinking makes its use imperative. When this occurs, keep in mind that climbing into the raft is only the beginning. You are not saved until all hands are either ashore or aboard a rescuing ship or aircraft.

When abandoning ship, be sure to attach the liferaft's painter before heaving the liferaft clear of the boat.

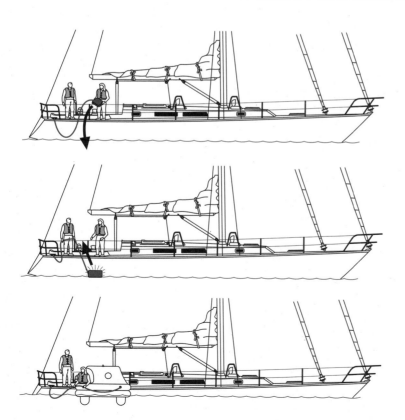

Any opportunity to attend a Safety at Sea Seminar involving hands-on liferaft experience should be sought with alacrity (for more information on Seminars, contact US SAILING or log onto its website at http://www.ussailing.org). Practicing deploying a liferaft correctly and taking appropriate actions once aboard can be the difference between life and death.

Launching the raft. It is assumed that by this time you have broadcast a MAYDAY signal and, hopefully, have received a response. If not, and crew numbers permit, have someone continue to send out distress messages at sensible intervals until the last possible minute.

Ensure that the painter is tied securely to something on deck that will not carry away.

Clear away lashings, then confirm that the water to leeward is not encumbered with wreckage. Check the painter again, then heave the raft over the lee side in its canister or valise. It will float.

Pull hard on the painter. This will run out of the raft's packaging until it reaches the end, usually at about 30 feet. There should now be a small explosion and the raft will inflate itself. If this fails to happen, tug hard on the painter until you hear the bang.

Drag the raft into the lee of the yacht. The last part to inflate will be the canopy. Once this is up, secure the painter as short as seas allow, and get ready for boarding. Don't worry if there is a noise like a deflating balloon. The cylinder contains more gas than is usually needed; the sound is merely the excess bleeding off.

Boarding the raft. Following is a checklist of food and equipment that should be brought aboard a liferaft used for an offshore passage. Many items should be pre-packed in a "grab bag" or packed into the raft during the periodic professional inspections.

- 406 MHz EPIRB
- waterproof handheld VHF transceiver and batteries
- extra flares: at least two red parachute and three red hand ones
- radar reflector or SAR transponder
- waterproof handheld GPS and batteries
- flashlight and batteries
- two "cyalume" light sticks or two throwable floating lights
- daylight signaling mirror and whistle
- spare sea anchor (drogue) and line
- extra PFDs
- safety knife
- warm clothing
- thermal protective aids (TPAs – these are like plastic space blankets)
- first aid kit
- fresh water in watertight containers (at least half a liter of water per person)
- plastic drinking vessel graduated in 10, 20 and 50cc
- food (chocolate/health bars and non-thirst-provoking rations and barley sugar or equivalent)
- two safety can-openers
- one copy of the illustrated table of life-saving signals
- waterproof plastic "sick bags" and nylon string bags
- seasickness medication, sunscreen, lip ointment, and other medications used regularly by crew
- Additional items should include ship's log, ship's papers, personal identification and money, and if there is time, other items such as more water and an open container to use as a "chamber pot."

The raft's entry point is generally beside the painter, so you have every chance of stepping in dry. This is most important, because wet people rapidly become cold, and being soaked lowers morale.

Before boarding, crew should be warmly dressed in full oilskins, wearing PFD and harness. You should also encourage crew to drink as much water as they can hold.

Contrary to what you might expect, send the strongest or fittest person into the raft FIRST to assist others less able. If this means you, let there be no false modesty about being the last to leave the ship. Brief everyone clearly and calmly, then get on with it.

Check everyone for sharp objects on their personal gear that could harm the raft.

If the raft has drifted beyond reach on its painter and the wind is so strong you can't pull it in, send the strongest across first, with harness clipped to the painter so as not to be swept away. The rest follow, one at a time, similarly clipped on for safety.

Righting a capsized raft. Sometimes a raft inflates upside down. Send your best swimmer to clamber up onto it and locate the gas bottle. Close to this will be the righting strap. The feet are placed on the bottle and the swimmer stands up, holding onto the strap or, if there isn't one, the boarding ladder. Leaning back against the pull will now flip the raft upright leaving the swimmer to work "out from under."

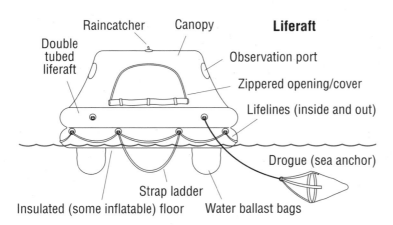

Raincatcher   Canopy   **Liferaft**

Double tubed liferaft

Observation port

Zippered opening/cover

Lifelines (inside and out)

Drogue (sea anchor)

Strap ladder

Insulated (some inflatable) floor   Water ballast bags

Imperative actions after boarding. Here is the recognized drill for clearing away from the ship. Memorize the headings.

Cut: Assuming the sinking of the yacht or her total consumption by fire is imminent, locate the folding safety knife which will be clearly marked and stowed near the entrance to the raft. Cut the painter with it. Unless you cannot find it, do not use any other knife. The raft's has no point and so is almost accident-proof.

Stream: Stream the drogue as soon as the raft has drifted clear (check for wreckage). The drogue serves three important purposes: it is attached away from the door, and so keeps the opening downwind. It sustains your position fairly close to that broadcast in the MAYDAY, and by holding the raft down it assists stability. If the drogue is lost, rig the spare as soon as possible.

Close: Unless the weather is fair, close up the entrance. Inflate the floor of the raft if this is a feature of its design. Doing so aids insulation. Now arrange the crew so that they are evenly distributed around the edge of the raft, facing inward. This is a critical part of the ballasting and must be adhered to. Classically, this discipline is one of the first to be lost if command breaks down. Uneven distribution of crew weight can encourage a capsize.

Maintain: Take stock. See what you have aboard. Check for damage to the raft, dry the floor, assure yourself that the EPIRB is activated and formulate a routine for survival.

Secondary actions in the raft.

Injuries: Injured crew are now a priority. Bandage or splint obvious injuries. Make them as comfortable as possible, reassure them and take what action you are able with the first aid kit.

Dryness: Work at mopping up the floor.

Body warmth: Watch for shivering, encourage huddling where this can be commensurate with raft stability. Issue the thermal protective aids (TPAs) which are in a SOLAS raft pack.

Seasickness: Distribute the pills to everyone, regardless. The motion is going to be awful. Do all you can to comfort sufferers. Place those vomiting regularly by the entrance so they can attempt not to soil the floor. If this is not possible, issue plastic bags. Vomit washing round can demoralize even the most optimistic.

Roll call: If your crew is numerous, check they are all aboard. If not, maintain a lookout for anybody missing. Even one chance in a hundred must be covered.

Watch routine: This is important to make sure you don't miss a chance of rescue, and also to sustain discipline and morale. The watch must ventilate the air under the canopy through the opening every 30 minutes or so to prevent a build-up of carbon dioxide. If there seems a likelihood of ship traffic, use the VHF sparingly within its battery capacity to broadcast regular MAYDAYs.

Rations: Issue no food in the first 24 hours, except for the very young and the injured. Thereafter, establish a routine. Watch children closely for signs of "fading." They have a greater tendency toward fluid and heat loss than adults.

Passing water: Urine retention is a real problem with liferaft survivors. People don't like relieving themselves for reasons of decency, but they must be encouraged to do so regularly. The "chamber pot" mentioned in the abandon ship kit helps the modest to overcome their scruples. Urine may well become dark and smoky after a day or two in the raft. This is normal and no cause for alarm.

As soon as help is in sight, make full use of the VHF and pyrotechnics. When using the red hand flares, make sure you hold them to leeward over the water to avoid dripping hot phosphor on the liferaft which could result in its sinking.

Rescue Scenarios. It is impossible to generalize about rescue scenarios. Each one is different, depending on numerous circumstances. If you are in mid-ocean, it is likely that the first contact you have with civilization will be a fixed-wing aircraft dispatched by the Coast Guard to pinpoint your position and, where necessary, to drop supplies or an additional raft. Next on the scene may be a ship. Far out at sea, this will probably be a merchant or deep-sea fishing vessel diverted to assist you. Her crew may not be rescue specialists, but they are all you have. They will probably maneuver to place you in the ship's lee, then either launch a boat or lower ropes and boarding netting. Communicate with them via VHF to advise of any special requirements, particularly injured or exhausted people. It's possible they will send someone down to assist.

Close to U.S. shores, the best option is a large Coast Guard cutter with full rescue gear, medical supplies and professional crew. Within 300 miles of the shore, you might even be sent a helicopter.

To help searchers find your liferaft, try to make it look larger, brighter and different from your surroundings (such as tying fenders, cushions and other flotsam to the painter).

Whoever comes to your aid, never forget that you are not saved until you are on board the rescue ship or aircraft. Possibly the most dangerous time of all is when making the transfer. Crew members may be tempted by their excitement to behave irresponsibly. The skipper's duty is to keep cool and maintain command right to the end. If control is maintained, there will be plenty time to celebrate later.

Heavy Weather Offshore

This chapter on heavy weather seamanship assumes the boat is far from land and that there are no sea room limitations. From time to time, however, particularly in higher latitudes, a gale comes up at the end of an offshore passage, leaving a yacht in a lee-shore situation. These are the most dangerous gales of all, and require the passagemaker to "stand up to" the weather rather than survive by giving ground.

Crew and Boat Considerations. In Chapter 14 the question of yacht stability was raised, and conclusions were drawn relating to different types of yachts. These factors may have a profound effect on survival tactics, but regardless of the sort of craft she may be, any offshore crew should take a

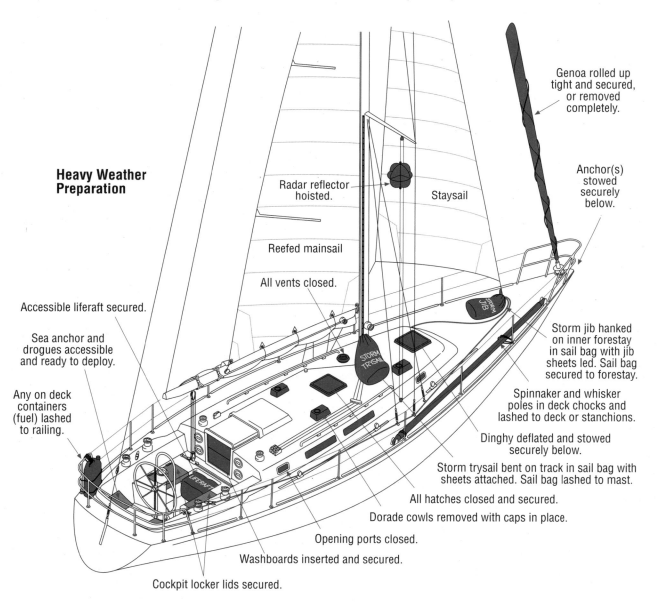

Heavy Weather Preparation

Genoa rolled up tight and secured, or removed completely.

Radar reflector hoisted.

Staysail

Anchor(s) stowed securely below.

Reefed mainsail

All vents closed.

Accessible liferaft secured.

Sea anchor and drogues accessible and ready to deploy.

Any on deck containers (fuel) lashed to railing.

Storm jib hanked on inner forestay in sail bag with jib sheets led. Sail bag secured to forestay.

Spinnaker and whisker poles in deck chocks and lashed to deck or stanchions.

Dinghy deflated and stowed securely below.

Storm trysail bent on track in sail bag with sheets attached. Sail bag lashed to mast.

All hatches closed and secured.

Dorade cowls removed with caps in place.

Opening ports closed.

Washboards inserted and secured.

Cockpit locker lids secured.

number of steps when it appears they are in for a serious "dusting:"

• Double-check all lashings on deck. The last thing you want is a five-gallon container of diesel taking charge at midnight. Is the dinghy secure? And the spinnaker pole?

• Rig the radar reflector if it is not permanently mounted.

• Go through the ship and ensure all openings are battened down. Following a period of fair weather it is not unusual to find an opening portlight unbolted, a mushroom vent fully open, or even the forehatch not secure. Fasten down all cockpit-locker lids and look under bunk cushions to ensure that turn buttons have been closed on hatches.

• Make sure storm sails are readily accessible as well as the drogue or sea anchor. These have a tendency to end up under spinnakers and light-weather sails which suddenly become heavy and awkward to move at 45-degree angles.

• General items stowed in the main cabin and around berths can fly loose at sea. It only takes a 60-degree knockdown to release anything that isn't solidly wedged in place. Check items in the galley, books in the navigation station, the tool boxes and companionway slides. Look around with a keen eye for anything that can go flying.

• If possible, give the engine a long run to charge the batteries up to the top. Doing this to keep the radar running on the second night of a hard spell is a nuisance.

• Make sure storm covers (deadlights) for large windows and other openings in deckhouses and hulls are readily accessible or in place.

• Cook a one-pot meal and clamp it down in the pressure cooker with the lid on. Fill thermoses with boiling water.

• Encourage the crew to take all the rest they can. Fatigue is a major concern in storm conditions.

Keeping Watch. Most people cannot handle a three-hour watch alone in 40 to 50 knots of wind, so watch cycles must be reconsidered in the light of individual crew strength, stamina and the severity of the weather. In all but the largest vessels, it is likely that if things become really tough, you will end up with nobody on deck at all, but there must still be a scheduled rotating watch to look outside and take charge while others rest. Chafe is a major issue in heavy weather, and the watch must keep an eye out for this, but the main task is to be aware of the sea state, changes in the sky, and particularly any shipping traffic that fate may send your way. The normal lookout based on an assumption of certain converging speeds is no longer relevant, because ships may now remain invisible until quite close because of spume, rain and high waves. The best precaution is to run radar (if you have one) and all your shipmates should be familiar with its operation before you get into this situation. Set it up for a 12-mile range, turn up the clutter, switch on the target enhancer and shut down the range rings so that any blip whatsoever is instantly visible. As soon as you see one, lay the cursor on it and turn the range rings back on. Follow it carefully, and if it is still on a collision heading at six miles work hard to sight the ship. If you see nothing at five miles, call up on VHF and tell them what's going on. Should there be no response, at least you can plan your avoidance tactics in plenty of time.

Radar watchkeeping is particularly important if you are caught in an area of higher than normal shipping activity. Use the stand-by facility to conserve

Below is a radar set up for storm watchkeeping mode

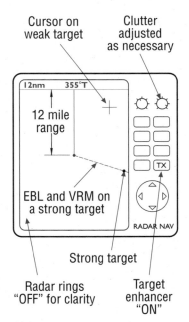

Cursor on weak target

Clutter adjusted as necessary

12mm   355°T

12 mile range

EBL and VRM on a strong target

TX

RADAR NAV

Strong target

Radar rings "OFF" for clarity

Target enhancer "ON"

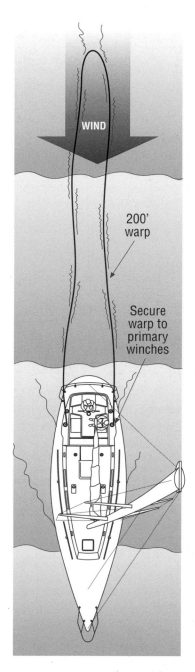

Running warps keep speed and steering under control.

vital battery power, then hit the "TX" button for a look round every ten minutes or so. Let the scanner rotate for at least two minutes to assess strong targets properly and to ensure that you don't miss any weaker ones.

Maintaining the Plot. In a mid-ocean storm, your exact position will often be of no more than academic interest, unless you need it to identify a ship you are calling up for safety reasons. Close to such ocean dangers as the Gulf Stream or the Grand Banks, however, questions as to which way to encourage the yacht to drift may become crucial to survival.

Away from such hazards, keeping an up-to-date position can form an important cog in the skipper's self-discipline. Today, thanks to GPS, knowing where you are is a matter of plotting a couple of coordinates every four hours or so. If the electronics are not functioning, however, you must revert to traditional means.

You will probably be running or drifting more or less in a straight line, so note its direction and plot accordingly. This presents no problem if the boat is under helm. It is simply a matter of working up a DR from logged distance and course steered — a two-minute job even with the boat laboring. If she is drifting hove-to or lying a-hull, the log will not work, so you must estimate the speed of her progress. The direction of drift is the reciprocal of a compass bearing taken on the slick left to windward.

Survival Tactics. In Chapter 14 the matter of yacht stability was discussed. Readers will have noted that all stability tests assume the worst-case scenario of a yacht lying beam-on "in the trough" of a wave, the position from which she is most likely to be rolled over. All storm survival options center around the issue of keeping the boat "on her feet" in an effort to avoid this vulnerable position.

The preferred survival technique in a given set of conditions depends on how vulnerable the yacht is to capsize, and her crew strength. Tactical alternatives can be divided into two categories, active and passive. Active methods require that the boat is steered, either by a self-steering mechanism — increasingly difficult to rely on as wind and seas build beyond the ordinary — or a human "driver." Passive techniques do not require anyone at the wheel. If you have an ample supply of strong crew members, active techniques may recommend themselves. Should you be a couple, or perhaps elderly or lacking in strength, think passive. Certain boats can look after themselves, while others are less able to do so. The factors of crew and yacht must be balanced correctly to handle heavy weather effectively.

In the following techniques, references will be made to the stability section of Chapter 14 and the boat types it describes. If you have not fully assimilated that part of the book, do so now before reading on.

Active Techniques. These can be used by any boat, but may be of special interest to skippers whose vessels are not noted for their ability to avoid a beam-on attitude without help. These will usually, but not always, be light-displacement craft with short keels and a shallow forefoot, and multihulls.

Running. The most obvious benefit of running before a storm is that if the weather is going your way, every mile you log is a mile made good. Further winnings accrue from apparent wind and sea factors. If it is blowing 45 and you are running at 6 knots, your speed is making appreciable inroads into the wind strength. The force of the seas is also eased and the boat is kept end-on to them. This effect is particularly noticeable for a multihull which will be making higher speeds.

On the negative side, someone is needed to steer and the yacht is exposed to the twin dangers of pooping and broaching. Pooping occurs when a wave breaks clean over the stern, sweeping the decks and filing the cockpit. When running off in survival conditions, all hands must assume that this will happen. People steering must be clipped on and companionway washboards or doors kept shut at all times when not in use. If a running boat is pooped two or more times in fairly rapid succession, alternative tactics should be considered.

When a running boat swings beam-on out of control, she is said to broach. This can happen for two reasons. An awkward cross-sea may pick up her stern, lifting the rudder out of the water and allowing the boat to "spin out." Or, if she runs so fast that she exceeds her "hull speed," the rudder alone may no longer be sufficient to control her. In either case, the force of her lurching round may add to the beam-on effects of wind and sea.

Controlling speed is initially achieved by shortening sail. However, there may come a point when she will be making too much way even under the minimum canvas you can set. At this point, you must douse all sail and continue under bare poles. Running under bare poles is surprisingly easy, given enough wind to keep the show on the road. For a rugged 35-footer, 50 knots would be more than enough, and some will manage at 40. If the stick alone is still driving the boat too fast, consider trailing warps to slow down and keep the stern "up" to the seas. Ease out your longest warp (200 feet is good) in a bight, with the ends secured to cockpit winches. If only one end is made fast, less drag is achieved and the whipping on the trailing end of the trailing line will be put to a terrible test.

Some skippers tow a drogue to create more drag than a warp alone. Lifeboats use these when crossing difficult bars, motoring against them to maintain directional stability. Try yours with a storm jib or, if you have a powerboat, do as the lifeboats do.

One final danger that may be

Right, a multihull is running with drogue rigged off the stern.

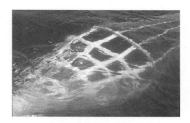

This Galerider® drogue provides resistance to seas and helps maintain proper orientation to the wind's force.

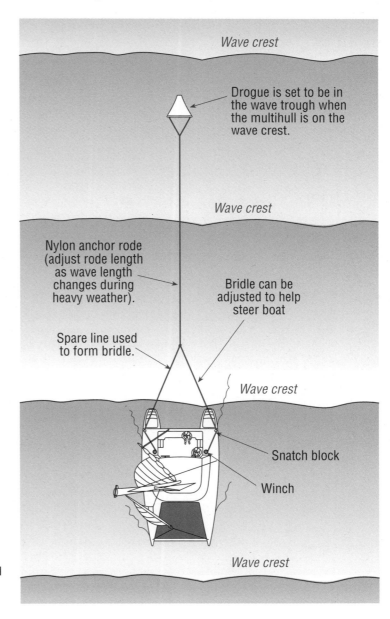

Wave crest

Drogue is set to be in the wave trough when the multihull is on the wave crest.

Wave crest

Nylon anchor rode (adjust rode length as wave length changes during heavy weather).

Bridle can be adjusted to help steer boat

Spare line used to form bridle.

Wave crest

Snatch block

Winch

Wave crest

Boat "idling" in a close reach attitude and drifting at 1.5 to 2.5 knots.

Jib trimmed on weather side.

DRIFT

WIND

Turn wheel to weather and lock.

Rudder hard over

encountered by those electing to run before heavy seas is "pitchpoling." This occurs when a wave picks up the boat and throws her end-over-end. The effects are dire, as can be imagined, and only the strongest vessels survive, often with serious crew injuries. A very high, steep wave is required to achieve this. Such phenomena are found in the Southern Ocean and the North Atlantic and Pacific in winter. In season, outside the Southern Ocean, you would be unlucky indeed to have this happen.

"Dodging" to windward. If you can't, or don't wish to run, the alternative is to offer the other end of the boat to the action, keeping her as near bow-on to the waves as possible. A powerful, agile yacht with a superb set of storm canvas might succeed in doing this under sail alone, given a first-class helm. The boat is steered "up" towards the crest of each succeeding wave, almost luffing; she then bears away down its back to build speed to sail up the next one. Race boats can do this successfully, but it is rarely a valid option for a cruiser, even if she possesses adequate performance, for the simple reason that steering is extremely exhausting.

For most offshore boats and crews, therefore, the motorsailing technique described for the coastal passagemaker in Chapter 11 offers a more realistic option, although limited fuel resources may make it a non-starter. If a blow is only going to last 12 hours, as many do in the summer, a dozen gallons of diesel burned at low revs may prove well spent.

This method of working to windward slowly under power, assisted where appropriate by a deep-reefed sail, is favored by deep-sea fishermen, some of whom call it "dodging." It also has the advantage of not giving away ground to leeward.

Passive Techniques. The success of the following survival options is dependent on how well a boat lies unattended.

Heaving-to. For a yacht that can manage it, this is the favored method in all but the most extreme of circumstances. It relies on losing all way by working the sails one against the other and balancing the effect with the rudder.

How to heave-to:
• Bring the boat to a close reach and trim accordingly.
• Tack, leaving the jib sheet made fast

4

Boat is in a hove-to state and begins to drift slowly.

Turn wheel to windward all the way as boat loses headway and ste erage.

3 Steer straight on close-hauled attitude after tack with jib trimmed aback on weather side.

Tack, leaving jib cleated.

2

WIND

Bring boat to close reach, trim mainsail accordingly, but trim jib tight.

Heaving-To

1

When heaving-to, jib is sheeted aback, main is "idling" in a close-reaching attitude, and wheel is lashed hard to windward. Drift will be across and somewhat downwind, typically at between 1.5 and 2.5 knots, depending on wind strength and boat type.

so that the sail comes aback as the boat comes through the wind.

• Steer straight ahead after tacking, with the boat in a close-hauled attitude, until almost all way has been lost. As the rudder loses its bite, turn the wheel all the way to windward (tiller to leeward). So long as she has lost way, the boat will refuse to answer the rudder, because her backed headsail will stop the bow from turning into the wind. The mainsail, on the contrary, is trying to help the rudder, and after a few seconds a dynamic equilibrium is reached.

Once hove-to, the yacht makes no headway but lies anywhere from 30 to 55 degrees from the wind and waves, drifting slowly across them and to leeward.

A wholesome boat hove-to under minimum canvas can stand a great deal of wind. Assuming the seas are more or less running with the wind, her attitude to them will keep her from falling beam-on. A comfortable ride ensues, and once the wheel is lashed to weather, no crew is required. This method is effective for most long-keeled craft but to hold the head up to real effect, the deeper forefoot is a big help. Ketches or yawls can aid their cause by using the mizzen instead of the main.

Multihulls and short-keeled monohulls often will lie beam-on when hove to, and some monohulls have been known to be so unstable directionally that they tack themselves. However, this doesn't exclude them from this most satisfactory of techniques. The parachute sea anchor has changed all that.

The parachute sea anchor. Given that "stopping" rather than "going" can be desirable in storm survival and that light, short-keeled yachts have problems making this happen, a method was sought to assist them. Multihulls experience similar difficulties, as do smaller yachts with otherwise good heaving-to performance. A proven solution for many of these craft is the parachute sea anchor.

A parachute sea anchor is made of lightweight nylon (the originals were literally ex-USAF parachutes) which packs very tightly. The ideal way for a monohull to deploy it is to heave-to as described above, then stream the para-anchor from the bow on a long rode. Two lines are tied into the end of the rode, either with bowlines or a swivel. One is led over the bow roller and cleated. The second is led amidships or further aft — ideally to a winch. The two lines are adjusted to encourage the boat to lie with the wind approximately 40 degrees off the bow, as she would if she were able to heave-to unassisted. You will need to experiment with sails, rudder angles and load-sharing between the para-lines before equilibrium is achieved, but many successful deployments are on record, particularly with smaller yachts.

In the case of a multihull, the parachute is set up to keep the vessel head-to-wind with no sail set. Some monohulls have also found this a better option. The only way to learn is to do it, so practice in a strong blow before you need the parachute in really tough conditions. Be aware that 50-knot winds and heaving seas are not ideal for crawling on the foredeck with an armful of parachute and coils of line. Rig ahead of time and lead the rode back to the cockpit, possibly securing along the rail with breakable ties until you decide to deploy the sea anchor.

Once the gear is set loads are enormous, so attachment points must be very strong indeed. Cleats should be well backed up as they would be for towing, but winches and windlasses are the preferred sites. If possible, use a

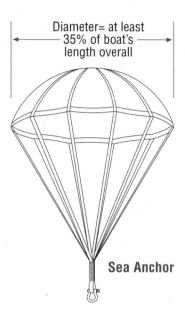

Diameter= at least 35% of boat's length overall

Sea Anchor

A parachute sea anchor (above) is shown deployed off a multihull's bow (below).

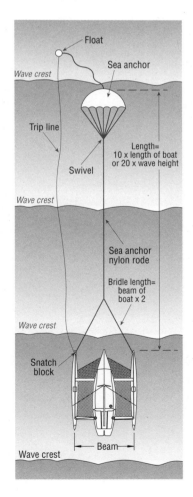

Float

Sea anchor

Wave crest

Trip line

Swivel

Length= 10 x length of boat or 20 x wave height

Wave crest

Sea anchor nylon rode

Bridle length= beam of boat x 2

Wave crest

Snatch block

Wave crest

Beam

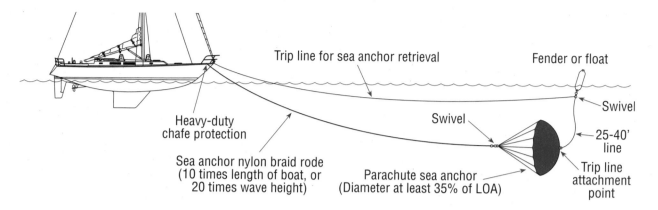

Trip line for sea anchor retrieval

Fender or float

Swivel

Heavy-duty
chafe protection

Swivel

25-40'
line

Sea anchor nylon braid rode
(10 times length of boat, or
20 times wave height)

Parachute sea anchor
(Diameter at least 35% of LOA)

Trip line
attachment
point

Above, a parachute sea anchor is shown rigged for a monohull.

braid or plaited rope, since a three-strand laid line inevitably "winds up" and "unwinds" as it stretches. Nylon is the best choice for strength and elasticity.

Provide chafe protection and replace as needed if conditions allow. The warps are stretching and contracting several times each minute, and every time they do, they rub in the fairleads.

Lying a-hull. Before even considering this tactic, you must be confident that your boat has moderate to heavy displacement for her length, good roll moment of inertia characteristics, a high angle of vanishing stability and a small area of "negative GZ" on her stability curve. Typical of such a boat would be a long-keeled, no-nonsense cruiser. When running is no longer a viable option, when she cannot heave-to owing to the massive weight of wind, if she has no para-anchor and her crew are too exhausted to think, she has no options left but to lie in the trough to take her chances unattended. This is called "lying a-hull." If the wind is strong enough to steady the boat, the situation is less uncomfortable than the uninitiated might imagine.

The dangers are obvious: beam-on, the yacht is the potential victim of any steep sea that happens her way. Even if she is extremely stable, she is clearly at risk from knockdown. Her people must have confidence that, should this occur, her rig has a good chance of coming through unscathed and she will rapidly roll back onto her feet. Many seaworthy yachts have ridden out serious gales lying a-hull, suffering an occasional knockdown of an acceptable 50 or 60 degrees. Some lightweights have tried and suffered 360-degree rolls.

If you opt to lie a-hull, lash your helm amidships. Turning the wheel to weather can help the boat point up somewhat, but if she should start sailing to leeward after the bow has blow off the wind, she can round up, lose way head to a steep crest and be thrown astern, risking rudder or steering damage.

Conclusions on Survival Options. New survival options are continually under review by the offshore sailing community. Nobody can say which method will be best for a particular boat in a particular storm. Only trial and (hopefully) not too much error, can tell you the answer. It is the responsibility of all skippers to educate themselves concerning these very real possibilities. Read books, discuss the subject with experienced people, attend seminars and genuinely try to become an expert, at least in theory. Only when you have a few gales and maybe a storm behind you can you really begin to know where you and your boat stand.

A Final Word

Passagemaking is one of the few real liberties left in a world of ever-increasing controls and legislation. Out at sea, whether ten miles from the coast on a brisk spring morning or running off the days through the impossible blue of the trade-wind ocean, we stand or fall by our own decisions. There is nobody to oversee how we manage our lives. No traffic police check our navigation, no hygiene officer pries into the way we clean the fish we catch, and the only "no-go zones" are those we define for ourselves. We voyage at will, in any manner that suits us.

The price of this unique independence is that we stand responsible for our own actions and must accept their consequences. A bad mistake, a moment of unguarded negligence, and the impartial sea will make us pay. The tools of the sailor's trade are constantly changing, not automatically for the better, but the sea remains unaltered. Only the thinnest skin of wood, fiberglass

or steel stands between our inappropriate, land-bound bodies and a great deal of salt water. By refusing to allow the machines and electronic devices of our invention to drive a wedge between us and this unarguable reality, we retain respect for the ocean's ultimate power.

In this book, we have kept an unblinking eye on the old ways while considering the benefits of the new. There is no nostalgia or self-indulgence in such a policy; rather a straightforward requirement to preserve ourselves in a world where tight modern boats and sophisticated equipment isolate us ever further from the unchanging foundations of our lives.

The final tests remain what they have always been: the storm wave and the lee shore. The pay-off for the self-discipline to confront these ancient enemies with confidence eclipses the ephemeral security promised by an electronic screen. It is the timeless freedom of a good boat lifting to a quartering sea with half her distance run, every sign of a fast passage, and a red sunset auguring a fine night ahead.

Additional Resources

GENERAL

United States Sailing Association:
www.ussailing.org

Basic Cruising, United States Sailing Association, 1995

Bareboat Cruising, United States Sailing Association, 1996

Coastal Navigation, United States Sailing Association, 1999

Safety Recommendations for Cruising Sailboats, United States Sailing Association, 1999

Safety Recommendations for Offshore Sailing: Including ORC Special Regulations, United States Sailing Association, 2000

US Coast Guard Boating Safety Office:
www.uscg.boating.org

Code of Federal Regulations:
www.access.gpo.gov

Student Certification Standards Details the student standards for each of the seven levels of US SAILING certification.

Any US SAILING publication can be ordered by phone, mail or on the US SAILING website (www.ussailing.org).

YACHT PREPARATION

Safety Recommendations for Cruising Boats, US SAILING, Portsmouth Rhode Island

Seaworthiness: The Forgotten Factor, by C. A. Marchaj, Tiller 1996

Desirable and Undesirable Characteristics of Offshore Yachts, John Rousmaniere, ed., W. W. Norton 1987

Gougeon Brothers on Boat Construction, by the Gougeon Brothers, Bay City, Michigan 1994

Spurr's Boatbook, by Daniel Spurr, International Marine, 1993

Sailors' Secrets, by Michael Badham and Robby Robinson, IM 1997

U.S. Coast Guard: www.uscg.mil

U.S. State Department travel and medical information: http://travel.state.gov/medical.html

RIGGING AND SAILS

The Arts of the Sailor, by Hervey G. Smith, Dover Publications 1990

The Complete Rigger's Apprentice, by Brion Toss, McGraw Hill 1997

The Complete Canvasworkers Guide, by Jim Grant, International Marine 1992

PASSAGE PLANNING

The Boater's Guide to Provisioning, by Dyan Farley, Arbaleste Publishing, Victoria, Canada, 1996

Boatowner's Legal Adviser, by Larry Rogers, International Marine 1997

Ocean Passages of the World, British Admiralty, 1987

The Mariners Handbook, British Admiralty, 1995

Atlantic Pilot Atlas, By James Clarke, International Marine 1997

World Cruising Routes, by Jimmy Cornell, McGraw Hill 1998

World Cruising Handbook, by Jimmy Cornell, International Marine 1996

Atlas of Pilot Charts North Atlantic, NIMA, 1992

The Atlantic Crossing Guide, by Anne Hammick, RCC Pilotage Found., 1998

Pacific Crossing Guide, Michael Pocock, ed., RCC Pilotage Foundation 1997

U.S. Centers for Disease Control: www.cdc.gov

LIFE ABOARD

The Cruising Chef, by Mike Greenwald, Paradise Cay Publications 1996

Cruising Rules: Relationships at Sea, by Roland S. Barth, 1997

Care and Feeding of Sailing Crew, by Lin and Larry Pardey, Paradise Cay Publications 1995

Sailing and Yachting First Aid, by John Bergan, M.D. and Vincent Guzzetta, M.D., United States Sailing Association

First Aid at Sea, by Douglas Justins & Colin Berry, Arlard Coles Nautical, 1999

My Old Man and the Sea, by Daniel Hays and David Hays, Harper Collins,1996

Sailing Alone around the World, by Joshua Slocum, Konemann 1999

Seabirds: An Identification Guide, by Peter Harrison, Houghton Mifflin 1991

WEATHER

The Weather Handbook, by Alan Watts, Sheridan House 1999

National Weather Service: www.nws.noaa.gov

Weather Predicting Simplified: How to Read Weather Charts and Satellite Images, by Michael Carr, International Marine 1999

Weather at Sea: A Yachtsmaster's Guide, by David Houghton, Fernhurst 1998

National Oceanographic and Atmospheric Administration: www.noaa.gov

PASSAGE NAVIGATION

Coastal Navigation, United States Sailing Association, 1999
Reed's Nautical Almanac, annual
Boater's Bowditch: Small Craft American Practical Navigator, by Richard Hubbard, International Marine, 1998
Celestial Navigation for Ocean Yachtsmen, by Tom Cunliffe, Fernhurst 1994
Sight Reduction Tables, Pub. 249, vols 1-3
The American Practical Navigator, Bowditch, U.S. Government 1995
Longitude, by Dava Sobel, Penguin 1996
U.S. Coast Guard Navigation Center: www.navcen.uscg.mil
U.S. National Information Mapping Agency: www.nima.mil

COMMUNICATION

Maritime Radio and Satellite Communications Manual, by Ian Waugh, Voyageur Press 1995
GMDSS for Small Craft, by Alan Clemmetsen, Fernhurst 1997
Mariner's Guide to Single Sideband, by Frederick Graves, SEA 1992

SYSTEMS

Boatowner's Mechanical & Electrical Manual, by Nigel Calder, International Marine 1995
Marine Diesel Engines, by Nigel Calder, International Marine 1992
Refrigeration for Pleasureboats, by Nigel Calder, International Marine 1991

SEAMANSHIP

Oceanography and Seamanship, William Van Dorn, Cornell Maritime Press 1993
Boater's Bowditch: Small Craft American Practical Navigator, by Richard Hubbard, International Marine 1998

EMERGENCIES

The Onboard Medical Handbook, by Paul Gill, Jr, M.D., International Marine, 1996
International Medical Guide for Ships, Second Edition, World Health Organization 1988
The Ship's Medical Chest and Medical Aid at Sea, DHHS Publications
Advanced First Aid Afloat, by Peter F. Eastman, M.D., Cornell Maritime Press, 1995
Adrift: 76 Days Lost at Sea, by Steve Callahan, Ballantine Books 1996
A Practical Guide to Lifeboat Survival, by Survival Center, 1997

HEAVY WEATHER

Storm Tactics Handbook, by Lin and Larry Pardey, Pardey Productions 1999
Adlard Coles' Heavy Weather Sailing 4th edition, Peter Bruce, International Marine 1999
Heavy Weather Guide, Richard Henderson, Naval Institute, 1984
Fastnet Force 10, by John Rousmaniere, W.W. Norton 2000
1979 Fastnet Race Inquiry, United States Sailing Association
Capsize Study, United States Sailing Association
DDDB: Drag Device Data Base, by Victor Shane, Para-Anchors International, Summerland, California, 1998

ANCHORING

The Complete Book of Anchoring and Mooring, by Earl Hinz, Cornell Maritime Press 1994

US SAILING publishes these valuable tools for coastal and offshore passagemakers.

Safety Recommendations for Cruising Sailboats
Minimum equipment and accomodation standards for cruising sailboats.

Safety Recommendations for Offshore Sailing
Including ORC Regulations Minimum standards for yachts sailing offshore.

Sailing and Yachting First Aid
A valuable first aid manual for cruising sailors. Written in layman's language.

Official Logbook of Sailing
A useful logbook for recording cruising, chartering and racing experiences.

Any US SAILING publication can be ordered by phone, mail or on the US SAILING website (www.ussailing.org).

Index